Holy

Practically *Holy*

Finding God in the Everyday

Carol Mead

Holy Ordinary
www.holyordinary.com

Scripture taken from the
HOLY BIBLE, NEW INTERNATIONAL VERSION®. NIV®.
Copyright ©1973, 1978, 1984 by International Bible Society.
Used by permission of Zondervan. All rights reserved.

Copyright ©2008 by Carol Mead

ISBN-13: 978-0-9746702-1-8 • ISBN-10: 0-9746702-1-9

Design by Cynthia Clark

Holy Ordinary
www.holyordinary.com

Dedication

I dedicate this book to God,
and to the loving people God placed in my life:
people who believed in me long before I believed in myself.

Table of Contents

Introduction 9

January 11

February 43

March 73

April 105

May 137

June 169

July 201

August 233

September 265

October 297

November 329

December 361

Index 393

Introduction

All of my life I have loved words and writing. This book, and all of my ministry of writing, brings me great joy because it allows me to combine my passion for God with my passion for words.

But that ministry could not have developed without the help of loved ones in my life. Jennet Lacey has been my faithful friend and supporter for 35 years, and she deserves much of the credit for anything I have accomplished in my life. The first book of these meditations, *Holy Ordinary*, came about because a dear friend, Randy Belton, believed in my writing ministry enough to help me produce the book. I will never be able to thank her adequately for her help in turning me toward God and for encouraging me to explore that relationship through writing.

I have also been blessed in recent years by the presence and guidance of another spiritual mentor, the Reverend John Stone Jenkins. His influence on my theology and his help in my spiritual discernment process have allowed me to explore territory—theological, personal, and academic—that I would otherwise not have had the confidence or skills to explore. I hope that, wherever my ministry takes me in the future, I will honor the gifts that God has given me through the guidance of John Jenkins.

My eternal gratitude, of course, goes to God, who put those marvelous, supportive, wise persons—and too many others to enumerate—in my life.

Practically Holy, the next step in a journey I have taken with God since December of 1999, is the second collection of daily meditations I have published. The response to the meditations has convinced me that people are hungry to know more about God, and to seek that knowledge of God in every aspect of life rather than only in traditional "religious" settings and experiences.

Since the days when I started writing these meditations, my life has undergone significant change. As I write these words, I am preparing to enter my third year of seminary at Yale Divinity School. And yet, despite my now traveling on a path of "professional" ministry, I still believe that God remains just as accessible to us in everyday experiences as in formal religious practice or theological study.

I have also come to believe that people long to think symbolically and metaphorically, and that we are in danger of becoming spiritually impoverished if we lose that way of thinking. This book is designed to remind people of the value of symbolism and metaphor, of the value of allowing our imaginations—and the Spirit of God within us—to "know" things that we cannot prove or articulate. I believe that this way of thinking about God allows our hearts to know what our minds can never comprehend.

I believe, too, that if we can nurture that imaginative way of thinking, we can be aware of and practice the presence of God even through the most ordinary events and symbols in our world. Religion and theology hold great value, but sometimes we human beings need something more down-to-earth, more useful in everyday terms, more "practically" holy. I hope that this book represents a translation of the holy into the practical, giving us all a way of seeing God in all times, all places, all persons.

We are mortal, flawed human beings, but we are also created in and infused with the image of God. That image of God, living within us, is not only a gift to be placed on a formal altar and reserved for Sundays and special days. The grace of God changes this day, this life. By opening the imaginations of our hearts and inviting God into the details of life, we find a practical gift. We live a life that is practically holy.

Carol Mead
November 2008

January

JANUARY 1

The day of grace

Pass through, pass through the gates! Prepare the way for the people. Build up, build up the highway! Remove the stones. Raise a banner for the nations. . . . Say to the Daughter of Zion, "See, your Savior comes . . . They will be called the Holy People, the Redeemed of the LORD; and you will be called Sought After, the City No Longer Deserted."

ISAIAH 62:10-12

There is something deeply hopeful about New Year's Day. Turning over that page on the calendar, from one year to the next, somehow reminds us of the power we have to change ourselves and our lives. This year I will be more loving, more successful, more studious, more in shape. This year. . .

I always have a mild sense of regret, too, on New Year's Day, knowing that the same power to change languishes in the drawer every day of the year. Every day, I can do better, start anew. Yet I can start fresh not because of my power, but because of the power of God living in me, and the grace of God embracing me.

Isaiah said that the power of God's salvation gives us hope for change every moment of our lives. Of those embraced by God, Isaiah says, "they will be called the Holy People, the Redeemed of the LORD, and you will be called Sought After, the City No Longer Deserted." Yes, this year, this day can be different. This person is redeemed, holy, "sought after."

This person can be different—today—by the grace of God.

JANUARY 2

So small

The Sovereign LORD was calling for judgment by fire; it dried up the great deep and devoured the land. Then I cried out, "Sovereign LORD, I beg you, stop! How can Jacob survive? He is so small!" So the LORD relented.

AMOS 7:4-5

On the road once, I traveled into the next time zone. I exulted when I realized that I "gained" an hour when the time changed on my way back home. Of course, time didn't change when I crossed that line; I changed in the way I measured it.

Just as I tried that day to make God's gift of time fit into my human construct, I often struggle to squeeze other attributes of God into small, human boxes. I demand justice, wanting others to pay for their sins, but the "time changes" when I'm headed home, when my own failures are at issue. I cry out "It's not fair!" when God forgives them, but praise His mercy when He forgives me. I forget (often) that God is God, that He metes out the justice and the mercy, and that, as Creator of the universe and of humankind, He certainly has the prerogative to change His mind about punishment and reward.

I can beg God, as Amos did, to show mercy, and hope that He will relent. I can hope that He will prevent my being devoured by the fire of selfishness and materialism that seems to be devouring us all on this earth today. Enveloped in my own darkness, I will continue to whisper desperately to my God, "Forgive them, Lord. They are so small."

We are so small.

JANUARY 3

A bit of bread and some fish

Jesus said to them, "They need not go away; you give them something to eat." They replied, "We have nothing here but five loaves and two fish." And he said, "Bring them here to me."

MATTHEW 14:16-18

I used go to one drive-through coffee place so often that they just waved me up to the window instead of taking my regular order. It was flattering that they remembered what I always got, but what if I wanted something more?

Such an attitude toward myself and my own potential can prevent my living the most abundant life possible. Aware of others' expectations of me, I think of doing something more or different, but catch myself thinking, "What will they think?" Oddly, at such times, I can articulate neither who "they" are nor why their opinions matter.

Miracles take place every day when ordinary humans put their lives fully in God's hands. Even if we have nothing more than five loaves and two fish, God can feed thousands with the gifts we offer. Whatever our gifts—and however modest they may seem to us—God requests simply, "Bring them here to me."

I could be so much more if only I could discard my low expectations of what can come from a bit of bread and some fish. The world expects little of me. I expect little of myself. Probably, more often than not, I will meet those low expectations and fail to participate in God's continuing creation, of the world and of me.

But what if I wanted something more?

JANUARY 4

Disarmament

"[The landowner answered] 'Didn't you agree to work for a denarius?. . . I want to give the man who was hired last the same as I gave you. Don't I have the right to do what I want with my own money? . . .'"

MATTHEW 20:13-15

North Korea finally agreed to implode a nuclear weapons facility in order to be removed from the list of nations fostering terrorism. Its feared lack of restraint in using such weapons meant it could only enjoy the full benefits of relations with other nations if it destroyed its nuclear capabilities.

Full participation in the kingdom of God, too, requires unilateral disarmament. God asks me to lay down the weapons of this world to help build a new world. But if I give up my weapons, the person I would have hurt benefits as much as I do. It doesn't seem fair.

But I am ultimately the one who benefits by not participating in aggression. I live the life of peace, as I no longer need to escalate aggression to feel as if I'm winning. I no longer need to hurt another to feel whole myself. I can love other persons whether they choose to help me or hurt me.

Jesus told a parable about workers who felt unfairly treated because latecomers were paid the same as those arriving early. God's standards will not feel fair by human standards; I would gladly disarm if I saw others do it first. Yet God asks me to do it regardless of what others do. It isn't fair.

But it is the way that peace breaks into a world enamored of war.

JANUARY 5

Grace

When the LORD your God brings you into... a land with large, flourishing cities you did not build, houses filled with all kinds of good things you did not provide, wells you did not dig, and vineyards and olive groves you did not plant—then when you eat and are satisfied, be careful that you do not forget the LORD, who brought you out of Egypt, out of the land of slavery.

DEUTERONOMY 6:10-12

I am embarrassed to say that I fell down twice in one day outside church, once going in and once coming out. The first time, people offered to help; the second time, no one saw me, but I knew I could get help from a church member if I needed it.

I think that falling and church are two concepts that go well together. Some people say they avoid church because it holds a "bunch of hypocrites." But I think church is the perfect place to go if you're prone to falling. Most of us in the pews know that we live by the grace of God, that we drink "from wells we did not dig" and are nourished by "olive groves we did not plant." We know that we are forgiven by that same grace when we fall away from God. And we know the sad truth, that we still often forget the Lord who brought us "out of the land of slavery."

Those of us in church know that we are saved, not by being perfect or by judging others as less than ourselves, but by the sheer, take-your-breath-away grace of God. Human grace may keep you from falling.

But divine grace helps you get back up.

Overnight sensation

After Jesus was born in Bethlehem in Judea, during the time of King Herod, Magi from the east came to Jerusalem and asked, "Where is the one who has been born king of the Jews? We saw his star in the east and have come to worship him."

MATTHEW 2:1-2

Often I have heard of people who, after years of work in the arts or in a sport, become an "overnight sensation." It isn't that their talent came instantly, but only *recognition* of their talent. Getting to that point of success, perceived by others as "overnight," often requires the journey of a lifetime.

In our culture, we have also come to think of an "epiphany" as something that happens in an instant, an insight which is the equivalent of an overnight sensation. In the church, we celebrate the "Epiphany" on January 6th. That celebration marks the arrival of the magi at the birthplace of the baby Jesus.

But the key word in the understanding of epiphany is "arrival." This epiphany, like any other important discovery, did not come simply in a moment; we only notice its arrival in a moment. Like an overnight sensation, an epiphany often requires years to materialize. The recognition of the importance and power of Jesus' coming may happen in an instant, in what we would call an "epiphany." But that epiphany comes after the journey of a lifetime. . .

. . . just like an "overnight sensation."

JANUARY 7

My, my, my

This is what the LORD Almighty says: ". . . What you brought home, I blew away. Why?" declares the LORD Almighty. "Because of my house, which remains a ruin, while each of you is busy with his own house."

HAGGAI 1:9

Several years ago I worked at my alma mater, and a donation came to the school from the family of a woman who had attended decades earlier. During her college years, a faculty member had given her $100 which allowed her to stay in school. Later she arranged to pay back the $100, plus the interest it would've accumulated in the meantime, knowing she could not have finished college without that loan.

I often wish I had such an enduring conscience, such faithful gratitude about paying back all that has allowed me to be what and who I am. I get so wrapped up in my own life—my activities, my relationships, my joys—that I neglect to remember that God is the source of every good gift. "Busy with my own house," I let the house of God and the worship of God within me go untended. I forget that I would be nothing without Him.

But the soul faithful to God remembers constantly that all good things are gifts from Him. The voice faithful to God speaks not of "my gifts," but of God's gifts. The heart faithful to God offers everything, principal and interest, back to God, knowing that life is not possible without Him.

The hands faithful to God build His house instead of a temple to the self.

Twins

Therefore, since Christ suffered in his body, arm yourselves also with the same attitude, because he who has suffered in his body is done with sin. As a result, he does not live the rest of his earthly life for evil human desires, but rather for the will of God.

1 Peter 4:1-2

At the mall I saw a young mother walking into a store with little bitty twin girls, about three or four years old. The two had obviously been instructed by their mother to hold hands and stay together, which was difficult. One twin kept wanting to go one direction while the other pulled to go somewhere else.

Sometimes I almost feel as if there are "twins" inside me, two people who look alike but continually pull against each other, one physical and one spiritual. The physical twin wants to go where there is abundance, applause, approval, where everything—good or bad—can be clearly seen on the exterior.

The spiritual twin, though, often pulls toward situations that are not as clearly defined, that are not as easy to solve, that live on the interior rather than on the exterior. Those places where the will of God rules are much more difficult to visit, but vastly more rewarding and meaningful. There, people grieve and exult, laugh and cry. There, human lives lean away from earthly desires and into the loving acts that are the presence of God incarnate in human flesh.

There, both sides of me touch eternity.

JANUARY 9

Why she smiles

But the angel said to her, "Do not be afraid, Mary, you have found favor with God. You will be with child and give birth to a son...." "How will this be," Mary asked the angel, "since I am a virgin?"... The angel answered, "... nothing is impossible with God."

LUKE 1:30, 34, 37

Using "emotion recognition" software, scientists scanned the Mona Lisa and estimated that her expression is 83 percent happy, 9 percent disgusted, 6 percent fearful, and 2 percent angry. The researchers did this particular analysis for fun, but it intrigues me that there is software—a scientific method—designed to "recognize emotion."

While I am skeptical, I myself frequently want to overuse logical, methodological approaches when trying to get to God, continually trying to "think my way there." Likewise, when Mary heard about the imminent birth of Jesus, she tried, understandably, to fit divine action into frames of human reason, asking "How will this be, since I am a virgin?" Like the Mona Lisa scientists, she struggled to apply human instruments to concepts that cannot be measured, because they live in the mind of God.

Although it makes no human sense, given my frequent indifference to Him, God loves me, a realization that makes me 100 percent joyful and zero percent fearful. The world is fractured and frightening, yet I am happy and whole.

It seems that nothing is impossible with God.

JANUARY 10

The big tip

Are you so foolish? After beginning with the Spirit, are you now trying to attain your goal by human effort? Have you suffered so much for nothing—if it really was for nothing? Does God give you his Spirit and work miracles among you because you observe the law, or because you believe what you heard?

GALATIANS 3:3-5

On the road, I stopped for the night and had dinner in a restaurant. Feeling generous, I left a big tip, and wondered fleetingly if that would help me get good service when I had breakfast there the next morning. Then I remembered that the tip is not to make something happen, but in gratitude for what has happened.

I fall into the same trap in my spiritual life. In my human instinct for cause-and-effect, I keep thinking that I am supposed to "do good" so that God will save me. As I did in the restaurant, I begin to think of my actions as a cause rather than an effect. I fall into "trying to attain my goal by human effort."

I know the truth, though. I didn't receive God's Spirit and see miracles worked in my life because of something I had done, but because God loves me and wants me close to Him. Like the Galatians, I struggle to maintain that distinction. My good works are not the cause of God's grace, but its effect. I love God and I want to do as He asks, not to *make* something happen.

But because something *has*.

JANUARY 11

Prime numbers

"Those who cling to worthless idols forfeit the grace that could be theirs. But I, with a song of thanksgiving, will sacrifice to you. . . ."
JONAH 2:8-9

I read an article saying that researchers have discovered the largest prime number, something that is over nine million digits long. The article reminded me that a prime number is a positive number that is only divisible by itself and 1.

This concept of prime numbers seems to convey purity, something reduced to its essence, its core. I know that, when I let many interests and anxieties "divide" me, I can no longer be the person I am designed to be. I "cling to worthless idols" and "forfeit the grace that could be mine."

Yet when I stop allowing my energy and attention to be pointed in many disparate and meaningless directions, I find my own, pure essence, "divisible" only by myself and the One who created me. I am who I am through God.

I finally see that dividing my priorities based on what the world thinks I should do or want or be can never work, as it puts my psyche, emotions, and physical self in a constant state of war. God is all that matters, and I know now to, "sacrifice to Him with a song of thanksgiving."

I do regret that it took me a half-century to come to the liberating understanding that I needn't worry about what everyone else thinks, that it took a half-century for me to feel undivided.

But maybe that's why it's called the "prime" of life.

Telling the truth

I will sing of your love and justice; to you, O LORD, I will sing praise. I will be careful to lead a blameless life—when will you come to me?
PSALM 101:1-2

"Tell the truth," my dad used to say. "Then you don't have to remember so much." I try to tell the truth, but in my heart I know that I often say things that cannot be true: unreasonable promises, New Year's resolutions, guilty reflections on mistakes, and prayers when I know I have let God down.

It is the truth, certainly, that I want to "lead a blameless life," but I have already proven I simply cannot do it. I have too much fear and pride, too little compassion and understanding, to do what I know I should do for God. So I say I will do better, and every time, I fall back to be less than the person God made me to be. Yet the worst mistake I can make is forgetting that God forgives me, dwelling in the past instead of the present.

So perhaps instead of "singing of God's love and justice," I will sing of God's love and mercy. God knows that I will fail again. But God also knows that I hold Him and His presence dear above all else in my life. I will always try to live a life that is compassionate, merciful, loving, kind, joyful, not allowing mistakes of the past to hold me down in the present. So in the moment of realizing my mistake, I tell the truth, but then I move on.

That way, I don't have to remember so much.

Ugly houses

The man answered, "Now that is remarkable! You don't know where he comes from, yet he opened my eyes... If this man [Jesus] were not from God, he could do nothing." To this [the Jews] replied, "You were steeped in sin at birth; how dare you lecture us!" And they threw him out.
JOHN 9:30, 33-34

Frequently when I see billboards proclaiming, "We buy ugly houses," I wonder about the advertising technique. While it's a hopeful thought in a way, a person wanting to take advantage of the offer would first have to admit owning an ugly house.

Spiritually, I suppose, every one of us owns "an ugly house," a place where we live but wish we didn't, a place that we can't believe we purchased at such a high price. Not one of us wants to admit having spent precious energy, desires, and gifts to acquire such an ugly place to live. And yet, the more quickly I admit I am living in an ugly house, the more quickly God can come in and turn the place into His temple.

It's frightfully easy, in the defensive and fearful human condition, to say as the disbelievers in Jesus' time said, "You were steeped in sin at birth; how dare you lecture us!" It feels good, triumphant, and self-righteous to throw out those who challenge us to see Jesus. It feels like winning to close our eyes and pretend we love living in this place. But that refusal to see our own flaws always, always brings the same result.

We keep living in ugly houses.

JANUARY 14

In the meantime

Again Jesus said, "Simon son of John, do you truly love me?" He answered, "Yes, Lord, you know that I love you." Jesus said, "Take care of my sheep."

JOHN 21:16

At the eye clinic one day, a woman and her two children were in the waiting room. The doctor chose to give the mother her eye test first. As she left the waiting room, she instructed the children, "Take care of each other."

Sometimes we get so absorbed in our own lives that we have to be reminded, like those children, to look out for one another. Jesus, like a parent asking children to care for each other, makes each of us responsible, one for the other. The instructions, "Take care of my sheep" do not apply only to Peter, but to every person who lives the life of Christ.

I have to admit that many people drive me crazy. I don't want to tolerate them; I want to absent myself from them, or win over them. The last thing I want to do is to take care of them. And yet, if the right person asks me to do better, to tolerate or even embrace those people who drive me crazy, I can rise above my own pettiness and begin to think of the bigger picture first.

Today's path could be filled with people I don't like much. But whether I like them or not, God asks me to love them. "I'm going to be gone awhile," God incarnate says to each of us. But He gives explicit instructions of what we must do until He returns.

"Take care of each other."

JANUARY 15

Aerial coverage

He guides the humble in what is right and teaches them his way.
PSALM 25:9

As I watched the NFL playoffs one year, I was amazed to hear that a company had provided "aerial coverage" (the blimp) for a game played inside a domed stadium. If a place is closed off, what's the benefit of a view from the sky?

I happen to know by experience, though, that we humans are sometimes that arrogant or that foolish, asking God to watch over us and yet being unwilling to let Him in. I want God to embrace me and forgive me, yet I often choose to remain closed to Him. Getting full "aerial coverage" would require me to let down my guard, something that is very difficult for me to do.

In order for God to help me fully, I would have to admit my failures, and admit exactly how small my heart can be. Besides, if I open myself completely to Him, there's a very good chance He will ask me to go somewhere I don't want to go. Yet it must be true that even the Creator of the universe, and of each human heart in it, cannot transform a place that is not open to Him.

Even the living, loving God cannot teach my heart to live and love if that heart is closed off from Him, either in shame or in arrogance. God "guides the humble in what is right," not those who are too proud or fearful to let Him in.

If a place is closed off, what's the benefit of a view from the sky?

JANUARY 16

The living Word

In the beginning was the Word, and the Word was with God, and the Word was God. He was with God in the beginning. Through him all things were made; without him nothing was made that has been made. In him was life, and that life was the light of men.

JOHN 1:1-4

A friend and his wife were once having a bit of trouble with their young daughter. She loved books, but at one point, she began tearing books apart, even library books. When her parents asked her why she did it, she said she loved the book's characters so much she wanted them to come out and play.

I encounter that same longing in wanting the "Word of God"—that is, the presence and power of God—to be not a theoretical story but a living, breathing encounter with the divine. Often I can slip into thinking of God as "out there" somewhere, removed from me, only a vague part of my life.

But the "Word" works within my life in a personal and powerful way. This Word of God steps off the page every single day of the human life. So we are spiritually impoverished, as Christians, if we think of the "word of God" as only printed words on a page. The Word of God engages us in the creation, as well as empowering us to rebuild ourselves—and the kingdom of humans—in the image of God.

Printed words about God, of course, hold great importance. But printed words cannot measure up to the living Word of God. When we strive to exist as loving human beings in a harsh world, we literally live the Word.

That Word comes off the page. It becomes the story of our lives.

JANUARY 17

Driving force

O LORD. . . You discern my going out and my lying down; you are familiar with all my ways . . . you have laid your hand upon me. Such knowledge is too wonderful for me, too lofty for me to attain.

PSALM 139:3, 5

During an ice storm, information ran on TV detailing places which would be closed. I was particularly relieved to see that the "Elite Driving School" would be closed. The roads, tough enough for experienced drivers, would be no place for those in training.

Many roads that a seeker of God is asked to travel are impassable, impossible for humans alone. God asks me to forgive people who have wounded me deeply. God asks me to love not only strangers, but enemies. God asks me to live in this frightful place without fear.

But God knows that such roads are too treacherous for someone like me to travel. God knows me intimately; He knows "my going out and my lying down," and He is "familiar with all of my ways." So when my weak or spiteful human nature prevents my going where God wants me to go, I ask God to do it for me. "God, forgive where I cannot. Love where I cannot. Bring peace where I find only fear."

Some wonderful acts—of loving, of compassion, of forgiveness—are often "too lofty for me to attain," so I ask God to do them for me. The one in training can stay off the treacherous roads.

The Teacher is in control.

JANUARY 18

All that glitters

Then the LORD said to Moses, "Go down, because your people, whom you brought up out of Egypt, have become corrupt. They have been quick to turn away from what I commanded them and have made themselves an idol cast in the shape of a calf. . . ."

EXODUS 32:7-8

Years ago I watched a TV show about frontier children who thought they had found gold in the bed of a stream. They "borrowed" the screen from a door and spent hours panning for the glittery stuff, planning all the good they would do with their newfound wealth, only to find out it was "fool's gold."

I certainly have brought home plenty of fool's gold. I become impatient, as the Israelites did while Moses met with God on the mountain, and I start seeking golden idols of all descriptions. I have thought, "This is it!" about some discovery, thinking I have found the treasure to make me rich. Every time, I find I have wasted time and energy panning for "riches" that are only fool's gold.

It has taken decades to learn that anything I can pan for myself is utterly worthless, that I have simply "made myself an idol." So now, I wait on God. This time I know I have found something to change my life for good, a treasure that makes me rich even when the rest of the world might consider me poor. This time I'm not wasting my time on something glittery and insubstantial. I have found God, and through God I have found myself.

This is *it*.

JANUARY 19

Matter

". . . Turn away from all your offenses; then sin will not be your downfall. Rid yourselves of all the offenses you have committed, and get a new heart and a new spirit. Why will you die, O house of Israel?. . . declares the Sovereign LORD. Repent and live!"

EZEKIEL 18:30-31

Long ago in a science class, I learned that "no matter is ever created or destroyed," that it only changes form. As I get older, I believe that precept holds not only in physical science, but also in the seeking of God and His eternal moment.

I have endured and precipitated many matters that I thought would create or destroy me: jobs or relationships that I thought would finally make me happy, and losses or failures that I thought would kill me. And yet, I look back at it all now and realize that things of this world cannot create or destroy me, but can only change me. Mistakes have become useful as an antidote to self-righteousness. Losses have turned the lens to make it very clear to me what is important in this world and what is not.

Still, it is critical to remember that I cannot live in the past, that I cannot stay there, either as a victor or as a victim. When I do—when I fail to move on and take advantage of the gifts of this moment—then like the house of Israel, I have chosen to die. God wants me to live instead. The burden of the past is gone the moment I turn to God; in His hands, that moment is transformed.

And so, it seems, am I.

JANUARY 20

The grace of God

To some who were confident of their own righteousness and looked down on everybody else, Jesus told this parable: "Two men went up to the temple to pray, one a Pharisee and the other a tax collector. The Pharisee stood up and prayed about himself: 'God, I thank you that I am not like other men. . . '"

LUKE 18:9-11

In my hospice chaplaincy, I saw a patient my age with a terminal illness and thought, "There but for the grace of God go I." I have said such words many times, but in my heart, I hope those words are nonsense.

That statement, meant as an expression of gratitude, implies that the person undergoing hardship on earth has been denied the grace of God. The natural progression of such logic is that a good prognosis for me signifies that God has given me *more* grace than the person in the next hospital bed, the next room, the next house.

Are those of us who have uttered those words, "There but for the grace of God" among those Jesus described as "confident of their own righteousness who looked down on everybody else"? Do we see God's grace as a badge to wear instead of a gift offered to all, deserving and undeserving?

Illness or misfortune is not a sign that God's grace was lost or withheld. In every place, in every person, the grace of God is offered equally and abundantly. So whatever today brings, I can make one statement with confidence.

"Here, amid the grace of God, go I."

Medicine

You, then, why do you judge your brother? Or why do you look down on your brother? For we will all stand before God's judgment seat.
ROMANS 14:10

Occasionally I have read of cases in which persons were poisoned because an industrial solvent had been mixed in with their medicine. Some instances were accidental, and the solvent was inadvertently used. In other cases, medicine counterfeiters used solvent in place of more expensive syrups. Either way, people needing medicine received poison instead.

In a less obvious but equally tragic case, people are poisoned every day by humans who act in the name of God and sit in judgment of others. Sometimes the intent is to help, but wrong-headed or self-serving judgment doesn't bring people to God; it chases them away. Whatever the intent, the so-called medicine can become a poison.

The problem of one sinner's judging another apparently is a timeless one; even in the first century, Paul asked, "Why do you judge your brother? For we will all stand before God's judgment seat."

For the most part, I don't think we mix the poison in intentionally. We simply fail to see that our words, spoken with human motives and human ineptitude, can give a person such a distorted idea of God that they run from Him instead of to Him. I want for people to see something in me that leads them to God, not something that chases them away from Him.

I want to offer medicine, not poison.

Love extravagantly

. . . Jesus . . . said in a loud voice, "If anyone is thirsty, let him come to me and drink. Whoever believes in me, as the Scripture has said, streams of living water will flow from within him."

JOHN 7:37-38

Traveling in the mountains once, I saw ice on sheer cliffs, and wondered how water moving straight down could ever freeze. I supposed that the water came down the cliff not in a rush, but in a trickle so slow it could succumb to freezing temperatures.

I also wonder how some people can remain closed off to the presence of God, totally self-involved, if they have ever loved or been loved. If you have witnessed and felt those "streams of living water," how can you stay angry? How can you continue to ignore the God who lives and breathes within the human heart?

Perhaps in both cases the problem comes from restricting the flow instead of allowing it to roar down the mountain. Some people are so hurt or so angry or so hate themselves that love dispensed drop by drop will never reach down to where they live. When love is rationed out, after all, it's easy to assume that it is not love at all, but the purchasing or rewarding of behavior.

Reaching some people requires loving extravagantly—in sloppy, generous helpings—letting love flow abundantly from God straight to those who need Him. To keep the water from freezing, we have to let it rush down that mountain.

Like "streams of living water."

JANUARY 23

Wounded grace

So Jacob was left alone, and a man wrestled with him till daybreak. When the man saw that he could not overpower him, he touched the socket of Jacob's hip so that his hip was wrenched as he wrestled with the man. Then the man said, "Let me go, for it is daybreak." But Jacob replied, "I will not let you go unless you bless me."

GENESIS 32:24-26

I attended a wedding reception with great music, where most of the people dancing were very agile young adults. Though I love to dance, I hung enviously around the room's edges, feeling too old, too uncool, too graceless to join the dancing.

I often feel equally awkward in seeking God. I hang around the edges, feeling so utterly graceless in His brilliant light that I know I don't belong there. And yet, that crippling encounter can become a blessing if I simply hold on long enough. My wounds and mistakes make me more compassionate and forgiving to others, and where compassion and mercy live, God lives. I walk away limping, yet blessed.

Jacob, too, found holiness in his crippling encounter. Though aware of his own lack of grace, he insisted to his opponent, "I will not let you go unless you bless me." He walked away limping, yet blessed. So it seems that the soul, where I long for God, is not at all like the human body in which I wrestle with Him. Wounded *bodies* cannot dance with grace.

But wounded souls often dance with the greatest grace of all.

The temple

So then, just as you received Christ Jesus as Lord, continue to live in him, rooted and built up in him, strengthened in the faith as you were taught, and overflowing with thankfulness.

COLOSSIANS 2:6-7

Not long ago I heard a person say of his religious practice that he could go to the temple and "leave the ordinary world behind." For a moment I envied that experience of moving completely from a secular reality into the sacred.

Later, though, I realized that I want to do the opposite. I want to carry with me such a sense of the holy that all becomes holy, even in the ordinary world. The beauty of Christianity is that God became incarnate in Jesus, and we can carry the presence of Jesus into everything we do, even the most "ordinary" things. As a Christian who has receiving the Spirit of God in Christ, I am "rooted and built up in him," and I can be a bearer of God in the everyday world.

I don't think God intends for us to seek Him only in a bricks-and-mortar place of worship. He wants me to seek Him in the need of the next human being I meet, in the compassion extended to a suffering stranger, in the patient listening of a friend. The presence of God in me allows me to see Him in all people, and to carry Him to all people.

As the body of Christ, we don't leave the ordinary world behind to step into the holy. We carry the holy with us everywhere we go. We don't go to the temple.

We are the temple.

The mystery of God's favor

This is what the LORD says: "In the time of my favor I will answer you, and in the day of salvation I will help you; I will keep you... to restore the land and to reassign its desolate inheritances, to say to the captives, 'Come out,' and to those in darkness, 'Be free!'"

ISAIAH 49:8-9

Many days I spent in the north, the weather was bitter cold. Puddles froze solid, and a thin layer of ice covered the entire pond out front. And even at a nearby large lake, the edges of the water turned to ice.

If we humans had our way, I fear that we would want everything about God and spirituality to freeze solid: completely knowable, utterly devoid of mystery. We want to solidify knowledge of God to make that knowledge portable, manageable, useful. But as with bodies of water turning to ice, the human ability to understand God is only solid in the small places, or in the areas around the edges.

Some people seem intent on speaking with great certainty about God's will and God's ways. I am content with the mystery, with not knowing. If God operated within my understanding, He would not bother to help me and restore me, because my life would be too insignificant. He would not say, "Be free!" to someone who chose to live so long in darkness.

We cannot know what lies in the deep center of God. All I can say with confidence is that God cares for me. I will never know why.

And, thanks be to God, I don't need to know why.

A stranger on earth

Do good to your servant, and I will live; I will obey your word. Open my eyes that I may see wonderful things in your law. I am a stranger on earth; do not hide your commands from me.

PSALM 119:17-19

When one African country was in conflict, poor residents attacked and killed anyone believed to be immigrants, viewed as criminals who lower wages and take jobs. As one immigrant described the violence, "They came at night, trying to kill us, with people pointing out, 'this one is a foreigner and this one is not.'"

It saddens me to think of anyone as being pointed out as a "foreigner," one to be attacked and marginalized, but it happens even in the supposedly safer territory of spirituality. And in the larger world, a moral, loving person who chooses to do right instead of getting ahead can be viewed as a foreigner.

Still, as a Christian, I hope to "live and obey" God's word, by loving God and loving neighbors. In making loving choices over self-aggrandizing ones, I may be a "stranger on earth." It can be unnerving to stop going along with the crowd, and too often I choose the easy way, one comfortable to me and others, rather than choosing the right way.

But our way, commanded by God, is to love, not to cull out those who are worthy and those who are not, those who "belong" and those who are foreigners. It bears repeating: our way, commanded by God, is to love.

For in the territory of God, there are no foreigners.

JANUARY 27

Down the mountain

> ... Jesus... led them up a high mountain by themselves. There he was transfigured before them... Peter said to Jesus, "Lord, it is good for us to be here. If you wish, I will put up three shelters—one for you, one for Moses and one for Elijah."
>
> MATTHEW 17:1-4

In a hotel room I found the following message: "This bottle of natural spring water is provided as a service to our guests. If consumed, $4.00 will be billed to your room. Please enjoy." I wondered, "Where's the service in having water that I cannot consume?"

I find myself with a similar question when I read of the transfiguration, and of Peter's desire to preserve the moment, there on the mountain, by putting up shelters and remaining there. What's the point? Why show me this God if He can't accompany me in my "real" life? Where is the salvation in a god whom I can only find by climbing the mountain, by staying in the high places?

Admittedly, it's often my instinct, too, to freeze God in a memorable, life-changing moment on the mountain rather than asking Him to continue to change me in the lower altitudes. And yet the true power of God is not how He looks on the mountain, but what He does in the valley. I worship God because He transforms the experiences I have down here, because He transforms me down here. After all, where's the salvation in a god that stays on the mountain?

What good is water I'm not allowed to consume?

JANUARY 28

God's ways

'In that day each of you will invite his neighbor to sit under his vine and fig tree,' declares the LORD Almighty.

ZECHARIAH 3:10

One day when I looked at the weather forecast online, the standard screen on the website called for "High, 28" and "Low, 28." In everyday language, we would never say such a thing, but sometimes the frames we have for communication are incapable of capturing the unusual or the out-of-the-ordinary.

Living as a Christian in a human world results in many days, many circumstances, that simply don't fit the frames with which we usually describe human behavior and human society. It makes no sense, in this world's eyes, to forgive a wrong. It makes no sense to stay connected to others when close human relations can bring such tragedy and such pain. In this world's eyes, it makes no sense for a person to "invite a neighbor to sit under his vine and fig tree."

Yet the world that God dreams for us—the world God dreams that we will help build—does not and will never fit into the easy descriptions and standard frames of human language. To do what God asks—loving Him and one another regardless of what others say—does not fit comfortably into our human frames of understanding and communication. But then, God's ways are not meant to validate this world.

God's ways are meant to change it.

JANUARY 29

Stilling the strings

. . . we constantly pray for you, that our God may count you worthy of his calling, and that by his power he may fulfill every good purpose of yours and every act prompted by your faith. We pray this so that the name of our Lord Jesus may be glorified in you. . .

2 THESSALONIANS 1:11-12

Once at a concert, I sat just a few feet from the person playing the harp. During the concert, she would play her part, and often would then flatten her palms against the strings to still them as another part of the orchestra took over.

Someday I hope to learn that move, the humility necessary for me to still the music I am making in order for the greater music to be heard. Unfortunately, often when I choose to do the right thing—to help someone rather than putting my own needs first—I'm still being selfish because I want "credit" for doing the right thing. I want the strings of my instrument to continue to hum, even if that sound distracts from the main message.

But I am only one part of the orchestra, and anything I do right is meant to glorify God, not to glorify me. So rather than continuing to make noise about what I have done, I need to realize that any good in my life comes through God's power, "that the name of our Lord Jesus Christ may be glorified" in me.

So yes, occasionally I do the right thing. Or, more accurately, God works through me for good. It's worth noting.

But there's certainly no need to harp on it.

JANUARY 30

One hundred percent

Do not love the world or anything in the world. . . The world and its desires pass away, but the man who does the will of God lives forever.
1 JOHN 2:15, 17

Online one morning, I saw a news headline which caught my attention: "Simple test helps predict chances of dying." My first reaction was that I don't need a test; if I am human, my chances of dying are 100%.

The difference for me as a Christian, of course, is not that my chances of dying are lessened, but that I find life beyond death. And that new life is not only the so-called "afterlife," but also the ability to find joy and depth when the things, people, and circumstances of this world have tried to kick the life right out of me.

Life after death isn't only about "going to heaven" when my days on this earth are done. It's also about living for God on this earth, a way of life that means the peace of God fills my heart instead of the anxiety produced by the worldly need for success, material things, power. It's about finding God in the smallest—and even the most painful—of human moments.

If I "love the world" and its things, then I lose that opportunity to transcend this world and all its worry and baggage. My chances of dying, as always, are 100%, but my chances of coming back to life after this world deals me a death blow are zero. A simple test can tell me my chances of living or dying.

Do I love God more than I love this world?

JANUARY 31

Nothing matches

I hate double-minded men, but I love your law. You are my refuge and my shield; I have put my hope in your word. . . . You reject all who stray from your decrees, for their deceitfulness is in vain.

PSALM 119:113-114, 119

Frigid weather requires me to bring out articles of clothing I seldom wear; on one occasion, my outside layer included a teal knit hat, red gloves, a navy coat, and a green scarf. I was warm, but nothing matched.

I often find myself having to put together a view of God which seems logically mismatched, but which protects me from the world. In one place a psalm celebrates the believer's "hating double-minded men" and "loving the law." Yet Jesus reminds me that the greatest law asks me to love God and neighbor, whether that neighbor is friend or enemy. Nothing matches.

I cannot find a totally consistent, systematic way of understanding God. I hear in one breath that God "rejects all who stray from His decrees." In the next breath, Jesus—God incarnate, the Word of God—tells me that God is love, that God has infinite mercy.

Yet even though such paradoxes confound my intellect, my heart implicitly understands that God is a God of hope, of tenderness, of boundless grace, of inexplicable mercy. True, the pieces of my rational understanding of God are woefully mismatched, but I don't worry.

He still keeps me warm in a terribly cold world.

February

FEBRUARY 1

God's toolbox

Away from me, you evildoers, that I may keep the commands of my God!

PSALM 119:115

Shortly after taking my car in for service, I found an object between the trunk lid and the body. At first I thought it was a broken or replaced part from the car, but the dealer told me it was a tool.

Frequently in my spirituality I encounter tools that first appear to be broken or useless junk. People who irritate me terribly are tools to show me an irritating trait in myself. People who hurt my feelings are often tools for repairing my relationship with God or for practicing forgiveness. The most unlovely of souls are tools to teach me the compassion and mercy that God shows me in my unloveliness.

My instinct is to look on such "tools" as junk, to toss them away without investigating their purpose in my life. I want to say to people who hurt or anger me, "Away from me, you evildoers, that I may keep the commands of my God!" But those people I call evildoers are the very ones to teach me the deepest command of my God: to love without condition even those whom I would cast aside. They remind me that God could just as easily toss me aside if worthiness figured into the equation.

I imagine that today I will stumble across something that looks worthless, or perhaps someone else will stumble across me. Then it's time to ask the question: Is it really a broken part, a piece of junk?

Or has God left me another tool?

FEBRUARY 2

Perfect pronunciation

> . . . *Jesus asked [the blind man], "What do you want me to do for you?" "Lord, I want to see," he replied. Jesus said to him, "Receive your sight; your faith has healed you."*
>
> LUKE 18:40-42

Our Greek professor continually encouraged us to read our homework aloud, as the sounds of words help discern meaning. The problem, though, was that most of the Greek we heard was read by students, so the pronunciation was halting at best and sometimes downright wrong. We all longed to hear correct pronunciation so we could try to imitate it ourselves.

That longing for the perfect example also fills the heart of the earnest Christian. I hear about God's perfect and unconditional love, and yet, all earthly examples I see of that love are halting, flawed examples. How can I speak the language of compassion if I have never heard it spoken correctly?

The love of Christ for each human He encountered gives us the perfect example of what God asks of us. Jesus did not demand, before healing the blind man, "What can you do for me?" Instead, He asked, "What do you want me to do for you?" The perfect example of love asks about you, not about me, and demands no price or reward in return. The perfect example of love says, "I love you. I want you to be whole. I need nothing from you to continue to love you." Perfect pronunciation.

Now I know exactly how the Word of God is supposed to sound.

FEBRUARY 3

Find some dust

[Jesus said] ". . . I tell you. . . there will be more rejoicing in heaven over one sinner who repents than over ninety-nine righteous persons who do not need to repent."

LUKE 15:7

In a TV show one night, a husband got annoyed when his wife mentioned personal business in front of the housekeeper. He said to the woman, who appeared to be eavesdropping, "Go find some dust."

Unfortunately, we have a plethora of dust-finders in our world, particularly spiritual dust-finders. We gleefully point out all that's wrong, convincing ourselves that we have made a contribution to the perfection of the world by pointing out its imperfection.

But pointing out others' deficiencies does little to replace the kingdom of man with the kingdom of God. Choosing to love others unconditionally despite imperfections (theirs and our own), however, does help perfect the world. Jesus told few stories about perfect people, but He did speak of the rejoicing in heaven when even one flawed and lost one is found and embraced.

We needn't point out imperfection outside in order to make the world better. We need to find the perfect love of Christ in our hearts. The problem is not finding the flaws; we have plenty of imperfection to go around, both inside and out. So the question is not whether we can "go find some dust."

The question is whether we'll help breathe the spirit of God into that dust.

FEBRUARY 4

The weather inside is frightful

"I gave you empty stomachs in every city and lack of bread in every town, yet you have not returned to me," declares the LORD.

AMOS 4:6

Once when I lived in the north and temperatures were bitterly cold, a friend joked, "I sure could use a little global warming right now."

While it was just a joke, it is amazing how often we humans are willing to sacrifice the precious in order to keep ourselves more marginally comfortable. Our frenzy to consume and our bottomless need for new experiences even threatens to shrink the expanses of potentially holy ground in our lives.

We don't take time to cultivate depth, but skate across the surface of experience. With no patience to tend messy relationships with flawed neighbors, we crave the latest "news" about celebrities who exemplify superficiality. We think of God not as our reason for living, but as one more means to an end.

It isn't a new trend, this frustration over the emptiness of the human condition when God is left out. Amos quotes the Lord as saying, "I gave you empty stomachs in every city and lack of bread in every town, yet you have not returned to me." Failing to appreciate the depth with which God loves us, we seek satisfaction by continually consuming and consuming and consuming. Meanwhile, the potentially sacred evaporates around us like a glacier receding year by year.

But at least the weather is warming up . . .

Ever

For I am convinced that neither death nor life, neither angels nor demons, neither the present nor the future, nor any powers, neither height nor depth, nor anything else in all creation, will be able to separate us from the love of God that is in Christ Jesus our Lord.

ROMANS 8: 38-40

During a classic sports match, one sportscaster described the match as "something none of us will ever forget for a long, long time." Use of the word "ever," though, seemed to make the phrase "long, long time" unnecessary.

Often we speak of "ever" and eternity as if eternity could be equated with a long, long time. But to me, eternity is outside of time, a transcendence of the need to participate in time at all. Such transcendence echoes through the words, "we are more than conquerors through him who loved us." Instead of promising that we'll be the best conquerors, God makes us "more than conquerors" by empowering us to step outside of this world into eternity through loving God and neighbor.

For one who loves, "neither height nor depth, nor anything else in all creation, will be able to separate us from the love of God that is in Christ Jesus." We are no longer subject to time, space and other mortal constraints; the love of God lifts us above them. I can't let this world weigh on me, knowing that nothing can separate me from the love of God in Christ Jesus. Nothing.

Ever.

FEBRUARY 6

He is not sleeping

"But you remain the same, and your years will never end. The children of your servants will live in your presence; their descendants will be established before you."

PSALM 102:27-28

I read once of a nation whose leader had been completely incapacitated by a stroke. Even though he was still alive, the nation grieved for him. One citizen said of the people's trust during his years of leadership, "They knew they could sleep at night because he was not sleeping."

I sleep well at night because I know God is not sleeping. It isn't so much that I think He will prevent all calamities from befalling me here. It is more that I know the worst of times here do not change the fact that I belong to God, and I am loved by God, and I have the capability to be with God at any moment I choose.

Whatever happens here, today, I have hope because I rest in God. I know that He "remains the same," and that His "years never end." I know that when I live in His presence, I leave a legacy of love that will endure forever, and that love allows the next person to also live in God's presence.

God watches over me, through the times of my life that are tragic, or joyful, or somewhere in between. So whatever happens today, and whatever might happen tomorrow, I can rest in the constancy, the tenderness of God's embrace. I know I will sleep well at day's end.

God has the watch for this night.

FEBRUARY 7

Melting the ice

. . . live a life worthy of the calling you have received. Be completely humble and gentle; be patient, bearing with one another in love. . . . There is one body and one Spirit. . . .

EPHESIANS 4:1-2, 4

In the movie *March of the Penguins,* the creatures, desperate for food after bearing their young, struggle to return to the sea where they can feed. All along the journey, the life-giving sea remains just a few feet below them, buried beneath impenetrable ice. If the ice were to melt, they could be fed immediately.

Some days I feel that I'm trudging across ice, desperately hungry, miles from anything that can fill me, not realizing I have the power to melt that ice. When I force myself, in a self-pitying moment, to think of another person instead of myself, I immediately connect to the life-giving presence of God and offer that presence to another. I choose to "live a life worthy of the calling I have received" to love in God's name. Part of the "one body, one Spirit" of God, I simultaneously feed myself and others in the body of Christ.

The nourishment I need is not miles away across a frozen ice floe, but right here, within a few feet of the place where I struggle. I need only move those few feet, to a person in need, to say, "God is here for you." Acting as the presence of Christ to another human being melts the ice completely, and I am not only fed.

I become part of the life-giving sea.

FEBRUARY 8

Tracking

... we constantly pray for you, that our God may count you worthy of his calling, and that by his power he may fulfill every good purpose of yours and every act prompted by your faith.

2 THESSALONIANS 1:11

After ordering a product online, I used the "Track Your Package" link through the company's website to follow the package's progression. It traveled through Utah, Colorado, Kansas, and Texas, and I knew exactly the day the package would arrive.

Unfortunately, such detailed "tracking" is not available to us spiritually. Once I express compassion for someone or share God's presence with another person, I have no way of knowing where that gift might go. It might go nowhere. It might change a life.

The good news is that I'm not responsible for results; I am only asked to be faithful to the tasks that God puts before me today. God is the source of my compassion, the source of any light shining through me. So any good which results from something I do is not my work at all, but God's, and it is God's concern where that gift goes from here. It is "by his power [that] he may fulfill every good purpose of yours and every act prompted by your faith." His power, not mine.

So I'm trying now to learn to turn off the need to track every action I take by asking, "Did it do any good?" I have been obedient. I have sent the gift.

The rest is God's business.

FEBRUARY 9

But it's cold out there

Then I said . . . "I desire to do your will, O my God; your law is within my heart.". . . I speak of your faithfulness and salvation. I do not conceal your love and your truth from the great assembly.

PSALM 40:7-9

When the temperature outside is in the single digits, and the wind chill below zero, I linger under the toasty covers. I finally get up, though, because I can't get much done by staying only where it's comfortable.

As religion has developed, I wonder if people saw God's law as that nice, warm safe, but confining place. It is comforting to hold the law within the heart, knowing exactly whether you have done right or wrong, and whether your neighbor has done right or wrong. It is also a very small place to live.

But when it becomes clear that living for God is about more than rules—that it's about loving beyond the rules, and even loving those who break the rules—the world becomes much bigger and in some ways much colder. It would be so much easier to say someone who broke a commandment gets no consideration. It is much more difficult to love persons—even ourselves—when the rules have been broken, to show God's "love and truth to the great assembly" by embracing all persons instead of just the rule-followers. Certainly I would love to stay in this small, warm place, but I have to go outside where it's cold.

God and I have things to do out there.

FEBRUARY 10

Plans

For I know the plans I have for you," declares the LORD, "plans to prosper you and not to harm you, plans to give you hope and a future. . . . I will gather you from all the nations and places where I have banished you," declares the LORD, "and will bring you back to the place from which I carried you into exile."

JEREMIAH 29:11-14

One of my nephews has gotten into the home-building business, an achievement that I simply cannot fathom. I cannot imagine looking at a piece of land, a set of plans and a stack of building supplies and turning them into a place to live.

I also often have trouble imagining what God can do with a life. I sometimes think nothing good can come of certain circumstances. And yet somehow, God in God's grace has wrought miracles in every possible combination of spiritual real estate and building supplies. He has done it because *he* has plans for each of us to live not in exile, but at home, where we can thrive and live in peace.

I have always found great hope in the idea that God would say to me, "For I know the plans I have for you . . . plans to prosper you and not to harm you." I should find hope, too, in knowing that God also has such plans for others. No matter what mistakes someone has made, or what limitations that person perceives, God can work miracles. God can look at any property and, with *his* divine plans, build a dwelling place. He doesn't do it only for us.

After all, when the place is built, God plans to live there with us.

FEBRUARY 11

All that stuff

In their fright the women bowed down with their faces to the ground, but the men [at the tomb] said to them, "Why do you look for the living among the dead?"

LUKE 24:5

A warning light keeps coming on in my car to indicate that the passenger's safety belt isn't fastened. Actually, there usually is no passenger; it's just that I carry so much weight in books and other stuff in that seat that the car's computer thinks it must be a person.

It's frighteningly easy to treat things with as much importance as persons, to confuse things with people. But despite all the time and energy I use on "stuff," I will never find life in inanimate objects, either in possessing them or controlling them. I will also never find or give God's love if I treat people like objects—tools to make my life better. In the great grand scheme, things don't matter at all; people do.

Trying to make myself feel better and more important by owning or controlling things or people is "looking for the living among the dead." Too much of the time, when I feel the weight of the world is on me, that weight comes not from concern over people, but from concern over things: getting them, keeping them, paying for them, displaying them.

That approach is not life-giving, but life-draining. Why do I do it? Why do I let the transitory things of this earth drag me down and keep me from being with God?

Why do I look for the living among the dead?

The unspoken Word

[Some Greeks] came to Philip... with a request. "Sir," they said, "we would like to see Jesus."

JOHN 12:21

On a TV drama, a worker chastised her superior for violating "an unwritten policy." He told her, "I'm the boss. I *write* the unwritten policy."

I find that it is easy to think in that passive way, to focus on what "is written" instead of asking who the writer is. It's easy and comfortable, for example, for me to tell someone, "You are loved." But I become vulnerable when I use the active voice, uttering the words, "I love you."

People, weary of hearing "of" Jesus passively, wanted to see him in the flesh. And they weren't interested in religious law or practice; they wanted to see this man who accepted and loved and healed the people whom society marginalized. So they came to Philip and said simply, "Sir, we would like to see Jesus."

We all want to see Jesus, God incarnate walking among us, touching us when others walk away. The Christian faith is a faith lived in the active voice, a faith of actively loving other human beings, not simply assuring them, "You are loved."

Human words don't reassure me nearly as much as do embraces, acceptance, forgiveness, compassion. Don't tell me I am loved. *Love* me. I don't want to hear words. I don't want directions to a church. I want to see the One who actively loves me. I would like to see Jesus.

He's the One who speaks the unspoken Word.

FEBRUARY 13

The unfinished puzzle

[The LORD] took him outside and said, "Look up at the heavens and count the stars—if indeed you can count them." Then he said to him, "So shall your offspring be." Abram believed the LORD, and he credited it to him as righteousness.

GENESIS 15:5-6

On an airplane one night, I leafed through the in-flight magazine. The back page held a crossword puzzle, about half of it finished. A note on the page suggested that the reader take the magazine rather than leaving it with a partially finished puzzle.

In seeking God, I am constantly asked to struggle with partially completed puzzles. Centuries of human scientific success have convinced us that everything is solvable, so we're not crazy about the idea of accepting mystery in seeking the divine. But in order to embrace God, I have to embrace mystery. Any so-called puzzle that I can solve entirely is simply not God, but something else. Something less.

Abram could not understand how he would receive the gift of children at his age. Yet he "believed the LORD," and God "credited it to him as righteousness." The puzzle made no sense to Abram, but he believed—he trusted—that God in His mystery would give him offspring as numerous as the stars.

How can such miracles happen? Why would God be so generous to me, despite my flawed human nature? Given the state of the world today, how can this puzzle possibly be completed and perfected?

It's a mystery to me.

FEBRUARY 14

True love

Now we see but a poor reflection as in a mirror; then we shall see face to face. Now I know in part; then I shall know fully, even as I am fully known. And now these three remain: faith, hope and love. But the greatest of these is love.

1 CORINTHIANS 13:12-13

So what's the story here, in our giving each other flowers and candy to celebrate Valentine's Day, the day we celebrate love for one another? What is the concept behind presenting sweet tastes and sweet fragrances in the name of love?

The truth, though, is that inviting true love—not the flawed, often manipulative love of humans but the pure love of God—does make life sweeter. If I know that I am truly, deeply loved, and that I cannot change that love by my mistakes, then I am truly, deeply free.

In those too-rare moments when I genuinely love another human being, with no thought of gain or self-interest, I allow God to be reflected in me. And when another human being loves and forgives me despite my mistakes and the things I have done to hurt others, I see the reflection—albeit imperfect—of the perfect love of God.

So we offer, on this day celebrating love, imperfect human offerings in an attempt to express the inexpressible to those we love. We don't quite know how to love fully and unconditionally, as God loves us. So we do the best we can. We send flowers. We give sweets.

Perhaps we're saying that nothing can make life sweeter and more fragrant than the knowledge that we are truly and deeply and unconditionally loved.

FEBRUARY 15

Loving the sad songs

When Moses came down from Mount Sinai . . . he was not aware that his face was radiant because he had spoken with the LORD.

EXODUS 34:29

From the day I got my first CD burner, I have been trying to make for myself a collection of such equally loved songs that I never want to skip a track or replay one. I want to make the perfect CD.

Now that I think about it, I'd like for my life to work that same way, to love each moment so much that I'm not rewinding to relive times I regret—or regret losing—and so much that I'm not "wishing my life away" to get to the good stuff. I want to remember constantly that I can be in God's presence, my face shining with His light no matter what's going on in my earthly life. Unfortunately, I'm not that faithful yet; I'm not even close.

Plenty of times, I feel radiant because "I have just spoken with the LORD," or have at least been very aware of His presence in my life. But plenty of other times, I have been down, trying to fast-forward, to skip difficult times to get to the good stuff.

And yet, I am learning that, in those strangely low but holy moments, God's nearness is palpable, as my ego and self-centeredness have been left aside. I am learning that even a face streaming with tears of sadness can shine with the radiance of God. I am learning that life in the valley can be just as holy as life on the mountaintop.

I am learning to love the sad songs, too.

Ruby red slippers

Record my lament; list my tears on your scroll—are they not in your record? Then my enemies will turn back when I call for help.

PSALM 56:8-9

I once saw a little girl wearing sparkly red shoes which looked exactly like the ruby red slippers Dorothy wore in *The Wizard of Oz*. I wondered if she had seen the movie and wanted the magical power always to click her heels and go home.

When I'm in trouble or feeling beat up, I, too, crave that magical power. I wish I could do something as simple as clicking my heels together to return to a safe place. And yet, as a seeker and lover of God, I do have that power through Him. It isn't magic, but simple trust that God will lift me above this world's frightening or hurtful circumstances.

I honestly believe that my "lament" is heard by God and answered with transcendence over this world, not at the end of life, but right here in the middle of it. I believe that He has "listed my tears on His scroll," that He cares for me now, today, in the midst of this world.

Trusting God is the power of transcendence over this world, the way to go home. When I click my heels and remember that nothing in this world can overcome God's power in my life, then my soul finds comfort, at home with Him. Suddenly, whisked away from my enemies to the place where God lives, I learn a truth every bit as life-saving as ruby red slippers.

There's no place like Him.

FEBRUARY 17

Day by day

Devote yourselves to prayer, being watchful and thankful.

COLOSSIANS 4:2

Though I can't remember the product advertised, I saw a commercial in which two longtime friends spoke of their weddings. One said she took two years to plan her wedding, while the friend took two weeks. The second friend lamented, "And we both ended up divorced."

Too often we worship the banner moments of relationships and fail to tend to the day-to-day aspects of those relationships. And it's true not only of glorifying weddings over marriages; that kind of prioritization happens in all sorts of relationships. The "falling-in-love" aspect, whether with an earthly partner or with God, is the fun part, while the work it takes to compromise and to love someone else above yourself is the hard part. The big moment takes panache, while the long-term relationship takes hard work and humility.

When we are admonished to "Devote yourselves to prayer," we are asked to value loving over falling in love, to tend, daily, our relationship with God. In prayer we find guidance, peace, and strength to get through the everyday hard work of loving God and loving neighbor. In prayer, we can be "watchful and thankful," constantly seeking God's will, constantly thanking God for saving us from this world and from ourselves. Everyone wants to fall in love.

But it takes courage to *love*, day after day after day.

Back seat

The LORD had said to Abram, "Leave your country, your people and your father's household and go to the land I will show you . . ."
GENESIS 12:1

On the road one day, I glanced over at a passing car and saw a child lying asleep across the front seat, his head on the driver's lap. While it was a sweet sight, it also made me fearful for the child's safety. I have heard too many stories about children who are unnecessarily hurt in accidents because they are not "properly restrained."

The place that the child wants to be is not always best for that child. Sometimes the parent has to insist that the child go somewhere or do something uncomfortable or unpleasant. I present my wishes to God, asking Him to grant them, but even I know that getting everything I would wish for—being "improperly restrained"—is often not in my best interest.

It could not have been easy for Abram to follow the Lord's instructions, to leave his country, his people, and his father's household to travel to a place he had never seen. Like the child asleep in the front seat, he must have wanted to stay somewhere comfortable and familiar rather than changing his entire life.

It's often uncomfortable, that place God asks me to go. I'd rather stay here, napping, oblivious to what the larger world holds. But God loves me, and He will not let me stay in a place that is not good for me.

So what I want has to take a back seat.

FEBRUARY 19

The open door

But since we belong to the day, let us be self-controlled, putting on faith and love as a breastplate, and the hope of salvation as a helmet. For God did not appoint us to suffer wrath but to receive salvation through our Lord Jesus Christ.

1 THESSALONIANS 5:8-9

One day I walked down the hall of a building, hoping a particular office would be open. Before I got there, though, I knew it was open, as I could see light from the office streaming out into the hall. I knew the door was open before I could even see the door.

I often feel that the peace and goodness shining out of one Christian heart can function in that same way. Someone else out there in the world may not yet be able to discern that there is a door to God, or even that there is a God. But a glimpse of light shining out may give a person, otherwise filled with despair or anger, hope that something better might exist.

Amid this world's darkness, salvation is not having to "suffer wrath" until life's end when God will save me. Salvation is knowing, in this moment, that the things of God overcome the things of this world, "For God did not appoint us to suffer wrath but to receive salvation through our Lord Jesus Christ." Sometimes I myself can't even see that door, but I can see the light of Christ, shining from God's people out into the darkness. The light tells me that door is there.

And that it is open, for me.

FEBRUARY 20

It has my name on it

... some people brought to [Jesus] a man who was deaf and could hardly talk, and they begged him to place his hand on the man. After he took him aside, away from the crowd ...

MARK 7:32-33

I saw a TV story about a homeless man who had to receive his mail at the address, "General delivery." Unlike the rest of us, who complain about junk mail, he enjoyed it. "It's something with my name on it," the man said. "I appreciate it."

I have days when I need to know that someone knows my name, to see anything with my name on it, even junk. In a world of mass production and marketing, knowing that another person is concerned about me—personally—can change the trajectory of the day. In extreme cases, for people who hurt deeply, feeling personally cared about may even change the trajectory of a life.

Jesus cared not about the crowd, but about the person. He performed acts of healing so personal that they had someone's name on them, although surely He could have invoked divine healing power on the entire crowd at once. When He encountered "a man who was deaf and could hardly talk," He chose to "take him aside, away from the crowd."

Christ heals me because He focuses His eyes and His attention on me, not on the illness, and not on the crowd. He sees all that has broken me, and He makes me whole. In other words, the healing that Christ brings to me has my name on it.

And I appreciate it.

FEBRUARY 21

Getting used to it

A man with leprosy came to him and begged him on his knees, "If you are willing, you can make me clean." Filled with compassion, Jesus reached out his hand and touched the man. "I am willing," he said. "Be clean!"

MARK 1:40-41

After brutal cold, snow, sleet, and then flooding rains, I said to a local resident, "I am so sick of being cold." She said, "You get used to it." But I don't want to get used to it. I want to go home. I want to be warm.

The human psyche has a remarkable capacity to "get used to it," to accept circumstances and live life with almost unimaginable burdens. In Jesus' time, a man with leprosy dared not even hope that his life could change, that he could stop getting used to it and become clean and whole. So he couched his request to Jesus with, "If you are willing . . ."

Implicit in that statement, for me, is a hidden question, "If you're willing—and able—to make me whole, why did I have to suffer in the first place?" The mystery of God's workings in the world escapes my intellect and my soul. The only answer I can manage is that God knows that whatever suffering I endure here is temporary, that I am protected and whole in God's arms, in this time and in eternity.

With God's peace in my heart, I can endure a great deal, perhaps even with minimal complaint. But honestly, I want to be home, with God. I want to be warm.

So no matter how cold this world can be, I refuse to get used to it.

FEBRUARY 22

Written on human hearts

You show that you are a letter from Christ, the result of our ministry, written not with ink but with the Spirit of the living God, not on tablets of stone but on tablets of human hearts.

2 CORINTHIANS 3:3

The first time I donated blood, I had an experience that was at once scary and reassuring. After donating, I became light-headed when I stopped at a restaurant on the way home. A family having their child's birthday party there helped me, bringing me something to drink, a cookie, fruit, then lunch. They would not let me pay them back.

I felt that I had caught a very personal and life-giving glimpse of the "Spirit of the living God, not on tablets of stone but on tablets of human hearts." Those people could have done much less. They could have done nothing at all. They could have accepted payment.

Instead, they cared for me, expecting nothing in return, then moved on without reward. I think it's the way the kingdom of God on earth is supposed to work. I had done my small part to help by donating blood, which left me a little shaky, and the next person came along to hold me up. I'd like to think that someone else will hold up those generous and loving people when they need help down the road.

All I know is that, on that day, I caught a glimpse of the Christ, the Spirit of the living God. I almost didn't recognize Him.

He was wearing a balloon animal on His head.

FEBRUARY 23

Hungry

"The days are coming," declares the Sovereign LORD, "when I will send a famine through the land—not a famine of food or a thirst for water, but a famine of hearing the words of the LORD. Men will stagger from sea to sea and wander from north to east, searching for the word of the LORD, but they will not find it."

AMOS 8:11-12

In the novel *The Kite Runner*, a man declares that all sins are forms of stealing. He maintains, for example, that murder steals a life, that adultery steals a spouse. Every sinful act goes back to stealing.

I sometimes think that all forms of hunger can be distilled down into one specific hunger: the hunger for God. Whenever I feel an emptiness and try to fill that void with food, with material things, with job success, with more human relationships, then I am hungering not so much for food, things, success, or human love, but for God.

That "mistaken identity" in the source of my hunger explains why consumption of so many other things leaves me still feeling empty. It explains why getting more and more of the things of this world leaves me only frustrated, not filled. It explains why my soul feels empty even when my schedule is maddeningly full. In an effort to fill a God-sized space with human-sized food, I "stagger from sea to sea and wander from north to east," and nothing on this earth can take away the hunger. Nothing on this earth.

Only God can fill me.

FEBRUARY 24

Getting home

I have been crucified with Christ and I no longer live, but Christ lives in me. The life I live in the body, I live by faith in the Son of God, who loved me and gave himself for me.

GALATIANS 2:20

While in seminary, I often had to fly home for visits, so, I had no car. Friends there not only allowed me to stay in their homes, but loaned me cars. Their generosity amazes and fills me with gratitude, knowing what such things would have cost me. In fact, if I had been forced to pay for those gifts, I could never have gone home.

My gratitude comes not only from the gifts themselves, but from the knowledge that those friends truly live in and embrace the presence of God in their lives. For when I or any other human does the good and generous and moral thing, it is not our gift that is in action, but "Christ [who] lives in me." We are flawed and mortal human beings, but we are made immortal and perfect when Christ lives in us.

There is, after all, no commandment that says, "Thou shalt open thy heart and home." There is the spirit of Christ, animating and empowering us to love with generosity and grace. By "drawing near to worship" God and embracing what God teaches us in Christ, my friends are being made perfect in that generosity and grace. I am, literally, eternally grateful for people who allow God to act through them in such ways. I am grateful for God's generosity.

If I had been forced to pay for such gifts, I never would have gotten home.

FEBRUARY 25

Up, up, and away

... God is light; in him there is no darkness at all. If we claim to have fellowship with him yet walk in the darkness, we lie and do not live by the truth. But if we walk in the light, as he is in the light, we have fellowship with one another. ...

1 JOHN 1:5-7

One day, the car in front of me had a helium balloon inside it. It bobbed insistently against the ceiling as the driver pushed at it to keep it out of the way. But the helium in the balloon was only trying to do what it was made to do: rise to the sky.

Sometimes I have that same frustration of wanting to fly but being held unnaturally down in a cramped space. I want to do the good and Godly thing, but some part of me also longs to win, to show I'm right, to bring someone else down so that I can look as if I'm rising. My soul is made for God, made to climb above this world, yet I allow obstacles to trap me here, on this earth.

That deep longing to rise and to lift others up is the lightness of God within me, bumping against the ceiling of living in this world. In answering the longing for God—loving a person I want to best or denigrate—I free myself from the cramped, human condition and join my Creator in the unbounded free place.

When I leave the junk behind, it's amazing how quickly my heart can escape the hurts of this world. Freed of ego and woundedness—healed and made whole in God—I can finally do what I am made to do.

I can rise to the sky.

FEBRUARY 26

Well qualified or not

For the message of the cross is foolishness to those who are perishing, but to us who are being saved it is the power of God.

1 CORINTHIANS 1:18

A car dealer's ads offered incredibly low interest rates as an attention-getter, but a footnote to the offer indicated that it was only for "well-qualified customers." In other words, a person struggling economically—the person most in need of a break—was much less likely to get that break than a financially successful person.

The world feels unfair most of the time. Those who have more get more, and those who have less lose more. As the body of Christ, though, we Christians are, at once, set apart from this world and living smack in the midst of it. We are to have an "otherness" about us, emphasizing only love of God and love of neighbor and eschewing worldly success if it compromises that way of life. And we don't have to qualify to be with God. Such an idea makes no sense to human ways; "the message of the cross is foolishness" to those who value things and relationships ahead of God.

I have an inordinate love for material things, but I know, by experience, that I only find peace when my self-image comes from within, emanating from the image of God within me. When I stop measuring myself by my acquisitive success, my heart is much more at peace, a peace available to me every day, every moment.

And not only if I have been declared "well qualified."

Don't blame me...

... Aaron answered. "[These people] said to me, 'Make us gods who will go before us...' So I told them, 'Whoever has any gold jewelry, take it off.' Then they gave me the gold, and I threw it into the fire, and out came this calf!"

EXODUS 32:23-24

I keep saying I don't have time to get needed new tires on my car. Someday soon, though, when I'm by the side of the road with a flat, I'll probably claim to be the victim of very unfortunate circumstances when in fact I have some control.

I employ the victim gambit often, ignoring the fact that there's much I can do to prevent being left by the side of the road. I could've prayed about decisions instead of making them precipitously. I could remember that I am defined by who I am in God, and not by who I am in the world.

Aaron tried the Old Testament version of the victim mentality, acting as if he had no control over his own plight. He protested, "Then they gave me the gold, and I threw it in the fire, and out came this calf!" He could've said to them, "Worship God, not gold," but he did not. He was no victim.

Like Aaron, we often forget that we exacerbate our own problems by failing to trust God, and by playing the games this earthly existence pressures us to play. The truth is that if we trust God above all else, we will never, ever have to play the victim again, because we will transcend this world.

But don't point that out the next time you see me stranded on the side of the road.

Reconciling

Hate what is evil; cling to what is good. . . . Honor one another above yourselves. . . . Bless those who persecute you; bless and do not curse. Rejoice with those who rejoice; mourn with those who mourn.

ROMANS 12:9-15

The more I see of God, the more my definition of the word "reconciling" has changed. Once I thought of admonitions to live a good life as payments to God to earn salvation, as in reconciling a checkbook or a financial account. Now, though, I have come to believe that "reconciling" means living in peace, becoming vulnerable and open to the other.

When we stop balancing the books and start living in gratitude for the grace of God, we begin subtly to "hate what is evil" and "cling to what is good." We help and honor each other, and not because we can balance the books or pay God for anything. We do it simply to remember and honor and express gratitude for the grace of God.

When we are reconciled to God, we find reconciliation with other human beings. We live in peace, and we are fully and graciously present to the persons in our lives, even those who persecute us. We "rejoice with those who rejoice," and "mourn with those who mourn."

The books were balanced long ago, in one man's decision, in AD 33, to value love above all else, even above his own survival. Those books have already been reconciled on our behalf. And because of that faithfulness, we, too, can be reconciled to one another.

And we can do it simply because of the magnificent grace of God.

March

MARCH 1

Dance lessons

But now, by dying to what once bound us, we have been released from the law so that we serve in the new way of the Spirit, and not in the old way of the written code. What shall we say, then? Is the law sin? Certainly not! Indeed I would not have known what sin was except through the law.

ROMANS 7:6-7

I have seen pictures of dance studios which had shoe-shaped outlines on the floor to indicate dance steps. The footprints were numbered so that the brand-new student of dancing could see, in graphic form, the places to move each foot and the order in which to make those moves. It's hard to look at those numbered footsteps, though, and think of dancing.

I wonder if God first gave people the law as numbered footprints to teach us how to live a life that holds meaning in eternity. In commandments, God has given us a starting place, a way of understanding in a step-by-step way how to begin this dance. Ultimately, though, we are called to "dying to what once bound us" so that "we serve in the new way of the Spirit."

When we finally begin to understand what God asks of us, we move far beyond what is called for by the law. We not only obey the rules, but we extend compassion and mercy to persons around us. We sacrifice the priorities of this world to be with God. The law teaches us the basic steps, how to proceed toward God in a stiff and rote kind of movement.

But it takes grace to look at those numbered footprints and see how to dance.

MARCH 2

Dare (the) devil act

[Jesus] shared in their humanity so that by his death he might destroy him who holds the power of death—that is, the devil—and free those who all their lives were held in slavery by their fear of death.

HEBREWS 2:14-15

A program on TV shows people braving "epic" conditions; the subjects of the show speak with exhilaration about intentionally confronting such challenges as sharks, extreme temperatures, and avalanches. They seem anxious to push their lives right up to the brink of death, all for a thrill.

To me, the true Christian life is more courageous than any other "daredevil" act. When I choose to be loving instead of being "right" or vengeful, then I go over the brink, dying a bit to myself and living more fully for God. Since Christ embraced the death of self fully and permanently, all Christians try to "die to ourselves" in order to live for God. Such choices make a person look weak or unsuccessful in others' eyes, so making those choices requires courage.

If I can completely let go of transitory priorities to embrace God fully, I am no longer "held in slavery by my fear of death." When I care only for God, then losses in this world do not hold me captive. I am free of living according to human whim. I am free of living in slavery to temporal and meaningless things. I am free of the one "who holds the power of death—that is, the devil."

So, how's that for a daredevil act?

Put us under

But Joseph said to them, "Don't be afraid. Am I in the place of God? You intended to harm me, but God intended it for good to accomplish what is now being done, the saving of many lives. . . ."

GENESIS 50:19-20

I once saw a movie in which a little girl, making up an initiation ceremony, invoked words from the marriage service. But instead of saying, "What God has joined together, let no man put asunder. . . ." she intoned, "Let no man put us under."

All of this world's human pain and thoughtlessness—the people who try to "put us under"—cannot ultimately triumph over God. But it can be difficult to think of God at all in this culture built on competition, in a continual battle against those who try to best us. In business, recreation, or relationships, someone is continually trying to put us under.

Joseph's brothers tried to vanquish him, and when their schemes failed, they feared that Joseph would bring revenge down on their heads. Instead, his refuge was God; he knew God would redeem him, and the circumstances, by bringing some good of others' attempts to hurt him.

While we will certainly experience pain and loss in this world, ultimately we will be with God. The transitory nature of all we know here will mean nothing when we stand in His presence. So yes, in the natural world, in the physical human sense, other humans can, and will, "put us under."

They just can't make us stay there.

MARCH 4

Mystery lesson

. . . God will save Zion and rebuild the cities of Judah. Then people will settle there and possess it; the children of his servants will inherit it, and those who love his name will dwell there.

PSALM 69:35-36

Several times I have seen a commercial for high-tech television featuring an airhead girl as spokesperson. She described the service available in very technical terms, then said, "I totally don't know what that means, but I want it."

That sense of confused longing captures exactly the way I feel when I read descriptions of God's plans for the future. In the present, I continually see scenes that make no sense: evil apparently being rewarded, good seemingly being punished, unnecessary suffering. So I can't figure out what God is doing in the present, much less decipher promises in Scripture about our future with Him.

And yet, somehow, the deepest part of me longs for that unknowable and mysterious life with God. I long for a place where everyone seeks God, where all creatures, including all human ones, know and live with their Creator. I choose simply to embrace the mystery of God, and the mysterious promise of a future in God's very presence.

I have no idea why God would allow unfaithful creatures like me to be with Him in eternity. Yet somehow I do believe that all of us who love His name will dwell with Him.

I totally don't know what that means. But I want it.

MARCH 5

A dollar's worth of Shakespeare

For he will deliver the needy who cry out, the afflicted who have no one to help. He will take pity on the weak and the needy and save the needy from death. He will rescue them from oppression and violence, for precious is their blood in his sight.

PSALM 72:12-14

One evening, I was approached on the street by a homeless woman who offered to recite Shakespeare for me if I would give her a dollar. Like all such encounters, it shook me, confused me, frightened me. It rattled my preconceptions of homeless people; they're not supposed to know Shakespeare. Should I give her money? Am I helping something or enabling something? Why do I want to run or turn my eyes away?

I suppose I want to run away from that kind of situation because I feel guilty that I have so much and others have so little. I read that God will "deliver the needy who cry out," and I have to wonder if He delivers them through me and other people frightened and confused by the condition of poor and homeless people in our society. And yet, knowing I can't save the world, I go into gridlock about saving one person from the cold of one night.

I have no answers. My deepest hope is that I will someday see such people with God's eyes, whatever that means, and that I will help as God would have me help. I can start by not thinking of them as "them," but as children of God whose "blood is precious in his sight."

But how can I see them if I always look away?

To be loved is no easy thing

Humble yourselves, therefore, under God's mighty hand, that he may lift you up in due time. Cast all your anxiety on him because he cares for you. . . . And the God of all grace, who called you to his eternal glory in Christ . . . will himself restore you . . .

1 PETER 5:6-7, 10

In one series of scenes in the movie *Elizabeth*, the queen's enforcers deal harshly with those who had plotted against her. One traitor is a man who had loved her; when she asks why he had betrayed her, he says, "It is no easy thing to be loved by a queen."

Sometimes it is no easy thing to be loved by someone powerful who knows our flaws and loves us anyway. It would seem to make life easy, to say that I am loved no matter what I do, but in fact it can make life very difficult. When I fail someone who loves me nonetheless, my disappointment and guilt are more profound than if I get what I deserve.

But even the burden of anxiety over being loved by my Creator no matter what I do is an anxiety that God carries for me. If I humble myself "under God's mighty hand that he may lift me up in due time," God will "restore me" and comfort me.

When I look at the mistakes of my past, and the mistakes of my present, I wonder why God continues to embrace me. If human measures were used, I would have been lost, but at least my life would be simpler. Dark, hopeless, tragic—but simpler.

It is no easy thing to be loved by the God of all grace.

MARCH 7

For good

When Jesus saw [the crippled woman], he... said to her, "Woman, you are set free from your infirmity." Then he put his hands on her, and immediately she straightened up and praised God.

LUKE 13:12-13

I have often wondered why, in English, we so often speak of a permanent change as something that has changed "for good." Why describe something lasting as taken care of "for good"?

Perhaps the phrase reveals our human instinct to equate eternity with good; in our depths, we ache to enter eternity by loving God and our fellow humans. I know that I have learned, after decades, that the things in my life cannot last. But taking care of other people lasts. Knowing that I am cared for by other people lasts. The spark of God within my heart, and within every human heart that loves, lasts.

The woman Jesus healed had been crippled for 18 years. When she was healed, "immediately she straightened up and praised God." She knew that the gift she received was not a temporary fix, but a result of God's goodness, a healing that would last "for good."

All of us suffer; some of us simply adjust to or hide our suffering better than others. And while we aren't all cured in human, physical terms, we can all be healed by the tender, loving touch of God through other humans. And such healing isn't temporal; through God, we are touched by eternity and healed forever.

We are healed for good.

Junkers

God is not unjust; he will not forget your work and the love you have shown him as you have helped his people and continue to help them.
HEBREWS 6:10-12

A few years ago, I saw an interesting sight way up on a hill overlooking the interstate highway. An advertisement for an automobile junkyard showed four or five wrecked cars stacked on top of each other. The business is designed to provide parts to help cars run, and yet it was advertised by cars that were damaged, seemingly beyond repair.

In that junkyard display, I saw the grace of a God who uses the imperfection of the human soul to give hope to other imperfect souls. God doesn't use perfect persons to display His grace and power. He uses flawed people like me, people who long for God but cannot sustain a way of life that is truly faithful to God.

God could easily have created perfect machines requiring no spare parts, no repair. But He chose to create us, knowing how imperfectly we will use the free will He gives us, knowing that even the best of us will fall away. God would love for us to love Him perfectly. He "is not unjust," though, and He will "not overlook your work and the love that you showed for his sake."

Despite the love we show for God's sake, we are all inept, and badly in need of repair. We are certainly not perfect machines.

We are, however, perfect advertisements for a God of grace, a God of forgiveness.

MARCH 9

The jab and the Cross

Grace, mercy and peace from God the Father and from Jesus Christ, the Father's Son, will be with us in truth and love. . . . I am not writing you a new command but one we have had from the beginning. I ask that we love one another.

2 JOHN 1:3,5

For a time, I went to the gym for instruction on boxing, as I thought that boxing (with a bag, not an opponent) would be a fun, vigorous way to get in shape. The instructor showed me techniques for several punches; my jab and hook are mediocre, but she said I have a great cross.

The experience brought to mind all of the ways that we defend ourselves emotionally and spiritually. We all have weapons—some more effective than others—to convince ourselves that we're okay and that our lives have significance. I usually rely on the jab: on biting, unspoken, but still very real criticism played out in my mind. I love people, but often in my insecurity, I disparage someone else to feel better about myself.

But the "Grace, mercy, and peace from God the Father and from Jesus Christ" mean that I need no weapons, no punches to bring others down. Thanks to the Cross and resurrection, I am a child of God. I can ascend to God, safely above the fight down here, by obeying the old command "that we love one another." Being a Christian makes it unnecessary for me to attack other people in order to feel more confident. So in this fight, I can safely leave my jab behind.

I can rely on the Cross.

Be loved

For [God] chose us in him before the creation of the world to be holy and blameless in his sight. In love he predestined us to be adopted as his sons through Jesus Christ, in accordance with his pleasure and will—to the praise of his glorious grace, which he has freely given us in the One he loves.

EPHESIANS 1:4-6

One day I started thinking about the word "beloved." I have long felt myself as the "beloved" of God, but I never thought about the word itself. I never really noticed the "be-" part.

In our fast culture, so occupied with impressing each other, we don't "let ourselves be" enough. When someone says they're busy, I want to prove that I'm busier. When someone expresses stress, I have to try to show that my stress is greater.

But I hate playing the "one-up" game. And since God "chose me in [Christ] before the creation of the world" and "predestined" me to be God's child through Christ, it means that I was loved by God before I did anything. So the key in feeling cherished is not found in what I do, but in being: being loved by God.

So if I don't measure up in the world's eyes, or in the eyes of the judgmental part of myself, I will not try to "win." I will not explain my excuses for not measuring up. I will not try to prove that someone else is wrong: that I do measure up.

I am not what I do. I am not what I own. I am not what others approve me to be. I am the beloved of God. Let me be.

Let me be loved.

The lake's secrets

So God created man in his own image, in the image of God he created him; male and female he created them.

GENESIS 1:27

Drought in Florida once shrank Lake Okeechobee so much that 3000 years of history were revealed, archaeological evidence long concealed by the lake's waters. When rains came to the area, much of that archaeological find was again submerged.

The times in my life which have seemed, spiritually speaking, "drought-stricken" are also the times in which the treasures of the past have been revealed. When my earthly life became so difficult and so desperate that I realized I could not save myself, I began to see the light of God. The presence of God, within me and around me, was simply not something I recognized when I thought I was the center of the universe.

Lying within the depths of my soul, though unrecognized for decades, was the image and power of God. When times were good, I convinced myself that I was in control. I saw no need for God. I saw no need for what might be in the depths when the surface waters were smooth and the worldly things seemed to be enough. Only in tragedy, in drought, did I seek God.

When things are going well, then, I have to remember the treasure that rests in the depths. I cannot afford to wait until the next drought reveals that presence of God. I have to be very intentional and purposeful about seeking God always, and returning to that image of God, always and ever within me. I can't wait for a drought.

I have to go deep.

MARCH 12

Waiting

Whoever loves his brother lives in the light, and there is nothing in him to make him stumble. But whoever hates his brother is in the darkness and walks around in the darkness; he does not know where he is going, because the darkness has blinded him.

1 JOHN 2:10-11

At the doctor's office, the person calling patients from the waiting room had a soft voice. For a few minutes I worried that I wouldn't hear my name, and that I would be delayed or miss my appointment with the doctor.

I spent years thinking a relationship with God worked that way. I thought I was waiting for Him to call me, that someone would let me know, "God will see you now." And what if I didn't hear that invitation? I had no idea that God was ready all along, that there was no need to wait for Him to call me.

I didn't realize that I had been seeing God for years, in the goodness of the world, in the compassion of other people, in the tender care given to me by friends and strangers. I didn't know that people who advance hate as a spiritual agenda do not see the light of God but live in their own self-inflicted darkness.

I didn't know that the light was available to me anytime I chose to look for it, not just in God Himself but in His people, for "Whoever loves his brother lives in the light." I didn't know that there was never a question of when, or whether, God would see me.

The question was whether I would choose to see God.

MARCH 13

Giving up the gold

The LORD preserves the faithful, but the proud he pays back in full. Be strong and take heart, all you who hope in the LORD.

PSALM 31:23-24

Some TV ads tell me to send in my scrap gold to a company, using their mailers; then supposedly the company very quickly sends me a check for my gold. It sounds like a terrible idea, to take something valuable, send it off, allow someone I've never met to name its value, and then wait for a check.

But don't I go through a form of that exchange of valuables every day? I offer the "gold" of my time, self-image, and other resources to unnamed people out there, allowing people I've never met to determine my status and my significance. I bow to the gods of success, and when I'm not favored by them, I feel less of a person.

On the other hand, when I love God, and place everything I value in God's hands, I am immediately rewarded. I can "be strong and take heart" when I "hope in the Lord." I don't have to wonder if I will ever see my valuables again. I don't have to worry that I will be disappointed in God's assessment of my treasures, because God values my experience, my life, my very self, much more than I do.

So I needn't trust my treasures to a stranger; I no longer need to embrace the gold standard at all. I have value now, and in eternity.

I live by the God standard.

The knowledge of the heart

"By what authority are you doing these things?" [the teachers of the law and elders] asked. "And who gave you authority to do this?" Jesus replied, ". . . Answer me, and I will tell you by what authority I am doing these things. John's baptism—was it from heaven, or from men? Tell me!"

MARK 11:28-29

A weather show once promoted its tornado preparation series by saying that it gives you "everything you need to protect your family" from tornadoes. The claim, a bit overblown (so to speak), probably should have said instead that the series "prepares you as much as possible" to be protected from storms.

Our success at gathering and using worldly knowledge has gradually led us humans to believe that all things are knowable, and that all forms of knowledge can be classified together. Yet while our knowledge can help us prepare better for a storm, we simply have no access to the most essential knowledge: exactly when and where (not to mention why) the storm will hit.

Some people of Jesus' time had the same trouble distinguishing human knowledge from divine knowledge, human authority from divine authority. They couldn't accept that some knowledge—like the love of God for humans—transcends all intellectual categorization. And they couldn't understand the most important truth of all . . .

. . . that the only essential knowledge can be known not with the intellect, but only with the heart.

March 15

What we worship

Then the LORD said to Moses, "Go down, because your people. . . have made themselves an idol cast in the shape of a calf. They have bowed down to it and sacrificed to it. . ."

Exodus 32:7-8

As gas prices continued to rise, car commercials suddenly started glorifying gas mileage as much as style and gadgetry. I would love to see the day when the "ultimate" is the car easiest on the environment. In truth, though, the main reason most of us want efficient cars is so that we can keep more of our money.

In our culture, though, moderation, humility and generosity get much less praise than do extravagance and wealth. Choosing to do the right thing instead of trying to outpace others is more likely to prompt sympathy than admiration.

The tragedy of building our own gods is that we become what we worship. We worship—and become—something with no chance of experiencing transcendence. We worship—and become—something that can be destroyed in an instant when the next storm or market crash comes by. We have not only sacrificed to such gods, but we have sacrificed ourselves for them, and any chance to glimpse eternity.

Besides, what will people think if I tell the truth, act with compassion toward a rival, or refuse to get by paying less than I owe? They will think that the world has been turned upside-down. But I will become what I worship: part of the eternal.

Now that's my idea of the ultimate.

MARCH 16

Finding reverse

... no one can enter a strong man's house and carry off his possessions unless he first ties up the strong man. Then he can rob his house.

MARK 3:27

After trading in a car, I had trouble finding reverse on the manual transmission of the new car. It wasn't located in any of the places it had been on my other cars, so every place I tried moved me forward instead of back. Where "reverse" used to be was now "forward."

In my spiritual life, too, many things that used to make me feel as if I were backing up now make me feel as if I'm moving forward. I no longer have to win over other people in every situation, because I no longer need that winning to feel of value. I used to have to prevail over other people in debates to feel good about myself.

But now, unless the topic is of great significance, I often don't even take up the debate. I can say to the other person, in my mind, "If you're trying to prove your smarter than I am, I'll give you that. You win." Once that attitude felt like "reverse," but now it feels like "forward."

If I totally depend on God and will give up everything for Him, no one on this earth can hurt me. I don't have to defend my territory, like a strong man being attacked by robbers. They cannot steal what I'm willing to give them. I can't lose if I no longer play the game.

What used to be "reverse" is now "forward."

MARCH 17

Have you ever?

"If you belonged to the world, it would love you as its own. As it is, you do not belong to the world, but I have chosen you out of the world."
JOHN 15:18-19

Some TV ads glorifying exhilarating, extreme experiences ended with the tag line, "Have you *ever*?" It's one more example of our desire to tie the significance of human life to uniqueness of experience. I can claim more status if I have done something no one else has "ever" done.

The trouble with measuring my value by extraordinary experiences is that the "rush" doesn't last; I have to look continually for another, bigger rush. This world loves the one who craves new experience, because measuring ourselves that way means we "belong to the world." But we belong to a world that cannot last.

So my concept of "ever" has changed. Instead of seeking experiences that no one else can match, I'm now more drawn to experiences we all share, and finding depth and meaning in those experiences. In being with others and seeking the depth of ordinary experience, I am drawn into eternity, as in "forever."

No, I believe that the substance of life experience is not in the extraordinary, but in the ordinary, not in the unique, but in the common. In loving others in shared experience and finding God in those experiences, we touch eternity and cling to something that lasts. So the important question is not, "Have you *ever*?"

It is "Have you *forever*?"

MARCH 18

Hope rises

But now he has reconciled you by Christ's physical body through death to present you holy in his sight, without blemish and free from accusation—if you continue in your faith, established and firm, not moved from the hope held out in the gospel.

COLOSSIANS 1:22-23

The temperature reached the 50s one spring day, and the sun was out. I judged it warm enough to put the top down on my convertible, but I saw one woman who wore a parka with the hood up. Spring wasn't really here yet, but I was ready to open up to the beautiful blue sky.

Such hope—of the "already but not yet"—rests at the heart of the Gospel. Even in the cold, the grace of God brings redemption, in the future and in the present. I try, as often as possible, to live out the hope of the Gospel even in the face of the stress and loss and grimness of this place. Some think the weather requires a parka; I wear short sleeves in anticipation of the warmth.

I have never understood Christians who seem to live in a shadow, with a judgmental, pessimistic, irritated attitude. How can you know what we know about the transcendence offered by God—today—and still default to harshness? How do we speak of a loving God and then let ourselves get "moved from the hope held out in the gospel"?

I suppose it has been a long winter. Some look up and think we're in for more bad weather, but I trust God. I choose to hope in God.

I choose to be open to the sky.

MARCH 19

I wouldn't want to live there

Sing to the LORD a new song, for he has done marvelous things; his right hand and his holy arm have worked salvation for him.

PSALM 98:1

I visited, in advance, the city where I would live for three years, searching for an apartment. I looked at one place that, on paper, should have been perfect. But I was uneasy there—frightened, almost—because the place felt dark and bordered on a shaky neighborhood. I decided not to rent it; I didn't want to live in a scary place.

For decades I shied away from God for a similar reason. I heard about His wrath and judgment, and I found no attraction in seeking a higher power who wanted me to live in a constant state of fear. Though I had done much wrong, I didn't want to live always in the dark shadows of a wrathful and angry judge.

I turned toward God when I saw that portrayals of Him as a perpetually angry judge don't do Him justice. The essence of God is not fear, but love; now I "sing to the Lord a new song," a love song instead of a song of fear. I sing that song every day because "his right hand and his holy arm have worked salvation for him." And for me.

Now I know that God's judgment is light to guide me toward Him, not darkness in which to banish me. He is a place of compassion, tenderness, love, safety. This God I glimpse in my heart's knowing is not a god who rules by fear. If He were, I would not care to know Him.

I don't want to live for a scary god.

Offense, defense

Jesus replied: "'Love the Lord your God with all your heart and with all your soul and with all your mind.' This is the first and greatest commandment. And the second is like it: 'Love your neighbor as yourself.' All the Law and the Prophets hang on these two commandments."
MATTHEW 22:37-40

On a college basketball game I once watched, the announcer said of one turn of events, "That was a great defensive possession." I criticized the word choice, since by definition the team with possession is the offense, not the defense.

Very often, though, our behavior shows that we have lost sight of our own definitions thanks to fear and self-interest. For instance, most of us Christians forget at one time or another that love of God and neighbor is the definition of Christianity.

When legal experts quizzed Jesus on "the greatest commandment in the Law," he told them unhesitatingly, "Love the Lord your God with all your heart and with all your soul and with all your mind . . . Love your neighbor as yourself." To follow Christ is simply to love—God and neighbor.

Sadly, often heavenly definitions don't translate well on earth. To make myself feel more important, I criticize others and lose the very definition of following Christ. Despite calling myself a Christian, my behavior can be incredibly petty and defensive.

But I feel sure God sees it as offensive.

Better weapons

They came to [Jesus] and said, ". . . Is it right to pay taxes to Caesar or not? Should we pay or shouldn't we?" But Jesus . . . said to them, "Give to Caesar what is Caesar's and to God what is God's."
MARK 12:14-15,17

In a documentary about the M-16 rifle, I learned that the weapon often jammed during the Vietnam War, endangering American soldiers. Experts now, though, speak of the efficacy that the weapons achieved once the rifle's problems were addressed.

I am constantly on the lookout for more efficient weapons, not for war but for competition in this world. I continually hope for better skills, more money, and more status, not because they hold intrinsic meaning, but because they give me an advantage over someone or something.

Jesus, in His cryptic reply about the things of Caesar and the things of God, warned humans about confusing the goals of two kingdoms: earthly and heavenly. When I wish or even pray for success in worldly things—success which prevents my caring for God and for other human beings—then I'm simply seeking a more efficient weapon.

The gifts of God don't bring success in this kingdom; they bring the ability to step out of it into His kingdom. I have to work hard sometimes to remember to "Give to Caesar what is Caesar's and to God what is God's." I have to work hard to remember that God doesn't want me to have better weapons of war.

God wants me to have peace.

MARCH 22

The machine

Be exalted, O God, above the heavens; let your glory be over all the earth.

PSALM 57:5

A credit card commercial I used to see showed a retail establishment operating like a giant machine, its efficiency resulting from all of its customers using credit cards in their transactions. That efficient machine ground to a halt when one person chose to pay with cash.

I continually marvel at the things and activities that we glorify. In this case, efficiency and buying on credit are glorified. Doing something as quaint and anachronistic as paying with cash throws a wrench into the machine of commerce and status. If you pay with cash, you're part of the problem.

Although I love God and cherish the awareness of His presence in my life, I certainly let the societal machine drive me far too often. Instead of exalting God "above the heavens" and declaring that I want to see His glory "over all the earth," I exalt success and march along with everyone else, one more cog in that immense worldly machine.

For many people today, the pursuit of God is considered increasingly passé; to exalt compassion over success threatens the efficiency of the machine. Anyone who seeks to reconcile rather than winning, to share rather than accumulating, threatens to slow down—or stop—the vast cultural and economic machine. If that happened, what would this world come to?

Or Whom?

MARCH 23

Stopping along the path

For we who are alive are always being given over to death for Jesus' sake, so that his life may be revealed in our mortal body.

2 CORINTHIANS 4:11

At a walking trail, I saw a young woman with a baby in a stroller. They stopped on the path so that the mother could point out to the child some squirrels playing happily in the trees.

Sometimes it takes a concerted stop on the path to appreciate something that otherwise would have gone unnoticed. I would have never appreciated some of the greatest gifts of God and man if I had not been forced to stop along the trail I ran every day.

I never would have known the eternal nature of living for God if I hadn't failed so miserably in living for myself. I never would have understood the presence of God incarnate in other humans if my mortal body hadn't faltered. I never would have appreciated the beauty of one ordinary day with ordinary people if I hadn't faced the loss of ordinary people and ordinary days.

Often the death of other priorities, the falling away of earthly treasures, has to precede a deep appreciation of the eternal life of God. "For we who are alive are always being given over to death for Jesus' sake, so that his life may be revealed in our mortal body." My life has been lived too much on fast forward. Occasionally someone has to stop me on the path, to point and say, "We have to stop running. Look, my child."

"There is God."

MARCH 24

It's the mirrors

Now about brotherly love we do not need to write to you, for you yourselves have been taught by God to love each other.

1 THESSALONIANS 4:9

Commercials for a high-definition television said that the TV's clear picture resulted from thousands of tiny mirrors inside the set. Those mirrors produce, as closely as technologically possible, the "exact mirror image of the source material." To explain the high-quality picture, the ads said of the technnology, "It's the *mirrors*."

We long for a clear picture of how God looks and acts, and each person has the potential to be one of those tiny mirrors reflecting God's image. If each of us lived only for God, then together we would produce a nearly exact mirror image of the Source. Sadly, most of us can barely reflect God's image accurately for one moment, much less a lifetime, so the image of God appearing through us remains distorted and broken.

Occasionally, though, when we get it right, a glimpse of God appears. When we show selfless love for another person, we reflect the perfect love of God, for we "have been taught by God to love each other." Minus egos and personal agendas, we could be small but clear mirrors of the way God loves. We are made in His image and taught by Him to love. So it's not that God chooses to remain completely hidden, as we have the potential to reflect him. The problem is not God.

It's the *mirrors*.

MARCH 25

Better

The LORD reigns . . . Mightier than the thunder of the great waters, mightier than the breakers of the sea–the LORD on high is mighty.
PSALM 93:1, 4

Sports equipment ads running during a basketball tournament showed athletes who challenged other athletes, saying things like, "My quick is quicker than your quick," and "My better is better than your better."

Nothing seems to get human energy going like competition: comparing ourselves—on or off the field of sports—with others. Unfortunately, we humans are so enthralled by comparison and competition that often, I fear, we think of God as in our category, only bigger and better.

The immensity and grace of God, though, far exceed human imagination. God is not simply bigger than we are, or more powerful, or simply better: God is the source of all being. Any words we use to describe God are inadequate, because God is beyond human comprehension and expression.

Still, we try to communicate about this God who means so much to us. We say such things as, "The LORD reigns . . . Mightier than the thunder of the great waters . . . the LORD on high is mighty." We use those comparative and absolute words because it doesn't feel very satisfying to say, "God is good," even in the sense that all good and all truth in the world belong to God and emanate from God. So it may be all we can say: God is good.

There is no "better."

MARCH 26

God's speed

Job continued his discourse: "How I long for the months gone by . . . for the days when I was in my prime, when God's intimate friendship blessed my house. . . . Whoever heard me spoke well of me, and those who saw me commended me, because I rescued the poor who cried for help. . . ."

JOB 29:2, 4, 11-12

I saw an ad for a company which touted its flexibility and relevance by claiming that it could "adapt at the speed of now." I loved the thought of "now" as a speed; what could be faster than "now"?

As people of God, I fear that sometimes we mistakenly focus primarily on future rewards, and we don't allow God to act with immediacy in our lives, to act "at the speed of now." We think of virtue as a vehicle, not as a destination.

Job mourned the lost days of his life in which "God's intimate friendship blessed my house." In those days, Job had "rescued the poor who cried for help." Job wore his righteousness like a badge, and he wondered why that badge was not buying him favor with God.

Somehow Job forgot that helping others in need is not the cause of God's favor, but the effect. He forgot that being the presence of God to another human being is stepping into the eternal, not then, in the distant future, when this life is over, but in the moment another is cared for, protected, embraced, healed. Loving doesn't get me to eternity; loving is eternity. Loving is God.

Experienced at the speed of now.

MARCH 27

Inside Out

Moses describes in this way the righteousness that is by the law: "The man who does these things will live by them." But the righteousness that is by faith says: . . . "The word is near you; it is in your mouth and in your heart. . . ."

ROMANS 10:5-6,8

Near my home I saw a huge store called "Outdoor World," a place which sells and allows demonstrations of equipment for hunting, fishing, and other outdoor activities. The paradox is that, though it's all about the outdoors, the place looked to be entirely indoors.

A paradox of outside/inside exists, too, in the Christian life. The word of God becomes internal to the heart pledged to follow Christ, and yet that word is also expressed in the actions of loving God and others on the outside. Something very interior also lives on the exterior.

And often the opposite is true. A friend once taught me that, when I feel I simply cannot muster forgiveness or compassion for another person, I still have to act forgiving and compassionate. When I make that choice, what is external—the "acting"—somehow becomes internal. Sometimes the heart prompts the action; sometimes the action prompts the heart.

I often miss opportunities to deepen my Christian faith by thinking that it is exclusively interior or exclusively exterior. The word is indeed very near me; God lives in my heart, and Jesus lives in my actions.

How can something so inside also be so outside?

MARCH 28

The keys

... our gospel came to you not simply with words, but also with power, with the Holy Spirit and with deep conviction ... you welcomed the message with the joy given by the Holy Spirit. And so you became a model to all the believers in Macedonia and Achaia. The Lord's message rang out from you ...

1 THESSALONIANS 1:5-6, 8

A man I know left his car to have the oil changed, then walked to a restaurant. Almost immediately, he got a call from the garage; he had forgotten to leave his car keys with them. Obviously they could not service the car if they couldn't get in it or move it.

For the longest time I wondered why God wasn't changing my life. Then I realized I hadn't given Him the keys: I had placed too many conditions on that transformation. I only wanted change within my comfort zone, and I clung to attitudes and habits that prevented authentic and Godly growth. If I honestly want to be changed, I have to open all of me to God instead of closing off parts of my life, reserving space to harbor pet resentments and vices.

On the other hand, if I allow God access to all of me—if I give Him the keys—then "the Lord's message will ring out from me," and the gospel will come not only with words, but with power. Power to change me completely, profoundly, irrevocably. Power to change the world, one heart at a time, when that message rings out from me.

But it ain't gonna happen if I don't hand over the keys.

MARCH 29

Goodness, greatness

The LORD will indeed give what is good, and our land will yield its harvest. Righteousness goes before him and prepares the way for his steps.

PSALM 85:12-13

I saw a commercial which declared that "Every child has the potential to do something great." Possibilities characterized as "great" included such impressive settings as the Oval Office, the cockpit of an airliner, an operating room.

Sometimes I fear that we are so anxious for greatness—both for ourselves and for our children—that we sacrifice "good" on the altar of "great." Goodness becomes incarnate when a teacher gives additional time to a troubled student, when a passerby stops to help a stranger, when an everyday citizen works on a Habitat for Humanity project. Goodness simply doesn't look as glamorous as greatness does.

And if we do nothing more than helping another person out of goodness, who will remember us? Well, the student, the stranger, the new homeowner will remember. They may even realize that, through a loving human being, they have been touched by the hand of God. After all, goodness at work in this world is nothing less than God at work, for "righteousness goes before him and prepares the way for his steps."

Perhaps every child of God does have the potential to do something great. But something more important and more lasting may await in our very next encounter.

We may have the chance to do something good.

MARCH 30

No simple season

The centurion replied, "Lord, I do not deserve to have you come under my roof. But just say the word, and my servant will be healed. For I myself am a man under authority, with soldiers under me. . . ."

MATTHEW 8:8-9

Finally one spring the trees and flowers began blooming, but then cold, windy weather came through. Strong wind blew the flowers off the budding trees; at one point the air was so full of white that I seemed to be in a snowstorm of petals.

Life would be simpler if the seasons divided more clearly. But very often, flowers bloom when it still should be winter. Snow gathers on daffodils in the spring. Something that looks like a burst of snow turns out to be petals from a flowering tree.

And the spiritual world is every bit as complex as nature's seasons. I would love to find a way to separate the good guys from the bad guys, but people are not labels. People we perceive as "good" make mistakes and point us away from God. Those we see as "bad" can be used by God to make the world a better place.

Jesus met a centurion, a man accustomed to power but one turned toward God in his own powerlessness, and Jesus saw in the soldier an example of faith. In other words, the world was not simple in Jesus' day. And much to our inconvenience, the world is not simple in our day, either. Any given day, someone perceived as an "enemy" may show us true faith.

Any given day, we may see a snowstorm made from the flowers of spring.

MARCH 31

Is this going to be on the test?

Even though I walk through the valley of the shadow of death, I will fear no evil. . . . Surely goodness and love will follow me all the days of my life, and I will dwell in the house of the Lord forever.

PSALM 23:4,6

One day while shopping I saw a teenaged kid wearing a T-shirt that read, "If it's not on the test, I don't care."

Don't we Christians spend an awful lot of time worrying about what's "on the test" theologically? We want to know about the doctrines, and to get them "right," so that we can pass along into the next world, the one where we spend an eternity with God. And yet, I don't think we're only supposed to study for what's "on the test."

To me, theology—thinking about God and reflecting on how He acts in our world—is important, but I don't think it's the lesson He most wants me to learn. To me, theology and doctrine are tools to teach me a way of living that is more about God than about me, more about love than about tests.

God wants me to look beyond what's on the test, to carry His presence to people who live "in the valley of the shadow of death." If I embrace other people instead of quizzing them, then goodness and love—a.k.a. God—will follow me all the days of my life. If the only lesson I learn is to love, then "I will dwell in the house of the LORD forever." Today I will try to love another person in God's name, not because it's on the test.

But because my God asks me to care.

April

APRIL 1

Length of days

The path of the righteous is like the first gleam of dawn, shining ever brighter till the full light of day. But the way of the wicked is like deep darkness; they do not know what makes them stumble.

PROVERBS 4:18-19

When I began living farther north, I realized that the spring sun leaves later and returns earlier, giving me extra light each day. I'm not sure if the change involves inclining more toward the sun or greater proximity to it. I only knew that I loved the new length of days and brevity of nights.

Light seems to dominate over darkness, too, when I rely more fully on God. I still experience darkness, but it doesn't seem to stay as long. When I am disappointed or even in despair, the light returns more quickly. More practiced at going back to God, the source of light, I realize more quickly the foolishness of trying to save myself and generate my own light.

I get in trouble when I welcome the darkness and its ability to hide my faults. In the darkness, I can blame too easily, complain too easily. And although I hesitate to call such behavior "the way of the wicked," I do deepen the darkness through my own self-absorption, and don't even realize "what makes me stumble."

Still, even on my worst days—my most selfish or despairing times—I remain hopeful. I can get through anything if I know the light will return.

I love this length of days and brevity of nights.

APRIL 2

Home Rage

"Do not think that I have come to abolish the Law or the Prophets; I have not come to abolish them but to fulfill them . . . until heaven and earth disappear, not the smallest letter, not the least stroke of a pen, will by any means disappear from the Law until everything is accomplished."

MATTHEW 5:17-18

In a disturbing trend dubbed "home rage," people whose houses are repossessed wreak destruction on those homes. They pound walls with hammers or scrawl graffiti, as if to say, "If I can't live here, no one else will, either."

The idea made me wonder if self-destructive habits we hang onto are a form of "home rage" in the sense of disquiet in our souls. We try so hard to be someone else, or to be what the world demands, that we cannot find peace in ourselves. It's almost as if we say, "If I can't be happy in this place, I'll damage it so God can't live here, either."

But the truth is that I cannot find happiness trying to be someone else or by trying to measure up to temporal yardsticks. And every time I try to take on those inauthentic measures, I destroy this dwelling place.

Jesus tried to tell people that the spiritual life wasn't a choice between law and Jesus, but a way of honoring God by fulfilling the law. God doesn't want to destroy my true self to build a different dwelling place; God wants to make me my truest self as a dwelling place. God and I want the same thing: for me to be home. . . .

. . . home to the living God.

APRIL 3

Life eternal

"Teacher," [the man] asked, "what must I do to inherit eternal life?" "What is written in the Law?" [Jesus] replied. "How do you read it?" He answered: " 'Love the Lord your God with all your heart and with all your soul and with all your strength and with all your mind'; and, 'Love your neighbor as yourself.'" "You have answered correctly," Jesus replied.

LUKE 10:25-28

One night, as I was trying to read, I was unable to concentrate because of noise outside. An ambulance flew past. A train rumbled by. A delivery truck stopped next door.

Though I was annoyed, the noises truly were a tiny inconvenience compared to their larger significance. Someone was hurting. People were trying to get somewhere. Supplies were being delivered where they were needed.

Too often I don't go far enough to "love my neighbor as myself." I am anxious to love my neighbor as long as there's little inconvenience involved. Or I am anxious to love my neighbor when I am so inconvenienced that everyone else notices my selflessness.

Amid the perceived noise of this world, it can be easy to pretend that loving others is impossible given the circumstances. But true love of God—expressed through love of neighbor—isn't a matter of convenience. Loving is the one thing I can do in this moment to live in eternity. So loving my God and my neighbor doesn't get in the way of life.

Loving God and neighbor is life.

APRIL 4

The horizon

A man can do nothing better than to eat and drink and find satisfaction in his work. This too, I see, is from the hand of God, for without him, who can eat or find enjoyment? To the man who pleases him, God gives wisdom, knowledge and happiness. . . .

ECCLESIASTES 2:24-26

I am fascinated with the horizon, with looking off in the distance, picking a spot, and thinking, "There the earth meets the sky." I know, though, that if I travel to that place, it would no longer be that meeting place of earth and sky.

Often the pursuit of God can have that same elusiveness; we think of God as distant, that we could see God and be with God if only we could reach that distant place. Or we think that we can be fully with God only after death, that all of this time on earth is a cosmic waiting room for heaven.

Now, though, I see God's presence as available and palpable in this time and place, not just in that distant place on the horizon. A person "can do no better than to eat and drink and find satisfaction in work," because "this is from the hand of God." Experiences that seem mundane become transcendent when we recognize and grasp that hand of God.

Yes, God is immense and transcendent, far beyond us. But God is also personal and near, right beside us. From some viewpoints, this place where I stand right now is that spot on the horizon. This place is touched by the hand of God.

In this place, earth meets sky.

APRIL 5

The music of eternity

For the perishable must clothe itself with the imperishable, and the mortal with immortality. When the perishable has been clothed with the imperishable, and the mortal with immortality, then. . . ." Death has been swallowed up in victory."

1 CORINTHIANS 15:53-54

At school one day I heard a snippet of gorgeous music which abruptly stopped. Another student had opened, then closed, the door to a music practice room. Those rooms are soundproofed, so music can only be heard from one when a door opens.

I picture those doors as the option each human has of experiencing eternity and gaining immortality through God. I do not create or control the music in that room; it plays whether I open the door or not. But I cannot enjoy the music unless I choose to, for God will not force the music upon me.

Continually in the perishable human life we have the opportunity to "clothe our lives with the imperishable, and the mortal with immortality." Each time I focus on tangible, physical things and presences, I keep the door closed and cling to the perishable. When I have the courage, though, to trust more in the things that I cannot physically see—like the love of God—then the door cracks open, and I hear the music of eternity.

Each of us walks this same hallway. Something deep within us tells us that music is playing here somewhere. Will we have the courage to try that door?

Will we choose to be blessed by that eternal music?

Giving up the oars

"We will never again say 'Our gods' to what our own hands have made, for in you the fatherless find compassion."
HOSEA 14:3

I saw a movie in which a man, adrift on a makeshift boat at sea, intentionally placed his oars in the water and let them float away. Apparently he had given up any chance of propelling the boat farther on his own. Not long after he gave up, a ship appeared and he was rescued.

Growth from spiritual surrender rarely appears in such a tidy Hollywood package with an overtly happy ending. And yet, it does seem that I have found the most peace when I have tossed away my oars and given up trying to control the sea.

It's a lesson I have learned not once, but repeatedly. I get a slightly bigger boat or a better set of oars, and I begin to think (again) that I can get wherever I need to be on my power, my own will, my own direction. Usually it isn't long before I am exhausted and frustrated. I toss the oars overboard one more time, declaring that I will "never again say 'My god' to what my own hands have made."

I have to continually remind myself that I have no control. Only then can God truly help me. Only when I am completely empty of myself can God fill me. As frightening as it can be at first, my only hope is to let go of those oars and admit that control is a dangerous illusion.

Only then can God save me from that vast and hostile sea.

APRIL 7

Stopped watch

You say, "I am rich; I have acquired wealth and do not need a thing." But you do not realize that you are wretched, pitiful, poor, blind and naked....

REVELATION 3:17

One day at work I glanced at my watch early in the day and realized that it had stopped, the battery dead. Throughout the day, I caught myself looking at the watch anyway. I smiled, thinking, "I'm doing it again—looking at a watch that has stopped."

I think that, as human beings living in a broken and chaotic world, we continually "look at watches that have stopped," measuring our lives by manmade timepieces that mean nothing in God's grand scheme. Some days, I look at my life—at some minor, fleeting success in work or relationships—and congratulate myself on how well I'm doing. And I realize that I'm doing it again—looking at a watch that has stopped.

I don't think the things and concerns of this earth are intrinsically evil, but they become evil when they get in the way of my relationship with God and my ability to love His people. When I focus on temporal things, I begin to think, "I am rich; I have acquired wealth and do not need a thing." Yet in God's eyes, in that moment of self-congratulatory materialism, I am "wretched, pitiful, poor, blind and naked." The moment I start to think how well I'm doing, the timepiece of this world has stopped, useless in marking time with God.

In other words, I'm doing it again . . .

The strong man

The righteous will see and fear; they will laugh at him, saying, "Here now is the man who did not make God his stronghold but trusted in his great wealth and grew strong by destroying others!" But I am like an olive tree flourishing in the house of God. . . .

Psalm 52:6-8

When reports appeared which identified major league baseball players who supposedly used illegal steroids and growth hormones, I was appalled. I like to think of myself as a fan of the pure game, and don't like to think that some of my favorite players may use such methods to boost performance.

But we sports fans do demand performance. Though quick to criticize players who use illegal methods to get to the top, those on top are the only ones whose jerseys or autographs or baseball cards we buy. If we're not careful, we see players not as people—as God's creation in God's image—but as machines measured only by their latest performance.

If we were truly the righteous ones in this deal, we fans wouldn't place sports performance above integrity and above compassion for others. Instead of valuing what God values and "flourishing in the house of God," we worship competition and winning, and we worship those who "grew strong by destroying others," and by destroying themselves. And by worshiping gods that are not God, we contribute subtly to the destruction.

Theirs, and ours.

APRIL 9

Loving lavishly

Simon Peter asked him, "Lord, where are you going?" Jesus replied, "Where I am going, you cannot follow now, but you will follow later." Peter asked, "Lord, why can't I follow you now? I will lay down my life for you."

JOHN 13:36-37

Years ago a friend and I, though inexperienced, decided to paint a room. We struggled with the border areas, where we needed to maintain very straight lines. A more experienced painter later told us that we could have solved the problem by having much more paint on the brush, as it is easier to paint a straight line with plenty of paint on the brush.

That idea of lavishing paint on the brush to draw a straight line keeps coming to me when I look at people who feel unloved and go through all sorts of performances to gain attention. Though such people irritate me, I try to love them in small measure, actually tolerating more than loving.

Peter thought he understood the kind of journey Christ was about to take, that Christ loved us in stingy human portions. He had no idea of the depth and breadth of love that his teacher and friend would offer.

Christ loves us in an unthinkably generous and selfless way. Loving, like bearing a Cross, is not something to be done in moderation. You cannot do it by dabbing on a bit here and there. Lavishing love on one another draws that straight vertical line from God to human, and a straight horizontal line from one human to another.

Love is lavish. Love is a Cross.

Bye-bye

But I am like an olive tree flourishing in the house of God; I trust in God's unfailing love for ever and ever.

PSALM 52:8

In a store one day, a little girl ran around playing while her father was at the cash register. When he got ready to leave and she wanted to keep playing, he started saying, "Okay, bye-bye." She panicked over his leaving and returned to his side. He seemed to feel that the only (or perhaps the quickest) way to get her to obey was to threaten leaving her alone.

I am grateful that my heavenly Father doesn't use such tactics to make me obey Him. I have made many bad choices, many thoughtless choices, many choices which landed me in trouble despite no unhealthy or mean intentions on my part. I hate the thought that each time I went away from Him, the only way God could bring me back would be to tell me, "I will leave you alone if you don't straighten up."

I believe God to be infinitely loving, forgiving, merciful; He keeps me by His side by assuring me that it is the one place I can be loved despite my mistakes. I don't obey Him because I'm afraid He'll leave me, but because I love Him and feel loved with Him. I flourish "like an olive tree" in God's presence because "I trust in God's unfailing love," not because He threatens to leave every time I wander. God knows I need Him, and I know I need Him. We have already established that I cannot save myself.

So no threats of "bye-bye" are necessary.

APRIL 11

Symptoms

But if . . . you seek the LORD your God, you will find him if you look for him with all your heart and with all your soul. When you are in distress and all these things have happened to you, then in later days you will return to the LORD your God and obey him.

DEUTERONOMY 4:29-30

I sometimes wonder why we never seem to speak of symptoms of health or symptoms of "ease" rather than the symptoms of disease. Of course, it makes sense that we aren't as focused on indications of good health, as the healthy person is in no danger.

Yet every day I wish that people who are not Christians would be overwhelmed by the "symptoms of ease" they see in people like me who claim to put our trust in God. Though I say I trust God, I then slip back into relying on my own abilities and accomplishments. If I accepted grace instead of seeing it as one more award to hang on the wall, maybe the symptoms of ease would become more apparent. Maybe then people who are in distress would see the source of all peace, and they would want to "return to the LORD our God and obey him."

Instead, I work overtime to whittle others down or build myself up. I trust in idols I have built, making human things and relationships my priorities and fitting God in as I have time for Him. I am frantic to prove myself, to win, to earn. I forget that I am God's beloved. No one can tell I have the peace of God within me.

They see no symptoms of my ease.

APRIL 12

Can you describe Him?

Then John gave this testimony: "I saw the Spirit come down from heaven as a dove and remain on him. I would not have known him, except that the one who sent me to baptize with water told me, 'The man on whom you see the Spirit come down and remain is he who will baptize with the Holy Spirit.' I have seen and I testify that this is the Son of God."

JOHN 1:32-34

I love crime shows, and they always make me wonder if I could give a detailed physical description of someone I saw commit a crime. I doubt that I would make much of a witness, though, as I couldn't even tell you the height, weight, and eye color of some of my very best friends.

Yet while I could not offer details to describe a person I had seen, I am confident I would know him if I saw him again. John the Baptist wasn't sure how to describe the Son of God, either. But he did feel confident that he would recognize Him as "the man on whom you see the Spirit come down and remain."

Like John, I certainly can't describe God, even though I have glimpsed Him often. He's the guy who changed my tire, the stranger who let me weep on her shoulder over the loss of my dad, the friend who gave me a ride when my car had been totaled. Can I tell you exactly what the presence of Christ looks like? No, I almost certainly cannot.

But I know Him when I see Him.

APRIL 13

Little sparrows

". . . Are not five sparrows sold for two pennies? Yet not one of them is forgotten by God. . . . Don't be afraid; you are worth more than many sparrows."

LUKE 12:6-7

I remember the day I learned that a friend of mine had died, having never recovered from being attacked at her home months earlier. She was well known and loved, and much of my hometown was up in arms about crime in the area. Before, crime statistics blended into the background, but my friend's death put a face on those statistics.

As with crime statistics, it's easy to discount talk of God as something that has nothing to do with me. But being helped by another human being puts a face on the overwhelming concept of God. At that point, I am no longer thinking about theology, but about God's tenderness for me. It changes not just my life, but my day, to be cared for and about, because sometimes I feel about as small and insignificant as a sparrow.

I will never read crime statistics the same way again; now when I read "victims of crime," I will think about a kind friend. And when I have been tended for, by friends like her and even by strangers, I will see those faces and think of God.

We're not lost like so many sparrows in the enormous cosmos; we are tenderly and intimately loved by our Creator. God watches out for us through the people who love us. God is here with us now.

And all of us little sparrows are mighty glad to hear it.

APRIL 14

God-finding

Sow for yourselves righteousness, reap the fruit of unfailing love, and break up your unplowed ground; for it is time to seek the LORD, until he comes and showers righteousness on you.

Hosea 10:12

I saw an old TV show in which a war veteran had pretended for years that he had participated in a charge up a hill, when in fact he had stopped along the way to care for a wounded comrade. For decades, only he and the man he saved knew the truth: that he had not been to the top of the hill at all.

We all dream of reaching the mountaintop, of an unparalleled experience with God that makes us feel glorious and noticed. Very often I have longed to go higher, to get to the top, as that kind of triumphant story is exciting and energizing to tell.

But the truth is that God-finding is done not only on the mountaintop, but along the way, where fellow travelers have fallen, too fatigued or fearful or wounded to go on. When we stop to help, in our compassion we "reap the fruit of unfailing love . . ." and the Lord "comes and showers righteousness" on us.

I hate to give up on making it to the summit, but God isn't only found in the immensity of the mountain. God is found as purely and as powerfully in the tears that one human being sheds for another in the lower elevations. I needn't climb the mountain to get to God. When I take the time from my "ascent" to stop and tend and heal and love, God comes to me.

And through me.

APRIL 15

Builder of bridges

And we pray this in order that you may live a life worthy of the Lord and may please him in every way: bearing fruit in every good work, growing in the knowledge of God, being strengthened with all power. . . .
COLOSSIANS 1:10-11

I generally procrastinate doing my taxes, partly because of a lack of expertise. But I also stall when I think I will have to pay additional taxes.

Generally, though, I don't complain about paying taxes, because they go, at least partly, to build things I need, like bridges and highways. I couldn't build a road, so without taxes, I couldn't get anywhere. Taxes are a much better deal than my being forced to go out and build a road or a bridge.

As much as I want to be a loving and compassionate person, I can't get there on my own, either. I want to take care of other people, but sometimes they frighten me, or anger me, or irritate the daylights out of me. So if I somehow "live a life worthy of the Lord" and love others unconditionally, as God loves me, it's only because of God. I could no more love unconditionally than I could build a bridge.

In some ways, I'd like to live a selfish life, one focused only on myself, instead of thinking of other people. Or, would I? Being separated from God would mean that I would have to make my own way, to build my own bridges and create my own roads.

And suddenly those taxes I pay are looking like a pretty good deal.

APRIL 16

Boss as brand

... we are confident of better things in your case—things that accompany salvation. God is not unjust; he will not forget your work and the love you have shown him as you have helped his people and continue to help them.

HEBREWS 6:9-10

In a class on leadership, a management professor spoke about "boss as brand," about the benefits and dangers of equating an entire brand or company with the persona of its CEO. The speaker said the public uses "boss as brand" as a form of shorthand to differentiate one otherwise faceless company from another. It's also easier, when things go wrong, to blame a person without considering the arduous and difficult systemic changes that are probably necessary for improvement.

For my part, though, I believe that our minds and souls are made to contemplate living beings, not things or anonymous organizations. God's incarnation in Jesus must be the ultimate version of "boss as brand." We can see, in a human being, what God asks of us in our own lives, and we can see in Christ his "work and the love you have shown him as you have helped his people and continue to help them."

And when the world goes awry, we are the hands and heart of Christ, the ones charged to lift this world up by helping God and His people. So this particular version of "boss as brand" isn't just shorthand: it is incarnation.

And it's our chance to be God's hands in creating a "brand" new world.

APRIL 17

Broken

To you, O LORD, I lift up my soul; in you I trust, O my God. . . Show me your ways, O LORD, . . . for you are God my Savior, and my hope is in you all day long.

PSALM 25:1, 4-5

Reports on a school shooting tried to determine if the school administration, gun laws, mental health laws, or some other part of the "system" failed. I wonder how many people feel that nothing on this earth failed as much as God failed to protect the people lost in such tragedies.

We Christians pray, "To you, O LORD, I lift up my soul; in you I trust, O my God." But down deep, don't we, too, wonder what part of the divine system failed when one human being can cause so much grief? Every time tragedy strikes, I endure a time of asking, "Show me your ways, O LORD," so that I can somehow reconcile my trust in God with the news headlines.

Ultimately, though, the truth is that God saves me, not in this world, but from it. Whatever happens here, I can trust God, knowing that this is not all there is. Of course, it's easy for me to say that I trust God when I'm not directly affected by such events. I hope my faith would hold fast if I were right in the middle of the tragedy.

Unthinkably tragic events have happened, and more will happen—somewhere—every week. The main conclusion we can draw from such circumstances is that this world is terribly, terribly broken. Does that mean God is broken?

No, but it certainly means God's heart is.

Sliver of a moon

From Zion, perfect in beauty, God shines forth.

PSALM 50:1

One gorgeous night a breathtakingly beautiful sliver of moon hung low in the sky. Though most of the moon was shrouded in darkness, I knew it was all there, because I had seen it shining, full and bright, on other nights. The heavenly body had not changed, but my ability to see it had diminished.

I know that God is present every moment, but I see more of Him on some days than on others. Though painful, inexplicable, unGodly things happen in the world, I know God is present. On days I cannot see Him well, the flaw is in my seeing, not in His being.

Like the moon, I am never a source of light, but only a reflector. When I listen closely to God, obey His will, when I seek to please only Him, then I become a brighter, more complete reflection of Him. When I listen to myself and try to win others' approval, the reflection of his light in my life shrinks to a sliver.

I don't want to be just another chunk of worthless rock hanging in a darkened nighttime sky. I dream of being a perfect reflection of my God, of being someone who loves other human beings so universally and so deeply that the Light of God shines forth as from Zion. I know I am, as a human, a poor reflection of God, fatally flawed, incapable of perfection. But I can dream of being all that God wants me to be.

I can look at the moon, and dream.

April 19

Nasty little tyrants

What good is it for a man to gain the whole world, yet forfeit his soul?
Mark 8:36

Once I read that the president and chancellor of Germany in the 1920s put Adolf Hitler in power because they thought they would be able to manipulate and control him. That selfish miscalculation changed the history of the world and resulted in millions of deaths. Millions.

I have put in power numerous tyrants—others' approval, money, competitive sports, and all forms of performance—thinking I could control them, only to find that they resulted in a less visible kind of death. Each time, if asked, I would have said, "I'm in control. That wannabe tyrant won't take over my life." Yet each time, a part of the real me, the part connected to God, died because I put an earthly need ahead of my relationship with Him. In trying to "gain the whole world" of human approval, in trying to achieve human success at all costs, I forfeited, at least momentarily, part of my soul. In my miscalculation, two needless 'deaths' took place.

My true self, defined only by God, dies, suffocated by those other tyrants I was so sure I could control. And the person of Christ in me dies, His life and death meaningless because I chose, in a moment or in a phase of my life, to love the kingdom of man more than the kingdom of God. Two more needless deaths.

And all because I thought I could control a nasty little tyrant.

APRIL 20

Singing for God

How good it is to sing praises to our God. . . . The LORD . . . heals the brokenhearted and binds up their wounds. He determines the number of the stars and calls them each by name. . . the LORD delights in those who fear him, who put their hope in his unfailing love.

PSALM 147:1, 3-4,11

One of my earliest memories is of a time when my mother asked me to sing an "Alvin and the Chipmunks" song to her mother, my grandmother. I didn't know at the time, but my grandmother was very ill. My mom knew that, despite my lack of musical ability, my singing that song with joy and abandon would make her mother smile.

Sometimes, in gratitude and awe for what God has done for me, I become frustrated, thinking there is nothing I could ever do to repay Him. He is, after all, the God who "determines the number of the stars and calls them by name," the same God who stoops to "heal the brokenhearted and bind up their wounds."

What gift could I ever give to a God who can do such things? This God who can count and name stars and heal wounds certainly doesn't need anything from me. But somehow I suspect that God would love a gift just like that goofy little off-key song I sang for my grandmother nearly five decades ago. It will make Him smile not because of the quality of the music, but because I "put my hope in His unfailing love." God doesn't care what I sing, or how well.

He only cares that I do.

APRIL 21

All eyes

The LORD reigns, let the nations tremble; he sits enthroned between the cherubim, let the earth shake. . . . Exalt the LORD our God and worship at his holy mountain, for the LORD our God is holy.

PSALM 99:1, 9

A reporter speaking of anxiety in world markets said one day, "All eyes are on Wall Street." The comment made me laugh, as it was the first time my uninformed self learned that there *was* a problem in the markets.

When my focus is on one part of my life, though, I believe that everyone is focused on that same topic. For instance, in times of unmanageable grief, I couldn't understand how everyone else could just go along as if nothing had happened.

Despite the events of my human day—events both ordinary and extraordinary—the Creator of the universe rises above those events to care for me and about me. "The LORD reigns," and his power can only be envisioned through something as awesome as when "the earth shakes."

I believe that, at my human core, God is all that I long for, the only presence capable of filling me. That explains why the salves of more money, better jobs, more friends have never quite helped me heal from wounds inflicted by this world. My heart, like all human hearts, aches for its Creator, not for more of this world.

Whatever happens to me today, the one assurance I have is that "the LORD reigns." So all eyes may be on Wall Street.

But all hearts are longing for God.

APRIL 22

One thing

As was the earthly man, so are those who are of the earth; and as is the man from heaven, so also are those who are of heaven. And just as we have borne the likeness of the earthly man, so shall we bear the likeness of the man from heaven.

1 CORINTHIANS 15:48-49

One state promoted a program which encouraged each person to do "one thing" to be more careful in tending the environment. Turning off a light or limiting water usage in even a small way was valued as a contribution to saving the planet.

If one thing I do can help save the planet, shouldn't I also be able to contribute, in small ways, to bringing about the kingdom of God on that planet? The problem, in both cases, is that the task seems so enormous that we can be fooled into thinking one individual human can have no effect. But that way of thinking is an earthly way, and as a human being I am called to think in a more cosmic, heavenly way.

I am a human, and a relatively obscure one at that. And like all of us, I struggle with feeling like a powerless part of a massive system. But having been made in God's image, "bearing the likeness of the man from heaven," I do have power. I can either perpetuate the ways of earth or help the ways of heaven break in. If I forgive today instead of judging, if I love those who dismiss or persecute me, I have made a difference. That difference may help begin to change the world . . .

. . . even though it's only one thing.

APRIL 23

Disposable lives

But our citizenship is in heaven. And we eagerly await a Savior from there, the Lord Jesus Christ, who, by the power that enables him to bring everything under his control, will transform our lowly bodies so that they will be like his glorious body.

PHILIPPIANS 3:20-21

One place where I have lived put great emphasis on recycling. At school, in fact, they had recycling containers for so many different kinds of material—paper, mixed paper, plastic, cans, bottles—that sometimes it seemed impossible to simply throw something away.

Connecting with God, too, makes it almost impossible to throw anything away, in one sense. While God's transforming power, through Christ, erases my past mistakes, God somehow redeems even mistakes into something valuable. At the very least, my sins become examples of God's mercy and reasons for eternal gratitude. The sins of others which harm me become opportunities to witness the transcending, transforming power of God.

So yes, God allows me to get rid of the past, never again giving that past power over my present and future life with Him. But in another way, nothing is lost, because God transforms not only our "lowly bodies" but all of our life experiences into His image and glory. Everything can go on to new and greater life. All can be redeemed. God simply will not allow us to casually throw something away.

Not to mention some*one*.

Too much light

Then God's temple in heaven was opened, and within his temple was seen the ark of his covenant. And there came flashes of lightning, rumblings, peals of thunder, an earthquake and a great hailstorm.

REVELATION 11:19

Frequently at my eye exams, the doctor dilates my eyes. On the way home, so much light enters my pupils that I can't see images clearly. Apparently having too much light is just as dangerous as having too little.

Are we prevented from seeing God face to face because our eyes simply cannot handle that much light? If I, as a mortal human being, saw God personally, so much light would be present that my own boundaries would disappear. We humans have always felt that to see God directly means destruction. Perhaps, though, seeing God face to face does not destroy the human, but causes that human's boundaries to be erased, and for all human concerns to disappear in the bright light of God.

Maybe the ultimate revelation is a new set of eyes that allow us to see clearly even in the brightest light. For now, full revelation of God is more than human eyes or minds or hearts can take. So He speaks to us in whispers. He appears to us in rumblings, peals of thunder, in religious temples, in the small but life-changing actions of one human taking care of another. In this life, we can see only glimpses of the Light.

God knows that too much light would be dangerous for our small human eyes.

Rolling away the stone

[The women] were on their way to the tomb and they asked each other, "Who will roll the stone away from the entrance of the tomb?"
MARK 16:2-3

One weekend a neighbor moving out had recruited some strong guys to help. One man asked what to do next, so she pointed to a woman struggling with heavy things and said, "Carry stuff for my friend."

The words could easily be a prayer I pray when people I know are in distress. I never know what to say in prayer, whether to ask for the earthly trial to pass or evaporate, or whether to simply ask for my loved one to have strength. Mostly, then, I pray for God to be present, and for the person in trouble to be aware of that presence.

The women who went to Jesus' tomb bore their own burdens. Their friend and teacher had been killed, and in their despair and grief they went to see Him. Even on the way, the more everyday, pressing concerns worried them, as they thought, "Who will roll the stone away from the entrance to the tomb?"

The answer to all concerns about ourselves and others, though, is the empty tomb itself. Earthly powers cannot overcome the power of God. Jesus is risen and present to us in our grieving and in our celebration. So when we don't know exactly how to pray, we simply open our hearts to that risen Christ. On behalf of our loved ones, we needn't worry about rolling away the stone.

All we need to do is say to God, "Carry stuff for my friend."

APRIL 26

Storm chasing

On that day there will be no light, no cold or frost. It will be a unique day, without daytime or nighttime—a day known to the LORD. When evening comes, there will be light.

ZECHARIAH 14:6-7

Unbelievably, a company exists that takes customers out to see tornadoes. The thrill-seeker pays a fee, then goes with the storm-chaser to an area likely to spawn tornadoes. I simply cannot imagine paying good money to see a tornado on purpose.

It seems sometimes that many Christians are storm-chasers in the sense of thinking that God's will for their lives will only involve tasks that are threatening, difficult, unpleasant. One friend even questioned whether she was truly following God's will because she was enjoying the experience too much.

Certainly God will ask me to go many places that I don't want to go. But I also believe that much of the work God asks me to do will be a joy, tailored to my passions and gifts. If every person did God's will, the world would fill with light, not the darkness of a demanding taskmaster god. "On that day there will be no light, no cold or frost. It will be a unique day."

I'll have the opportunity in this lifetime to weather plenty of storms in God's name and with God's strength. But I honestly don't think that seeking out storms makes me a more faithful or more devout Christian.

I can't believe that God wants only foul-weather friends.

Seeing God's face

The god of this age has blinded the minds of unbelievers, so that they cannot see the light of the gospel of the glory of Christ, who is the image of God. For we do not preach ourselves, but Jesus Christ as Lord, and ourselves as your servants for Jesus' sake.

2 CORINTHIANS 4:4-5

Once I was asked to take photographs of a group posing in front of a large window, but light coming in from the window "fooled" the camera's meter. The flash didn't activate, so faces in the photo were too dark to see. The problem wasn't a lack of light, but light coming from the wrong direction.

For many of us in today's culture, the light often seems to stream in from the wrong direction in terms of our priorities. While it's popular to pray for the poor and disenfranchised, sometimes I think that those of us who are comfortable may need prayer more. When life goes well, we think we are capable of doing all that needs doing. A comfortable life can become the "god of this age" blinding us. We can easily forget that we need God. We certainly don't care for the idea that we could be "servants for Jesus' sake," or anyone else's.

I want people to enjoy worldly abundance. But I fear that material abundance has become the "god of this age," obscuring the presence of God. Material things are wonderful, but to rely on them for meaning is to allow the light to come in from the wrong direction.

And the face lost in the darkness is the face of God.

APRIL 28

Soul memory

When all the people were being baptized, Jesus was baptized too. . . . And a voice came from heaven: "You are my Son, whom I love; with you I am well pleased."

LUKE 3:21-22

My sole memory of my maternal grandfather hurts to this day. When I was three or four, he snapped at me and hurt my feelings. Sadly, he died weeks later, so I always thought of him as mean and harsh, though others told me he was very loving.

Clearly, one experience can taint the memory of a person or an event irrevocably. That experience makes me wonder how many people have associated an equally bad memory with the thought of God, something so painful or frightening that they never cared to know Him at all.

I wonder, too, how many more people would seek God and love God if they had experienced an early, positive encounter with Him and His people. What if the first words the human heart knew of the divine were, "You are my child, whom I love"?

I suspect that many people who have no interest in God had a harsh, stinging experience early in life, one that they mistakenly associate with Him. And even though that unpleasant memory "of God" isn't of God at all, but someone's false picture of Him, they never recover from that one painful experience. Thinking of him as I did of my grandfather—as mean and angry—they cower away from Him. That sight must break His heart. They are His children, whom He loves.

If only they knew . . .

PRACTICALLY HOLY 133

Present

And now, O Israel, what does the LORD your God ask of you but to fear the LORD your God, to walk in all his ways, to love him, to serve the LORD your God with all your heart and with all your soul . . . ?
DEUTERONOMY 10:12

A major computer firm once ran commercials in which four of a company's workers were panicking about a project demanded by their bosses. The timeline was critical: "Soon. Yesterday. Now."

Yet only the word "now" creates true urgency. If someone demands something soon, it is unformed, in the future. If they want it "yesterday," the timeline is already impossible to meet, so we're off the hook. But to do something now requires will and action in this moment: not tomorrow, not yesterday. *Now*.

"And NOW . . . what does the LORD your God ask of you . . ." As a Christian, I am asked now to love and fear God, "to walk in all his ways" and to serve God "with all my heart and with all my soul." To the person standing in front of me in need of comfort or forgiveness, the words, "soon" and "yesterday" mean nothing. A person who hurts or grieves or errs needs the presence of God now, so each person who longs to serve God has that opportunity in the now.

The timeline of God is neither the impossibility of "yesterday" nor the postponement of "soon." To embrace, forgive, soothe, heal, tend—these are actions of the heart moved by the love of God, actions that show God is present.

And "present" means "now."

APRIL 30

A walk to remember

That which was from the beginning, which we have heard, which we have seen with our eyes, which we have looked at and our hands have touched—this we proclaim concerning the Word of life. The life appeared; we have seen it and testify to it, and we proclaim to you the eternal life. . . .

1 JOHN 1:1-2

Four thousand feet above the Grand Canyon, a glass and steel horseshoe-shaped walkway called Skywalk allows visitors to stand above the canyon and appreciate its enormity and grandeur. It's a way of seeing earth from the vantage point of heaven.

A human life infused with the love of God holds the opportunity to tread a "skywalk" suspended between earth and heaven. Each time I make a loving, moral choice over a selfish or hurtful one, I am in that elevated place. I haven't relinquished my mortality and humanity, but I have a way to stand on solid ground and know how it feels to be with God in the heavens.

Perhaps loving God and neighbor is not something to learn, but something to remember. If I could go back to "that which was from the beginning," I would see that I am made to be with God in eternity and have simply forgotten how to do it. Then, when I care for someone and experience a transcendent, skywalking moment, that image of God within me becomes not only something I can see and touch, but something I have *heard*: a memory of my beginning.

Can it be that I was made to see earth through the eyes of heaven?

May

MAY 1

Feeding the volcano

[Demetrius] said, ". . . this Paul has persuaded and drawn away a considerable number of people by saying that gods made with hands are not gods. And there is danger not only that this trade of ours may come into disrepute but also that the temple of the great goddess Artemis will be scorned. . . ."

ACTS 19:25-27

In portions of Indonesia, active volcanoes form part of not only the landscape but the culture. Despite the threat of death from an erupting volcano, many people live near them; some cultures have developed elaborate rituals to placate the gods believed to inhabit the volcanoes.

It sounds crazy, to remain near something so dangerous, but I do it every day that I tie my self-image and my sense of worth to the things of this world. At any moment, an eruption can occur, destroying everything—even my idea of who I am. To put my sense of significance in temporal things and circumstances amounts to living in the shadow of a volcano.

Like those cultures choosing to live near the volcano, I continually toss in offerings, believing that I can appease the god that lives in that frighteningly unstable place. I give up more and more time to the job, or to the sport, or to some other god of worldly status. I somehow begin to believe that if I only do the things of this world just right, that those things will be enough to sustain me.

All of the appeasement I can muster will not allow the "gods made with hands" to save me. When the volcano erupts, only the God of love and forgiveness can save me.

Only the God of love and forgiveness can lift me out of the volcano's way.

MAY 2

Missing

For this is what the LORD says—he who created the heavens, he is God; he who fashioned and made the earth, he founded it; he did not create it to be empty, but formed it to be inhabited. . . .

ISAIAH 45:18

At a favorite breakfast place, I sat, on one occasion, at a table removed from my usual spot. Later another of the "regulars" told me everyone thought I hadn't shown up that day; he said to me, "You were missed." Those three little words warmed my heart. Of course, I am a fixture in the place, so perhaps it was more as if a piece of furniture was not where it belonged.

But I like to think that the missing was more than absence, but incompleteness, a loss of what I could bring to the place. I think of heaven and earth that way, that anyone who doesn't live with God leaves the scene incomplete, and the rest of us just a bit poorer, because we have lost what that one soul could have brought to us.

When God "created the heavens" and "fashioned and made the earth," He had to hope that nothing and no one would be missing, or missed. When I separate myself from God, through sin or neglect, I like to think that He says, on my return, "You were missed." I like to think that life in heaven is fuller if we are all there, rather than just a few who have walked a fine doctrinal line. I like to think that my presence with God matters not just to me, but to Him, and to the others who are with Him.

I like to think I would be missed.

MAY 3

The forest and the trees

I love you, O LORD, my strength. The LORD is my rock, my fortress and my deliverer; my God is my rock, in whom I take refuge. He is my shield and the horn of my salvation, my stronghold.

PSALM 18:1-2

I love to drive through the mountains, to look at far slopes covered with what appears to be a blanket of green, and then to see the bases of the trees themselves as I get closer. What looks from a distance to be a smooth blanket turns out to be millions of trees that can be hiked around, sat under, leaned upon.

My view of God and theology used to look, to me, like that blanket of green: beautiful but impenetrable, and generally irrelevant to my everyday life. I didn't see what use any of it could be to me, particularly when I was hurting or frightened.

But now I have studied incarnation, and see that theological concept in terms of Godly people who hold my hand and comfort me. I have studied redemption, and I see how apparently negative circumstances in my life have been turned into something positive. I have studied the Trinity, and see the different ways we have named God as we have perceived Him in our world.

So I was wrong when I thought God and concepts about God didn't matter. I once imagined a blanket, beautiful if seen from the sky but otherwise useless. What I see now, though, is somewhere to find shade, something to lean on when this world makes me too weary to go on.

I love you O LORD, my strength.

MAY 4

Glimpses of God

Then [Jesus] turned to his disciples and said privately, "Blessed are the eyes that see what you see. For I tell you that many prophets and kings wanted to see what you see but did not see it, and to hear what you hear but did not hear it."

LUKE 10:23-24

Windows lined the halls I walked in seminary every day; through those windows I could see a quadrangle of grass crisscrossed with sidewalks. As I walked the halls one day, I wondered what was going on in the quad. People were gathered there, but I only caught a brief glimpse of the activity each time I passed a window.

Every day holds such brief glimpses of the face of God, if I will only pay attention. Lately I have had many such opportunities to see God: in the embrace of someone who saw my tears, in kind words, in friends who let me talk away my hurt. In each of those "windows," I was able to glimpse God.

The tangible image of God is a sight human beings have always longed for as deeply as we have longed for food or water or oxygen. Jesus reminded His disciples that they were privileged to see God working in the flesh, something many God-seekers in millennia before them had not been allowed to see.

I know that my eyes are "blessed" to see God in the people of my everyday life. After all, it isn't everyone who gets to see God. It isn't every day that we remember to look for Him.

Even prophets and kings long to see such things.

MAY 5

Inclination

". . . Light has come into the world, but men loved darkness instead of light because their deeds were evil. Everyone who does evil hates the light, and will not come into the light for fear that his deeds will be exposed. But whoever lives by the truth comes into the light, so that it may be seen plainly that what he has done has been done through God."
JOHN 3:19-21

From time to time, I have tried desperately to grow a little plant in my apartment, though growing anything outside the refrigerator has always been a challenge. The plant's brave little shoots try valiantly to grow; as they break the soil's surface, they naturally incline toward the sunlight.

I don't think that inclination toward light is limited to plant life. Even the most complex creation, the human soul, inclines toward the light of God just as surely as that plant bends toward the sun. Sometimes we get used to living in the dark, and even think of the dark as preferable, in our fear. Or we "love darkness instead of light" because we know we are evil. But without the light, nothing can grow.

If I remain fearful, away from the light and insisting on self-reliance, I lose all hope of lasting life. But if I bend toward the light, asking God to take the mistakes I have made and somehow redeem them, I can grow. It is a simple matter of surrendering my will to God's will.

Today, will I be like the plant that leans toward the light? Will I incline my heart in God's direction?

Or will I decline?

MAY 6

One across

No one has ever seen God; but if we love one another, God lives in us and his love is made complete in us.

1 JOHN 4:12

One day I saw a woman relaxing and working a crossword puzzle. She would read one clue, shake her head, and then read the clues from the other direction to get hints about the first word. Slowly she persisted and worked through the puzzle, one word, one small success leading to the next.

It seems that I work the puzzle of loving God in a similar way. If I try to picture God "up there in the sky," I have no clue how to start loving Him. "No one has ever seen God," so how can I possibly express my love for Him when I am accustomed only to loving other human beings? But when I love another person, I am in the presence of God, filled for the moment with Him. "God lives in me, and his love is made complete in me." So when I help another person, I am loving God.

At other times, when a person who needs help seems abjectly unlovable, I look to God to help me, and He teaches me to love the unlovable, as He loves me. In this puzzle, I fill in the horizontal spaces by asking God to help me love those whom I cannot love on my own. I fill in the vertical spaces by loving another human being when I can't quite figure out how to get my arms around God. The word reading across, from one human being to another, is love. But that same word, reading down from the heavens to the earth, is something else.

Three letters. Starts with "G."

The unruly child

But you, O LORD, have mercy on me; raise me up, that I may repay them.

PSALM 41:10

In a restaurant, I saw a little girl watching a slightly younger boy. The older child was being very good, while the little boy drew great attention and delight by being louder and more conspicuous. I wondered if the little girl felt hurt; she got much less attention by following the rules than the unruly little boy did by breaking them.

Children of God often struggle with that same kind of rivalry. People who generally obey the rules must feel somewhat victimized by others who continually rely on God's mercy. When I follow the rules, I sometimes want those who break the rules to "get theirs." I'm too superficially pious to actually add vengeance to my prayers, but I have to admit that sometimes my deepest thoughts include, "O, LORD, have mercy on me; raise me up, that I may repay [my enemies]."

But repaying enemies is the human response, not the divine one. The words which ask vengeance to be rained down upon others is not God's decision, but our hope of using God for our own vengeance.

It seems impossible to love others as God loves them, to see that "younger child" of God and not complain about the extra attention received. And yet somehow, we're supposed to change our prayer of vengeance into a prayer of compassion.

O LORD, have mercy on me; raise me up, that I might love my enemies.

MAY 8

God be with you

"Because of your great compassion you did not abandon them in the desert. By day the pillar of cloud did not cease to guide them on their path, nor the pillar of fire by night to shine on the way they were to take. You gave your good Spirit to instruct them."

NEHEMIAH 9:19-20

I often hear people mention a change made "for good," meaning it was a permanent, lifelong change, and I started wondering about the phrase. How did the words "for good" come to describe something that lasts forever?

Perhaps just as "goodbye" has come from "God be with you," the words "for good" originated in the phrase "for God." I have made changes in my life that I thought were "for good"—trying to end bad habits or take up new ones—but if I left God out of the equation, those changes didn't last. In all my efforts to change myself for good, God has never "abandoned me in the desert." When I have a base human instinct to hurt someone else, He "gives His good Spirit to instruct me."

Eventually, when I practice following His will instead of my own, I do find positive, lasting change in my life. Absolutely nothing of this world is lasting, although many things that exist in this world will last forever: the love of God; the compassion of hurting with others; the joy of exulting with others. Such gifts will last into eternity, not because I have decided they are "for good."

But because they are for God.

MAY 9

Road ends

[Do not live as those who] are darkened in their understanding and separated from the life of God because of the ignorance that is in them due to the hardening of their hearts. ... You ... were taught ... to put on the new self, created to be like God in true righteousness and holiness.

EPHESIANS 4:18, 20, 22

In a small town I saw a side road which stopped abruptly at a guardrail with a sign reading, "Road ends." There was no advance warning; the sign "Road ends" didn't appear until there were no other options. The road wasn't ending; it had ended.

I have been on spiritual and emotional roads that ended every bit as abruptly. Either there were no advance signs or I ignored them, because I suddenly found myself staring at a "Road ends" sign, wondering what had happened, wondering where to go. I didn't realize that I was "darkened in my understanding," and I certainly didn't "separate from the life of God" intentionally. I simply got on a road that I thought would go forever.

Then I learned suddenly that people, relationships, things, lifestyles go away, leaving nothing but me and my wounded soul staring at a sign that reading, "Road ends." Now, though, I am eternally grateful for the day that I had no choice other than to turn back toward God, the day I finally made room for Him in my heart. I bless the day I saw the sign that said, "Road ends."

It might just as well have said, "God begins."

Nothing for something

Mary . . . sat at the Lord's feet listening to what he said. But Martha was distracted by all the preparations that had to be made. She came to him and asked, "Lord, don't you care that my sister has left me to do the work by myself?" . . . "Martha, Martha," the Lord answered, "you are worried and upset about many things, but only one thing is needed. Mary has chosen what is better. . . ."

Luke 10:39-41

A handheld game system which came complete with video games and learning tools was supposedly ideal for people with a little extra time on their hands. The slogan for the system was, "Do something with your nothing."

In our society, filling a schedule to the brim is a competitive sport; importance is measured by busy-ness. The busier I am, the more important I must be. Time with "nothing to do" is seen as a sign of weakness or insignificance.

That instinct to measure worth by activity has been around a long time. When Jesus visited Mary and Martha, Mary "sat at the Lord's feet listening to what he said" while Martha "was distracted by the preparations that had to be made." Jesus described the quiet attention—not the frenetic activity—as "better."

God can't speak clearly to me when I fill every possible moment with activity. Yes, it's true that when I choose a moment of quiet with Him, "something" will remain undone.

But sometimes God asks me to do nothing with my something.

MAY 11

Reflections

. . . since we have such a hope, we are very bold. We are not like Moses, who would put a veil over his face to keep the Israelites from gazing at it while the radiance was fading away. . . . But whenever anyone turns to the Lord, the veil is taken away . . . we, who with unveiled faces all reflect the Lord's glory, are being transformed into his likeness. . . .

2 CORINTHIANS 3:12-13, 16, 18

One day on a walk I saw bits of a mirror which had been smashed. The pieces reflected the blue sky, but in different distortions depending on each shard's size and the angle of light.

Every human being who seeks God is such a piece of mirror, a bit of reflection of God at work in our world. People of Moses' time believed that seeing God would cause them to die, so Moses wore a veil to protect them. Yet we are allowed not only to see the face of God but also, in a small human way, to *be* the face of God to others. So we, "who with unveiled faces all reflect the Lord's glory, are being transformed into his likeness."

And maybe, in a way, we do "die" if we regard the face of God. If we fully understand and take to heart the love that God feels for us, our egos and anxieties and temporal priorities simply cannot survive. The "I" disappears, replaced by the glory of God's image. When we all see that truth, God's kingdom will finally overwhelm this kingdom. We will live as those made in God's image are meant to live, fully reflecting that image.

And the mirror will be whole once again.

MAY 12

Beneath the surface

Remember your word to your servant, for you have given me hope. My comfort in my suffering is this: Your promise preserves my life.
PSALM 119:49-50

At a museum I visited, I was especially fascinated with one painting; about one-third of the surface was without color, simple lines on neutral canvas. That portion of the painting had originally showed a royal wedding scene, but layers of paint had been removed to show beautifully intricate drawings of Mary, Jesus, and John the Baptist.

Often I feel that layers of worldly images have to be removed to show the person I truly am, the person God intended me to be. The images on the surface are not authentic, but put on from the mild despair of trying to fit in, trying to look successful. I have painted layer upon layer over the image of God that lies within me.

Ultimately, though, the image of God within guides and sustains me. When life here on earth gets to me, God and I can peel away the layers of paint to reveal the hope of knowing that He is in me, that His "promise preserves my life." I have to remember that the image I often project to the world is only a surface. No matter what I do to cover them, the life and hope given by God are always there within me.

Sometimes, though, it's painful to remove that old paint.

Unoriginal sin

There is no difference, for all have sinned and fall short of the glory of God, and are justified freely by his grace through the redemption that came by Christ Jesus.

ROMANS 3:22-24

Often I go to online to an internet search engine and type in what I consider to be a very weird or offbeat question. Invariably, I find that many other people have already asked that question, so I have easy access to an answer. Sometimes, though, I find myself a bit disappointed that my question is not "original."

I experience that same battle between encouragement and discouragement when I think of the mistakes I have made in my life. It is comforting to know that others have made the same mistakes I have, but sometimes I also cling to my mistakes as more "original sins." I think to myself, "I know God is forgiving, but even God cannot forgive this."

The truth, though, is that I say I cannot forgive myself. And in that failure to forgive myself, I put myself in God's place, as if I get to decide what is forgivable and what is not. In fact, "all have sinned and fall short of the glory of God, and are justified freely by his grace through the redemption that came by Christ Jesus." My sin is no different from anyone else's. And I am not justified by my own forgiveness of myself, but by God's grace.

God loves me, no matter what I have done, no matter what I will do. So will I claim to be different, and continue to separate myself from God?

Or will I let God be God, and embrace the one who forgives my unoriginal sin?

MAY 14

Remade in God's image

Some men brought to [Jesus] a paralytic, lying on a mat. When Jesus saw their faith, he said to the paralytic... "Get up, take your mat and go home." And the man got up and went home.

MATTHEW 9:2, 6

One spring, a tornado nearly wiped Greensburg, Kansas off the map. The town, as it rebuilt, decided to reinvent itself as an environmentally friendly, energy-efficient place. Because of tragic loss, the town had the opportunity to remake itself in a wonderfully new image.

No one should have to endure such loss, but I think most of us would welcome, at least occasionally, the opportunity to remake or reinvent ourselves. What if we could wipe the slate clean of fears rooted in the past, of others' expectations that we have allowed to shape us, of value systems that we do not believe in but continue to obey?

The most profound losses of my life allowed me to remake my life in a way I would never have done if the storm of tragedy had not come. As a Christian, though, I needn't wait for storms to wipe away my past. By the grace of God, my slate can be cleared at any moment; mistakes and value systems of the past can be vanquished.

Like the paralytic healed by Jesus, I have been given by God the power to get up and simply walk away from the past. So even without the storm, I have the opportunity, by the grace of God to be reinvented, to embrace a new-old image.

I can be restored in the image of God, the image in which I was created.

MAY 15

The thieves of light

[The Jews and Greeks living in Ephesus] were all seized with fear, and the name of the Lord Jesus was held in high honor. Many of those who believed now came and openly confessed their evil deeds. A number who had practiced sorcery brought their scrolls together and burned them publicly.

ACTS 19:17-19

I bought a device which locks onto my car's steering wheel to protect it from theft. But the thing sat on the floor of my apartment for weeks, where it probably didn't do much to deter car thieves. Rather than doing something about potential theft, I simply hoped each night that it wouldn't happen.

I'm continually amazed at how many tools we have available to us that go unused, both in everyday human terms and in spiritual terms. For instance, I know that God is not only willing to help me, but that He is actually aching for me to go to Him with every concern of my life. And yet, I often choose God as a last resort, praying to Him for guidance only when all else has failed.

Unlike the people of Ephesus who were willing to sacrifice their former priorities for God, I try to live in both worlds. I keep my other little "gods" hidden away, and even pray to God Almighty for help with them. My unwillingness to go to God first makes me easy prey for the forces of this world, the thieves of light.

I have the tools—the presence and peace and strength of God—to keep this world from stealing my heart and soul. But my failing to use them leaves me open to anxiety, fear, loneliness.

I hope those thieves don't come this night.

Possibility

For the secret power of lawlessness is already at work; but the one who now holds it back will continue to do so till he is taken out of the way. And then the lawless one will be revealed, whom the Lord Jesus will overthrow with the breath of his mouth and destroy by the splendor of his coming.

2 THESSALONIANS 2:7-8

On a TV drama, one character lamented of another's disappointing behavior, "People can be broken by the weight of possibility." The idea rang true, that we human beings can be every bit as damaged by our best potential as by our worst.

Sometimes I wonder if I delayed pursuing God because I was afraid of the "weight of possibility," of the depth of good that could come if I allowed God to change me completely. "The secret power of lawlessness" was the comfort I found in not living up to my potential. My greatest fear was (and often still is) that I might live up to my fullest potential and still not be much of anything. Yet, if I will but crack open the door, the light of God will come in and destroy the darkness of my fears "by the splendor of His coming."

Sometimes I am still paralyzed by the thought of the potential of God's power working in me. But only by living into God's dream for me can I be whole and holy. After all, I have already seen the grace with which God can lift my worst self; maybe it's time to see what He can do with my best.

Scary, scary thought . . .

The needy and the greedy

Since they had nothing to eat, Jesus called his disciples to him and said, "I have compassion for these people; they have already been with me three days and have nothing to eat."

MARK 8:1

On TV one night, I heard a father tell a son, "We're giving to the needy, not the greedy." I didn't know the context of the remark, but I certainly like its sentiment. The world seems terribly skewed, with too many resources going to the greedy and not enough to the needy.

The trick to making the world right, it seems, is determining what we really mean by need. Is the rich person who spurns God in need, or not? What about the economically poor person who craves no material things and puts the love of others first?

God chooses, though, to shower grace on all, both the needy and the greedy. I picture God looking at us, saying, "I have compassion for these people," and longing to satisfy our hunger. And that grace of God is offered equally to those who know they cannot make it on their own and those who think they can do everything for themselves.

Such magnanimity doesn't make sense if seen through human lenses, but it is the way of the abundant grace of God. The truth of the Gospel is that Jesus has compassion for the human condition, and He wants to feed the hungry.

And it doesn't matter whether they're rich or poor. . . .

The Lord rains

I will be careful to lead a blameless life—when will you come to me?
PSALM 101:2

During a water crisis in India, the inhabitants continued to dig wells deeper, which in turn depleted the country's groundwater supply dangerously. They were not short-sighted; they were desperate.

Far too often in my life, I have believed that I can handle things for myself if I only "dig deeper" and work harder. Like the psalmist, I continue to cling to the belief that, if I lead "a blameless life," I can convince God to come to me.

But, as in the thirsty lands of India, that tactic cannot work for long, as I will deplete my reservoir of energy, and with still no hope for a better future. In my fatigue and despair, I not only fail to save myself, but I lose the strength to seek God.

The truth is that I don't have to ask God, "When will you come to me?" He is here, waiting for me to turn to Him. He is here, now, ready to quench my thirst if I will only ask.

God doesn't save me because I have led a blameless life, but because I am His beloved child. Salvation is not my reward; it is God's gift. Only when I remember to stop digging deeper wells and start looking to the skies will I be saved from myself and from the rest of this arid world. On that day that I look up, my thirst will be quenched forever.

On that day, God's grace will fall like rain.

MAY 19

Regaining the joy

See to it, brothers, that none of you has a sinful, unbelieving heart that turns away from the living God. But encourage one another daily, as long as it is called Today, so that none of you may be hardened by sin's deceitfulness. We have come to share in Christ if we hold firmly till the end the confidence we had at first.

HEBREWS 3:12-14

When I was 12, I fell in love with the game of golf. I soon started playing tournaments, and I became so obsessed with winning at golf that I forgot how much I loved to play the game. I traded away joy for performance.

The human psyche can easily get so wrapped up in performance or competition that we forget why we took up an activity in the first place. I first learned to love God when I realized that He loves me despite all I have done—and will do—wrong. Yet I still catch myself wanting to display God like one more trophy on the mantel. I lose "the confidence I had at first" and "turn away from the living God" to worship myself and my pursuit of God.

As Christians, we have to continually remind each other of the grace of God so that we worship Him instead of the trappings with which we surround Him. We can remind each other of that grace by forgiving where resentment might be our first instinct. We can remind each other by loving other persons whether they can benefit us or not.

We can trade in the performance and regain the joy.

MAY 20

Good and great

Knowledge puffs up, but love builds up. The man who thinks he knows something does not yet know as he ought to know. But the man who loves God is known by God.

1 CORINTHIANS 8:1-3

One business guru has said, "Good is the enemy of great." A good leader or organization may stop short of the heights it could achieve if it took risks. That need to maintain the good can prevent accomplishment of the great.

For me, spiritually, though, "Great is the enemy of good." As a human being in need of continual reinforcement about my own worth, I once wanted to do something great, for someone to think of me as great. I wanted to make the grand gestures to convince myself that this life of mine has meaning. Then I would finally know myself, and my own worth.

Now, though, I see that no matter how "great" I become, someone else will be greater, smarter, more famous, more accomplished. And in comparing myself to others, I will have lost sight of my true self as defined by God. I think I know something, but that proves that I do not yet know what I need to know.

Knowledge and besting others only "puffs up" the ego; it does nothing for the actual value of a human life. I have worth not because of what I achieve, but because I am the beloved of God. Would I love to be famous, to make a "great" difference in the world? Of course I would.

But only if "great" doesn't become the enemy of "good."

MAY 21

Fireproof

Deep calls to deep in the roar of your waterfalls; all your waves and breakers have swept over me. . . . I say to God my Rock, "Why have you forgotten me?. . . "

PSALM 42:7-8

Once I was hired by a man to write the story of a company he had established. For the work, he provided a heavy-duty, fireproof filing cabinet to protect irreplaceable documents I was using.

Often I have wished that God would provide me with an indestructible vessel to bear the precious gift of His image in my life. If He wants to give me something so very precious, shouldn't He also give me a way to protect it, a way to ensure that nothing harmful can get in?

But "deep calls to deep," and God's presence cannot touch me, or anyone else, if that presence is sealed up in an indestructible container. Relating to people deeply in the name of God requires risking harm to the human heart—carrying this most precious cargo in a vessel that is vulnerable and wide open to a scary world. If I can't be hurt when I speak of God, then He has no relevance in this world.

Still, it all makes me wonder, "Why have you forgotten me?" But God hasn't forgotten me when I am hurt doing His work. He is speaking to me in the deepest, most difficult, most tragic places so that the God of heaven can live with us—and in us—on earth. God has no intention of keeping my heart from catching on fire.

In fact, it's what He's hoping for.

Flowers along the road

. . . some men came from the house of Jairus. . . . "Your daughter is dead," they said. "Why bother the teacher any more?" Ignoring what they said, Jesus told the synagogue ruler, "Don't be afraid; just believe."

MARK 5:35-36

Driving on the highway, I saw a woman lugging a pailful of flowers, just picked from the roadside, back to her car. The flowers must have been beautiful, because the woman had to slog through mud and weeds to get to them.

Sometimes clinging to the hope of God in this world requires an equally heroic effort. This world says that people only help others for selfish gain, that I had best protect myself rather than being vulnerable in loving others, that I should be self-reliant instead of letting others help me. I have to get past that mud of human doubt and skepticism, past the junk of selfishness and fear, to love God and allow myself to be loved by God.

A man of Jesus' time, told that his daughter was dead, could have listened to human logic which said, "Your daughter is dead. . . . Why bother the teacher?" But Jesus tried to tell the frightened man to hold onto hope, to work his way past flawed human understanding, past skepticism. "Don't be afraid," Jesus told him. "Just believe."

How and why would the God of the universe come to help me today? Human logic says He would not. But my heart says He will, and that He has. "Don't be afraid," Jesus tells me.

"Just believe."

MAY 23

Elsewhere

If I speak in the tongues of men and of angels, but have not love, I am only a resounding gong or a clanging cymbal. If I have ... a faith that can move mountains, but have not love, I am nothing. If I give all I possess to the poor and surrender my body to the flames, but have not love, I gain nothing.

1 CORINTHIANS 13:1-3

On the news one night was a story about a proposed affordable housing development in a nearby town. A group of people whose property bordered the land said they hoped the development would go elsewhere, but the developer said, "There is no 'elsewhere.'"

For many people who struggle, there is no "elsewhere" in our world. We say we want to help, but it certainly is easier to write a check and keep that person in need at a distance, out of "my backyard." But if I'm truly going to love God and love my neighbor, it's going to get messy. I can't always take care of other people in ways that are comfortable or tidy.

All of the religion in the world will not bring me as close to God as will a genuine interest in taking care of others. I don't love others because it's the right thing to do societally. I am to take care of my neighbor because in that uncomfortable instant of being present to another human being—that untidy place where one flawed human embraces another—I find God. I encounter God in that specific time, in that particular place.

For me, and that person, and God, there is no "elsewhere."

The broken seal

But no one in heaven or on earth or under the earth could open the scroll or even look inside it. I wept and wept because no one was found who was worthy to open the scroll or look inside.

REVELATION 5:3-4

In an article about human rights in one nation, a lawyer there said, "People across this country are awakening to their rights and seizing on the promise of the law. But you cannot be a rights lawyer in this country without becoming a rights case yourself." It is an example, it seems, of becoming both the giver and the gift; the one using the law to save is also the one being saved.

The Christian life strikes me much the same way, that when we offer help, we have to also be willing to be helped. When we seek to love, we have to be willing to admit that we long to be loved, to be willing to let love in, from God and others. Personally, I am much more comfortable, in some ways, giving help than accepting it. I suppose somewhere in me is the feeling that I don't deserve to be loved until I've paid some price to earn it.

The life-giving, liberating truth, though, is that "no one in heaven or on earth or under the earth" is capable of giving or receiving love until the hand of God touches us. With that touch, we learn to love, and we learn to allow ourselves to be loved. We become the love of God incarnate. In God's hands, the seal to the eternal now is finally broken.

And the giver becomes the gift.

MAY 25

Say the Word

[Jesus] was not far from the house when the centurion sent friends to say to him: "Lord. . . I do not deserve to have you come under my roof. That is why I did not even consider myself worthy to come to you. But say the word, and my servant will be healed. . . ."

LUKE 7:6-7

As a teenager, I made my mom laugh one day by pronouncing the word "khaki" as if it were spelled "ka-HEE-kee." Though I had read the word silently many times, saying it aloud certainly was a different experience than saying it to myself.

The centurion who met Jesus knew the power of a word spoken aloud. He came to Jesus on behalf of a servant, saying, "I did not even consider myself worthy to come to you. But say the word, and my servant will be healed, . . ." A moment of healing grace occurred because one man overcame his own doubts to come to Jesus on someone else's behalf.

Jesus is not the only person capable of effecting healing by the spoken word. As a human being in a broken world, I see opportunities daily to heal by simply "saying the word." When I get angry but choose to speak in a way that rises above that anger, I have said a word that begins to heal. When I am hurt and offer a word of forgiveness or spiritual generosity rather than retribution or resentment, my words may bring healing.

Many chances for spoken grace may come today. Will I be willing to say the right word, so that someone may be healed?

Even if I am that someone?

MAY 26

What I know

The people walking in darkness have seen a great light; on those living in the land of the shadow of death a light has dawned.

ISAIAH 9:2

At one semester's end, I had long final exams in two classes; no matter how much I studied, I never felt that I knew enough. When it came time to take the exams, though, I felt better by focusing on what I did know instead of focusing on what I didn't know.

I took a rocky, circuitous route to God, largely because I insisted on emphasizing what I don't know. I do not know how to explain God. Given my record, I certainly don't know why God would continue to care for me and forgive me.

And yet, I do know that God loves me, and that my life means something in His eyes even though it sometimes feels insignificant to me. I know that I once lived in great darkness, but that now I feel filled with life and excited about what tomorrow brings. I know that light has come to the very darkest places in my life.

Much remains that I do not know, and that I will never know. But I know that I belong to God, and with God. I know that living for God allows me to live in eternity instead of within time. I know that I am loved, protected, embraced, lifted up.

So in tough times, I focus on what I do know rather than on what I don't know. I know that, not so long ago, I was "living in the land of the shadow of death," but now "a light has dawned." That light is the presence of God: this much I know.

And it is enough.

God looks on the heart

But the LORD said to Samuel, "Do not look on his appearance or on the height of his stature, because I have rejected him; for the LORD does not see as mortals see; they look on the outward appearance, but the LORD looks on the heart."

1 SAMUEL 16:7

Anais Nin once wrote that, "We don't see things as they are. We see them as we are." All of our preconceptions and experiences go into the way we see in this world.

I'm afraid that very subjective way of seeing also applies when a human being tries to see God. Oftentimes, I don't see God as God is, but as I am, even as I am at a particular moment. The upshot of such distorted seeing is that I can think of God as petty and vengeful, as I can be. I make God, if not in my image, in the image I need at the moment.

But when my fears and prejudices are overcome, I know that God is not petty and vengeful. I can't even see God correctly when I think of God as "just," because my human understanding of justice involves humans' getting what we deserve. I believe that God is mercy, and forgiveness: that God is just in God's way, not in human ways. God knows that, despite my mistakes, my heart longs for only Him.

Samuel questioned the man chosen to be the next king, as he didn't much look the part. Yet God told him, "mortals . . . look on the outward appearance, but the LORD looks on the heart."

I have been wrong so many times, but I have hope that I can always be with God. God doesn't see things as they are. He sees them as they could be.

In other words, God looks on the heart.

The burden of lost baggage

But because of his great love for us, God, who is rich in mercy, made us alive with Christ even when we were dead in transgressions—it is by grace you have been saved.

EPHESIANS 2:4-5

One ad for travel services offered by a credit card company asked, "Are you burdened with lost baggage?" I couldn't help wondering how baggage that is lost, leaving nothing to carry, could be a "burden."

And yet, I am often burdened by lost spiritual or emotional baggage. In certain times of my life, I have seen and defined myself through the baggage: frightening experiences, mistakes, personal losses. If I'm not careful, I hang onto the loss and start to think of myself only in terms of those negative times. The "bad old days" can somehow become part of me that I'm strangely afraid to lose. So I guess I can say I have been "burdened by lost baggage."

But to define myself only through the darkness—either through a failure to forgive myself or through staying unnecessarily in the memory of tough times—sacrifices the present on the altar of the past. So I need to stop saying, "God cannot forgive this," because God can. God *has*.

"God, who is rich in mercy, made us alive with Christ even when we were dead in transgressions." It's time to embrace God's mercy, forgiveness, grace. It's time to let God do God's work.

It's time to stop being burdened with lost baggage.

MAY 29

Looking for the light

How, then, can they call on the one they have not believed in? And how can they believe in the one of whom they have not heard?

ROMANS 10:14

Whenever I stay in unfamiliar places, a first priority is always to find the light switches. Too many times I have forgotten to locate the switches in the light of day, and I find myself groping along walls when the darkness comes.

When I first began looking for God, something told me, despite the hard times I was experiencing, that God exists and God would care for me. I didn't have the sense to look for God in the light, though. So eventually I found myself inching along a wall, knowing a switch was there somewhere, but finding it only with great effort.

Now I see others struggling in the dark, many of them unaware that a relationship with God could save them from the dark of desperation, many others unaware that they're in the dark at all. I think of them, and of myself just a few years ago, when I read, "How can they call on the one they have not believed in?"

I'm convinced that simply telling people about the light and life of God will do little good. People have to see the light and peace of God in us. They have to see people who are more willing to embrace than to exclude, more willing to forgive than to condemn. Eventually, they may begin to ask about the source of that light and peace.

But why look for a light switch if you don't even know you're living in the dark?

MAY 30

There has been a sighting

"Teacher," said John, "we saw a man driving out demons in your name and we told him to stop, because he was not one of us." "Do not stop him," Jesus said. "No one who does a miracle in my name can in the next moment say anything bad about me . . ."

MARK 9:38-39

Once I read that the words "sighting" and "siting" can be used in very similar ways. "Sighting" means catching a glimpse of something, while "siting" means identifying something with a particular place, or locating it. So a "sighting/siting" of Bigfoot could mean either a glimpse, or an experience of situating him in a particular place.

The difference can be critical, it seems, in speaking of God. Each time we see God's hand at work in the love of one human being for another, we sight— or glimpse—God and become closer to God. Yet each time we think we can "site" God—fully describing or understanding God—we move further away through our own arrogance.

Jesus' disciples walked that same fine line of seeing God but never fully locating God; they wondered what to do about people who claimed to "drive out demons" in His name. Good work, though, is the work of God, no matter what humans choose to call that work. So while we cannot completely capture or completely understand God, we can confidently identify good work as God's work. We can, every day, experience a sighting of God.

But we can never claim a "siting."

Untoward

They would not be like their forefathers—a stubborn and rebellious generation, whose hearts were not loyal to God, whose spirits were not faithful to him. . . . They forgot what he had done, the wonders he had shown them.

PSALM 78:8,11

I have always liked the word, "untoward," which the dictionary says can mean "troublesome" or "improper." It seems to be something we say when we know something simply isn't right, but can't think of a specific word to describe its wrongness.

More literally, though, the word seems to mean "away from." To move "toward" is to approach, so something "untoward" must be moving away. Perhaps the ultimate version of untoward behavior is that which distances us from God.

It's a very old story—this moving toward and away from God. Even the psalms describe people who were "a stubborn and rebellious generation, whose hearts were not loyal to God, whose spirits were not faithful to him." Like many of us, those people once had great appreciation for the gift of God's presence, but then "they forgot what he had done" and acted against the will of God. Their behavior was "untoward."

If I had the courage to do it, I would examine each action I take, each word I utter, and measure it according to this standard. Does this action or word help me to move closer to God?

Or is it, well, "untoward"?

June

JUNE 1

Unnamed storms

O LORD. . . You discern my going out and my lying down; you are familiar with all my ways. . . .If I go up to the heavens, you are there; if I make my bed in the depths, you are there.

PSALM 139:1-3, 8

Today is the first day of the official hurricane season. About this time each year, the National Hurricane Center releases a list of names to be used for that season's hurricanes. Anyone who doubts that those names will endure needs only to mention the names "Camille" or "Katrina" to Gulf Coast residents.

I'll bet that people who endure loss as a result of tornadoes and other weather events—"unnamed storms"—wish the cause of their grief also had a name, rather than just a description of a date and time that disaster came.

Much of the loss and grief we endure goes unnamed or otherwise defies description in human terms. We offer instant sympathy to one whose storm is named, but we are less likely to listen patiently to a story of loss with no name, or a prolonged story of how lives were changed.

The only place we can go in such indescribable grief and loss is to God. When I experience grief over a circumstance other humans don't understand or over something long ago, God understands, and holds me close. I know that God understands "my going out and my lying down," and that, "if I make my bed in the depths," God is there.

We humans can be impatient, wanting others' grief to fit into neat names and sound bytes. Only God can hear us in those ineffable moments. Only God understands the depths to which my soul can plunge.

Only God can hold me close, even when the storm of my loss has no name.

The big event

". . . My people come to you, as they usually do, and sit before you to listen to your words, but they do not put them into practice. With their mouths they express devotion, but their hearts are greedy for unjust gain. Indeed, to them you are nothing more than one who sings love songs with a beautiful voice and plays an instrument well, for they hear your words but do not put them into practice."

EZEKIEL 33:31-32

An acquaintance, returning from a trip where he proposed to his girlfriend, described arranging the dramatic moment, the exotic place the wedding will take place, and the cost of the cake. He never once mentioned anything substantive about the woman he would marry.

Perhaps the man's fervor for his beloved can be assumed from all that he is spending to marry her. But while it's simplistic, it does seem that, as in many human relationships, the emphasis is on the big, dramatic event instead of on the day-to-day-ness of loving another person.

The prophet Ezekiel heard similar accusations when God asked him to speak to the people about their lack of faithfulness, saying, "to them you are nothing more than one who sings love songs . . . for they hear your words but do not put them into practice." God does not want love songs, but love. God does not want events of high drama, but quiet moments of devotion. God doesn't care about a big wedding.

God wants us to speak of our Beloved.

JUNE 3

What we gave away

Thomas said to him, "Lord, we don't know where you are going, so how can we know the way?" Jesus answered, "I am the way and the truth and the life."

JOHN 14:5-6

When I moved to seminary, I gave away many things I thought I wouldn't need. Later, I sometimes thought about replacing some of those things. I found myself saying, "I wish I hadn't given that away."

I have come to believe that every human soul has that same feeling of letting something valuable get away and longing to get it back. Deep within each of us lives the sense that we are made to be with God, and a faint remembrance that we are made in God's image. Time living in this brutally indifferent world and fear have made us forget that we are made by God, for God, and that we can return to God at any moment.

Like the disciples who saw the risen Jesus, though, we slip into believing that following God is a mystery we cannot solve, something that requires a strength and wisdom we cannot muster. So we ask, as Thomas did, "Lord, we don't know where you are going, so how can we know the way?"

The truth, though, is that the God of Jesus Christ needn't be found, because God lives in us, in our lives, today. Our hearts and souls once knew that truth. Our hearts and souls once knew the way. Despite all of the noise in our human lives, we still know the way. We needn't wish we could get it back.

The love of God is the one thing we cannot give away.

Best-kept secret

What I tell you in the dark, speak in the daylight; what is whispered in your ear, proclaim from the roofs. Do not be afraid of those who kill the body but cannot kill the soul. Rather, be afraid of the One who can destroy both soul and body in hell.

MATTHEW 10:27-28

A marketing expert I once heard said that no company or product wants to be known as the "best-kept secret." The lure of inside knowledge aside, those marketing to us want their products to be widely known, not secrets.

Sadly, in our culture, the saving grace of God can be considered the world's "best-kept secret." Though the presence of God in my life gives me peace, I am tragically hesitant to speak of that presence as central in my life. If others notice peace or patience in me, I am more likely to pass it off to "having a good day" or to "being happier with myself" than to give God the credit.

Considering the difference in my life since I began inviting God into that life, I should "proclaim from the roofs" what was "whispered in my ear." I know that God not only holds the meaning of life, but is the meaning of life. I live in peace amid the chaos because I know that this world can "kill the body but cannot kill the soul." And yet, why am I so timid about telling others about God?

This is one piece of wisdom that is best (not) kept secret.

JUNE 5

The small picture

When you make a vow to God, do not delay in fulfilling it. . . . It is better not to vow than to make a vow and not fulfill it . . . do not protest to the temple messenger, "My vow was a mistake."

ECCLESIASTES 5:4-6

Off from school my last summer of seminary, I vowed to spend some of it exploring New England. I was determined to take advantage of that gift of time and place, as I knew that I might never be in that territory again.

It's easy to make sweeping vows, but actually fulfilling such a promise, even to myself, will require daily vigilance in the small things. I have to schedule work carefully. I have to avoid being lazy and postponing a trip until another day. I have to choose these small trips over other appealing, but less singular, opportunities for fun.

Vows—whether made to myself, to other persons, or to God—are never fulfilled in a big picture, but by faithfulness in the small picture. I can always find excuses or rationalizations for not fulfilling something overwhelming, so I have to focus on being faithful one detail at a time. And by taking care of those small tasks, I show my faithfulness to God in this time, and this place, regardless of what the future holds.

God has given me many gifts, the most precious of which is His very presence in my life. With God beside me and within me, I can move today toward my vow of living life abundantly.

After all, I may never be in this territory again.

JUNE 6

Stormy weather

. . . as servants of God we commend ourselves in every way: in great endurance; in troubles, hardships and distresses. . . [we are] sorrowful, yet always rejoicing; poor, yet making many rich; having nothing, and yet possessing everything.

2 CORINTHIANS 6:4, 10

A TV special commemorating D-Day described a brief break in bad weather that allowed the Allies to go on with the invasion. The invasion caught the Germans by surprise, in part, because they didn't expect anything to happen in such stormy weather.

I would expect that people become more conscious of God in good times, so I've been surprised, like the Germans on D-Day, to first become aware of God when the weather felt absolutely forbidding. God surprised me, as God has surprised many of us, by coming right into the middle of the storm.

Perhaps God is seen more clearly in storms because people who love and worship Him step up to help in difficult times. Though realistic about this world, we offer a glimpse of a love and a life that transcend present troubles. Because we know God will lift us above this life, we are "sorrowful, yet always rejoicing; poor, yet making many rich; having nothing, and yet possessing everything."

The human forecast, seeing storm clouds, says that nothing good can come of frightening weather. The divine forecast, though, sees something different. True, the dark clouds are here.

But so is God.

JUNE 7

Exploring inner space

As he approached Jerusalem and saw the city, he wept over it and said, "If you, even you, had only known on this day what would bring you peace—but now it is hidden from your eyes. The days will come upon you when your enemies will build an embankment against you and encircle you and hem you in on every side. . . ."

LUKE 19:41-43

Sometimes I read about our efforts at space exploration and wonder what benefit those expensive efforts offer. In earlier times, though, I suppose research which would become life-changing or life-saving must have looked irrelevant to small human eyes.

As humans often obsessed with conquest and accomplishment, it can also be hard for us to understand the benefits of exploring our own inner motives and inner longings. We have so much to do on the outside that we neglect exploring the inside. We wonder what possible good it can do to look inward when our outward to-do list overflows.

As in Jesus' day, we humans struggle to know "on this day what would bring us peace." Enemies on the outside seem intent on "encircling us and hemming us in on every side." The human psyche believes that salvation is on the outside, that the only way to best those enemies encircling us is to fight them on their own ground.

The truth, though, is that we "win" in this world only by refusing to participate in it. We find peace by opening our hearts to the grace and presence of God.

Ultimately, it's the exploration of inner space that will allow us to get out of this world.

The broken key

The man without the Spirit does not accept the things that come from the Spirit of God. . . . The spiritual man makes judgments about all things, but he himself is not subject to any man's judgment. . . .

1 CORINTHIANS 2:14-15

Long ago, in a hurry to open my front door, I broke the key off in the bolt lock. If I put my piece of the key in just right, I could get the lock to open. Until my roommate arrived with her key, I had to leave the broken key in to have access.

I think each of us stumbles through this life, a broken key in our hands, wondering where to find the other piece. I have finally realized that the door to peace in living the human life cannot be opened with only the piece of key I hold.

For years, I thought the missing part of the key was "more"—more relationships, more possessions, more success. Yet all of those things left me empty, no matter how much of them I had. Then I found the other part of the key by seeking God first, finally integrating my spiritual life more fully with my physical life and letting God's dreams for me become my own dreams.

Now I do a better job of "making judgments about all things" in God's light, rather than letting myself be "subject to man's judgment." The spiritual and the physical no longer work against each other, but with each other. The piece of key in my hands fits perfectly with the piece in the door, and the door has swung open.

I have finally found that missing peace.

JUNE 9

Feeding the hungry

While Jesus was having dinner at Matthew's house, many tax collectors and "sinners" came and ate with him and his disciples. When the Pharisees saw this, they asked his disciples, "Why does your teacher eat with tax collectors and 'sinners'?"

MATTHEW 9:10-11

Food, medicine, and fresh water weren't getting through to victims of the a cyclone because of the government's restrictions. One aid agency official said of the obstacles put in place by the bureaucracy there, "It's a race for time, a race to save lives."

Sadly, we humans often set up roadblocks when people are starving, physically or spiritually. Though asked simply to love God and love neighbor, too often we want to raise barriers to filter the deserving from the undeserving. Or we claim to know God's will and ways and declare that some of "us" belong with God and some of "them" don't. Fearful and defensive, we act as if grace is our property. We argue about how to structure the system of aid; meanwhile people are starving.

But if we are truly to follow Jesus' example, we will embrace everyone, pouring the love of God out abundantly and letting God sort out the details. If we were to lavish the love of God on every person we meet, we might even "eat with tax collectors and sinners." We might feed someone, and in the process, find nourishment for ourselves. What a scandal!

What kind of God would allow such things?

JUNE 10

Judgment

Follow the ways of your heart and whatever your eyes see, but know that for all these things God will bring you to judgment.

ECCLESIASTES 11:9

I love to watch golf, especially the men's U.S. Open golf tournament. I consider myself a pretty good golfer, but the game those people play reveals how little I really know how to do. Still, seeing the game played right made me want to go play, to practice, to do better.

I think that the judgment of God works that same way. In the perfect light of God, we see our own flaws. We see what we could be if we were to live the life God asks. We see how much better—how very eternal—this world could be if each of us lived a life faithful to God.

In those moments of revelation—of seeing how this life is truly designed to be—I find both despair and hope. When I have "followed the ways of my heart" without consulting God, I have made mistakes and hurt God and others. The realization of the hurt I have caused brings me despair.

But I also have hope in seeing what I am capable of, as a human saved and empowered by the grace of God. When I see judgment in that way, I see that light as a way out of the despair. Yes, the light of judgment feels harsh because it shows me what could have been.

But ultimately, the light of judgment brings mercy, because it teaches me what still could be.

JUNE 11

Big little words

Are not all angels ministering spirits sent to serve those who will inherit salvation?

HEBREWS 1:14

In Greek class I struggled most with prepositions, small words which can dramatically alter the meaning of a sentence. Is the action happening *for* someone, *to* someone, *in* someone, *with* someone? Those little words can make a big difference.

Even before I knew anything about religion, I knew that, to the spirit, little words can make a big difference. The big fancy words of theology didn't draw me toward God. The love of God's people, expressed through small acts of kindness or concern, made me want to know more about Him. Something in my heart told me that the people who helped me through the darkness were angels, "ministering spirits sent to serve those who will inherit salvation."

The smallest act—of tending to someone, being with someone, standing up for someone—might open the door for one lost soul to step into God's presence. The smallest act of kindness can make someone begin to believe that God not only exists, but cares personally about us and for us.

I have lived that storyline, of seeing life change because of the seemingly insignificant moments in which I was ministered to by angels. I know from direct experience that one small act can change a life or even, in the spiritual sense, save a life.

Small acts, like small words, can change everything.

The sound of thunder

If only I knew where to find him; if only I could go to his dwelling!
JOB 23:3

In a classroom building one day, I was shocked to hear thunder, as the day's forecast had called for clear skies. But I wasn't hearing thunder at all; noisy movers on the second floor were making the noise pushing heavy furniture around.

Am I the only person who struggles to tell the difference between the sounds coming from the heavens and sounds made by humans? Many people in my life seem absolutely certain that they hear directly from God, and they seem to know a great deal about his nature and his will. Do they truly hear the thunder of the skies—the voice of God—or are they hearing manmade noise? How can they tell? Why can't I?

Job, the prime example of the human need to understand God and God's will, begged for a hearing with the Almighty. In his misery, Job lamented of God, "If only I knew where to find him; if only I could go to his dwelling!" I often have a mild version of that same lament, wishing God would speak directly to me about what to do.

Are our "encounters" with God truly about God, or about seeking affirmation for doing what we want to do? The human imagination and the need to control can be powerful enough to convince me that I'm hearing God when all I'm really hearing are echoes of my own will. Sometimes I do hear sounds I can't identify. Is that a sound made by noisy humans?

Or am I hearing something from the heavens?

JUNE 13

Show me a picture

He is the image of the invisible God, the firstborn over all creation. For by him all things were created: things in heaven and on earth, visible and invisible, whether thrones or powers or rulers or authorities; all things were created by him and for him. He is before all things, and in him all things hold together.

COLOSSIANS 1:15-17

A dear friend once served, during a summer, as costume mistress for a Shakespeare festival. When I asked her what that meant exactly, she said, "The director would show me the picture of a costume, and I had to make it."

Generally a picture is helpful, but most of us require both a picture and some kind of pattern to use in guiding us in the construction, piece by piece. In the incarnation of Christ, we get both: the picture of how this Godly life looks in a human being, and a pattern of how we might make such a life. The pattern lives within us, as each of us is created "by him and for him."

How do we live, in this great drama of life on earth, and reveal the divine which calls to us from above, and from within? We look at a picture, in the life of Christ, and we allow that logos—that creative force of Christ living in us—to guide us piece by piece in living that life.

God's son became incarnate and lived among us. And because he did live among us—and continues to live among us—we can begin to understand and build a life of peace. So God doesn't just show us a picture of a life. God also shows us how to make it, piece by piece.

To peace.

JUNE 14

Infrequent flyer

Brothers, stop thinking like children. In regard to evil, be infants, but in your thinking be adults.

1 CORINTHIANS 14:20

On a flight home, a passenger who had requested a seat with a "view" sat next to me. She looked out the window the entire flight, often even checking a map to see where we might be. She took great delight in the experience, as an innocent child might who never imagined humans could touch the sky.

Seeking God, we are often urged to be more like children, with a sense of wonder and awe, of openness to the good of the world. We're asked, "In regard to evil, be infants, but in your thinking be adults." We follow God with as much openness as we can muster, not allowing ourselves to become cynical about the evil we see in the world.

I often wonder how to make that combination work in a world that can be frightful and victimizing. I would like to help people more often—strangers on the street—but that stance can be dangerous. Perhaps, then, to be "infants" in regard to evil is to live in the world without trying to beat the system or take advantage of others. And yet, "in thinking (as) adults," we are to be on guard for those who would victimize us.

The trip we take with God each day can be breathtaking. Others, more cynical, have no appreciation for the gift, but we know how awe-inspiring it is for a human to have access to God.

Like children, we never imagined humans would be allowed to touch the sky.

What we consume

[Jesus] said, "I tell you the truth, one of you will betray me—one who is eating with me." They were saddened, and one by one they said to him, "Surely not I?"

MARK 14:18-19

Preparation for U.S. Olympic participation in China included shipping food over for the team. Some foods sold in China were so full of steroids that consuming those foods could have made the athletes test positive for illegal steroid use.

Often the ways we contribute to the ills of the world can be that insidious and that subtle. I may not overtly oppress another person, but through thoughtlessness and self-interest, I encourage a skewed system to stay in place. In other words, what feeds me may turn out to be just as toxic as if I had directly hurt another person. If I consume more and more goods out of selfishness, I add to the world's refuse, not to mention adding to the mistaken notion that we are what we own.

Jesus' disciples were appalled to hear that one of them would betray him; when he spoke of betrayal, "one by one they said to him, 'Surely not I?'" Something in them hinted that they were capable of such betrayal. Perhaps each wondered how desperate he could become if his own interests were at stake, or how often his own selfishness had caused someone else pain.

So who is responsible for the upside-down priorities of this world if not those who benefit from and perpetuate the system?

Surely not I . . .

JUNE 16

Near and far

[Jesus] entered Capernaum. There a centurion's servant, whom his master valued highly, was sick and about to die. The centurion heard of Jesus and sent some elders of the Jews to him, asking him to come and heal his servant.

LUKE 7:1-3

After years of playing golf in contact lenses, I tried to hit some golf shots wearing bifocal glasses instead. It was tough going at first, as I had trouble switching between the close vision and distant vision parts of the lenses.

The way we see God, too, can be that confusing and unsettling combination of close and far vision. We know of God as the Creator of the universe, but we begin to know God more in the personal relationship. The centurion began to see God only when Jesus came close enough to heal the man's dying child. A far vision of God, as Creator, probably would not have converted the man, but the near vision of seeing his child recover allowed him to see God in Jesus.

As human beings—part of the Creation—trying to see our Creator, we will always struggle with near and far vision. The creation of a universe, an unimaginably enormous task, looks small when your own little world is falling apart. And yet the healing of a loved one—just one person among billions—looms large. So is God in the far heavens, or near on the earth?

Yes.

Preventive medicine

This is what the LORD says—your Redeemer, the Holy One of Israel: "I am the LORD your God. . . . If only you had paid attention to my commands, your peace would have been like a river, your righteousness like the waves of the sea. . . ."

ISAIAH 48:17-18

While in seminary, I caught a virus one week. The doctor gave me, on the way out, a book designed to teach me how to live more healthfully. At that moment, I wasn't interested in preventive medicine. I needed help getting through that particular day.

Christianity sometimes must look like nothing more than preventive medicine, especially to those who don't know about God and find themselves in acute pain. A person in trouble seldom wants to hear how that trouble could have been avoided "if only" some other course had been taken. Like the Israelites, we don't want to hear how our lives could be better and more manageable, "If only you had paid attention to my commands." When drowning in trouble, it is hard to imagine "peace flowing like a river."

And yet, I believe that God does help even those who haven't yet embraced Him or who have turned away from Him. The person in pain, having spurned the preventive medicine, is still helped by other people who already know Christ, people whose "righteousness flows like the waves of the sea." If only everyone knew God, we could all find peace despite this world's pain.

If only. . .

Human doings and human beings

Yet I am poor and needy; come quickly to me, O God. You are my help and my deliverer; O LORD, do not delay.

PSALM 70:5

Sometimes I catch myself simultaneously listening to music, voicemail messages, and the GPS device's directions. In truth, I'm not listening to anything, but I congratulate myself on everything I can do at once.

It saddens me that our culture has convinced me that busy-ness indicates importance. We measure ourselves by all we are doing. I feel greater confidence if I'm "in demand" enough to be maniacally busy. And yet, in all the noise, I lose the connection with God, and consequently lose the connection with my true self.

Even in prayer, I hurry, admitting that "I am poor and needy," but then urging God, "come quickly to me, O God," and "do not delay." I hurry along, asking God to do something, or to help me do something, so that I can feel good about my busy self.

When I stop long enough to think in depth, though, I know that I have value not because my daybook is filled with important appointments, but because God's heart is filled with grace and tenderness for me. Obviously I want to thank God by doing what I can to make the world better and closer to Him. But being busier doesn't give me more value. So I can take a deep breath, inhaling the grace of God and bringing peace to my chaotic life and heart.

By the grace of God, I can stop "doing" for a moment and simply "be."

Eclipse

What business is it of mine to judge those outside the church? Are you not to judge those inside? God will judge those outside.
1 CORINTHIANS 5:12-13

In a lunar eclipse, the earth passes between the sun and the moon, blocking the sun's light. Apparently the moon is still visible, but it darkens and changes color. "Moonlight" dims, since that light actually comes from the sun and is only reflected in the moon.

Sometimes human nature struggles to distinguish the light source from the reflector. We are supposed to judge each other in the sense of helping each other be transformed into God's image. But too easily, that "judging" can become denigration of others, and we begin to think we know which persons deserve God's favor and which ones don't. We are called to respond in fairness, to learn—and to teach others—how to respond in grace. But we are not called to exalt judgment over mercy. When we judge in that way, in order to exclude or marginalize others, we eclipse the light of God rather than reflecting it.

After all, the whole point of the church is finding God, and being changed by God's presence into the image of Christ: an image of mercy, of grace. This day, and this night, I have a choice. I can choose to reflect the light, or I can cast a shadow by getting in the way. Either way, I have to remember that I am the moon, not the sun.

The light does not belong to me.

JUNE 20

Send pictures

"We are witnesses of everything [Jesus] did in the country of the Jews and in Jerusalem. They killed him by hanging him on a tree, but God raised him from the dead on the third day and caused him to be seen...."

ACTS 10:39-40

After moving to a new place, far from home, I took many photos of school, of the area, and of my apartment. Friends back home seemed to feel better when they could picture where I was and what I was doing, when they could see the context of my new life.

I think of Jesus as a picture God sent us to show us exactly what He wants of us in our "new life." For millennia, God spoke of such concepts as holiness, mercy, forgiveness, of loving God and neighbor, but our hearts and minds longed to see a picture of those ideas in the context of a human life.

Jesus, a man who walked this earth, showed us that loving God and neighbor means embracing those marginalized by others. Healing means not only physically curing others, but also forgiving them and helping them to move on, whole and holy. Redemption means finding divine good in the worst of human circumstances.

I believe in the risen Christ because God "caused him to be seen" in my life, in the healing touch of others, in the forgiveness offered by one I have wronged, in the ability of a person to find wholeness despite abuse or manipulation. Because of Jesus, I know what God looks like. I have seen the pictures.

I have seen the Christ.

Giving back

Does not wisdom call, and does not understanding raise her voice?. . . she cries out: "To you, O people, I call, and my cry is to all that live. . . Hear, for I will speak noble things, and from my lips will come what is right; for my mouth will utter truth. . . ."

PROVERBS 8:7

In several programs, pharmaceutical companies provide assistance to people who cannot afford their medications. The cynical part of me asks why the firms don't simply lower prices, or says it's only a public relations move. Still, the people who receive the assistance appreciate the companies' efforts to give something back.

Human "wisdom" might lean more toward keeping all we have, but acknowledging gifts of grace by "giving something back" embodies the wisdom of God. That wisdom cries out "to all that live," telling us that nothing we have of value comes from our own efforts. The wisdom of God speaks of what is right and truthful—not what is profitable.

So what response do success and abundance prompt? The human instinct to survive and thrive might mean that we want to hoard grace. But God, living within us in the form of spiritual wisdom, speaks "noble things." Such wisdom reminds us that we are deeply and abundantly blessed by the hand of God, not by our own hand and not by the hand of those we are able to help.

That's why sharing our abundance is called giving something "back."

JUNE 22

Do you want to get well?

One who was [by the healing pool] had been an invalid for thirty-eight years. When Jesus saw him lying there and learned that he had been in this condition for a long time, he asked him, "Do you want to get well?"
JOHN 5:5-6

I play racquetball against much more experienced players, and they frequently victimize me with the same passing shot. Sometimes, though, the problem becomes one of laziness, not inexperience. It was much easier for me to resign myself to losing, saying they are better players, than to move and cover the court as I have learned to do.

Part of me can become incredibly complacent, frighteningly comfortable with staying in a place where I can play the victim and continue to whine about my circumstance. In situations more important than sports—situations involving learning, standing up for what is right, taking care of the gifts God gives me—I find it much easier to complain than to allow the power of God to challenge me, work within me, heal me.

My first instinct is to deride the man who lay by a healing pool for thirty-eight years without asserting his potential to be whole. But in truth, I too have languished, in many cases for years, rather than seeking the healing touch of God. Yet if I stop whining and listen closely, I can make out a quiet voice of compassion, of gentle inquiry, whispering to me.

"Do you want to get well?"

JUNE 23

Unhappy medium

When men tell you to consult mediums and spiritists, who whisper and mutter, should not a people inquire of their God?

ISAIAH 8:19

I would love to be able to read music–not all of the complicated symbols, but simply to identify which sound goes with which mysterious dot. Instead, I am forced to listen to the voices around me to find the pitch, as I have no absolute standard.

My decision-making process often falls into that same trap. When facing a dilemma, I listen to the voices around me. I consult, without success, modern versions of "mediums and spiritists, who whisper and mutter." I ask advice. I look in reference books. I Google the question in hopes of finding an answer without revealing my ignorance and anxiety.

I fumble for the right notes, relying on voices around me when my heart knows how to read the music itself. My heart knows that God will hear my prayer. For whenever I have gone to Him in the past, even in the most painful and frightening moments, He has given me peace. He has calmed the dissonant voices, even when I didn't quite know who or what He was.

Sadly, even now, knowing that God's redemption is available moment by moment, I often fail to go to Him. It makes no sense to consult all of these other sources when I could put all of my questions before my Creator and find peace amid the noise. After all, "Should not a people inquire of their God?"

Should not a *person* . . . ?

Holding the umbrella

The reason the world does not know us is that it did not know [God]. Dear friends, now we are children of God, and what we will be has not yet been made known. But we know that when he appears, we shall be like him, for we shall see him as he is.

1 JOHN 3:1-2

On a rainy day, I saw a father walking in the rain with his small daughter; he had allowed her to carry the umbrella. But she was so small that she couldn't hold the umbrella high enough to cover dad, who walked in the rain. He had allowed her to do the important job of carrying the umbrella, even though he could have done it much more effectively and stayed dry.

I wonder if someday all of us who consider ourselves children of God will learn of such gifts that God has given us. Will we come to know, when we truly join God, a higher appreciation of the incarnation of Jesus? Will we know then all that God has sacrificed in the storm so that we could feel we made some contribution to the world?

It seems we will not know the answers to such questions in the human life because, though we are children of God, we still live in a world of merely human knowledge. And "what we will be has not yet been made known." Somewhere, sometime, will we know the whole story? Will we "see him as he is" and truly appreciate what he has done for us?

Will we have the chance to thank God for letting us hold the umbrella?

JUNE 25

Saturday in the Park

You, my brothers, were called to be free. But . . . serve one another in love. The entire law is summed up in a single command: "Love your neighbor as yourself." If you keep on biting and devouring each other, watch out or you will be destroyed by each other.

GALATIANS 5:13-15

I spent one Saturday afternoon in New York's Central Park. It amazes me that such large green expanses can survive in the heart of a crowded city. The park property must be worth untold amounts on the commercial market, yet it survives, offering respite amid the urban frenzy.

Embracing God offers an internal, spiritual place of rest amid the fast-forward pace of the human world. The forces of this world—-materialism, my own ego, competitiveness—threaten that space every day. Such open, restorative space constantly faces seductive offers of being bought out and converted from the kingdom of God to the kingdom of humans.

But because, at my core, I am free of worldly concerns about proving myself, measuring up, or "winning," I can "serve another in love." I can love my neighbor because, in that place of rest and re-creation within me, I can stop "biting and devouring" others in an effort to perform.

In the midst of my human existence remains a wide-open, beautiful place that resists being bought, a place that restores my soul. It must be worth a fortune on the commercial market, but it remains free.

And in it, so do I.

JUNE 26

Knowing (about) God

The LORD said to Job: "Will the one who contends with the Almighty correct him? Let him who accuses God answer him!" Then Job answered the LORD: "I am unworthy—how can I reply to you? . . . I will say no more."

JOB 40:2-5

I saw a display of Audubon's *Birds of America* folio book. Our guide said that Audubon produced the drawings by killing the birds, arranging them on pins in natural poses, and then drawing them life-sized.

When I heard of the process, I couldn't help thinking of our human inquiries into the nature and presence of God. After an invigorating experience of God's presence, I want to repeat it, to tell others about it. So I try to take the living God and pin Him to a frame for closer examination.

Job desperately sought to understand his struggles, given what he had always believed about a faithful and loving God. But at some point, Job's desire to know about God got in the way of his knowing God. Ultimately, he gave up his need to explain God, saying, "I put my hand over my mouth. . . I will say no more."

I do believe that God wants me to seek Him with my mind and my soul. He just doesn't want my pursuit of facts about Him to replace my need for His very presence. In other words, a list of facts about God can never heal my heart as God Himself did. Knowing about God doesn't compare with *knowing* God.

A creature pinned to an examination board cannot compare with one that takes flight.

Disarming

In God, whose word I praise, in God I trust; I will not be afraid. What can mortal man do to me?

PSALM 56:4

I learned in a documentary that, in the Middle Ages, the possession of weapons was a sign of the freedom of individuals. In that time, slaves were not permitted to carry weapons, so anyone bearing one was known to be free.

In the kingdom of God, on the other hand, those who are truly free carry no weapons at all, while those enslaved to the opinions of others continually carry arms and strike out to defend themselves. I want to be one of the unarmed, the free, one who trusts "In God, whose word I praise." I want to say with complete confidence that, because of that trust, "I will not be afraid. What can mortal man do to me?"

And yet, often that complete freedom seems distant, if not impossible. I become so overwhelmed with insecurity that I feel the need to attack others. I pick up weapons—the defensive armor of letting no one in and the offensive sarcasm that cuts others to pieces—because I don't yet live the free life of God.

Yet when I live for God, I can lay down my weapons, for human criticism won't bother me. When I see myself through God's eyes—as his beloved child—I won't need to slash away at others to make myself feel bigger or more important.

Someday God's way will replace the way of humans. Until then, we'll know the free citizens of the kingdom of God who live among us now.

They're the ones without the weapons.

JUNE 28

The price

"Suppose one of you wants to build a tower. Will he not first sit down and estimate the cost to see if he has enough money to complete it?. . . In the same way, any of you who does not give up everything he has cannot be my disciple."

LUKE 14:28, 33

As the crisis in gas prices escalated, an economist with a petroleum interest group lamented that part of the public resentment over gas prices came from the conspicuous signs declaring those prices. He said, "It clearly evokes a visceral response because we're the only industry that has our prices in two-foot-high letters on the street corner."

I often long for such a clear statement of the cost of decisions I'm considering in my life. If I could see, in two-foot-high letters, the cost of indifference to other humans—a cost borne both by me and by them—then I would be much more loving in my interactions with others.

Jesus tries to tell us in advance the cost of following him, saying, "any of you who does not give up everything he has cannot be my disciple." God asks nothing less than all of me. He asks for me to embrace Him so fully that I cannot cling to things and relationships incapable of lasting in eternity.

The cost of loving God is everything, but how much does our "everything" mean in eternity? So those huge letters in the sky tell us to give up chaos and temporality in order to be filled with peace.

In other words, no matter the size of those letters, this goodbye will be the ultimate good buy.

Happy endings

Already you have all you want! Already you have become rich!. . . . We are fools for Christ. . . . When we are cursed, we bless; when we are persecuted, we endure it; when we are slandered, we answer kindly.

1 CORINTHIANS 4:8,11-12

At the end of the mob show *The Sopranos*, the Soprano family—the center of a violent mob machine—sat in a diner while mob members were brutally attacked. Maybe the show's producers were asking those of us who glorified the violent criminals, "Can you really expect a happy ending from a life like this?"

While extreme, it does highlight the incongruities we humans often try to reconcile. Can a mob boss have a "fluffy" family scene to close his story? Can material things—which can't even outlast rust or fire or a market flutter—save us? And yet, as persons made in the image of God, we frequently find ourselves in conflicts of the human and the divine.

To this culture, Christianity looks like foolishness: to bless when we are cursed or to answer kindly to those who would slander us. It looks like foolishness, but it is the ultimate wisdom to put trust not in things that pass away, but in the eternal.

True foolishness is to look for the happy ending in a life spent pursuing temporal things. Such priorities cannot last, no matter how good we are at them. Only in God can I live happily ever after.

And happily ever before, for that matter. And happily ever now.

JUNE 30

The river

Jesus answered her, "If you knew the gift of God and who it is that asks you for a drink, you would have asked him and he would have given you living water."

JOHN 4:10

I once read an article about an area of China where residents used to get water from a river that had become filthy. Rather than continuing to use the dirty water, many of them linked long elaborate plastic tube systems to a single well in order to have access to clean water.

We humans need water to live, and rather than die of thirst, we will even drink that river water. The world offers many ways to assuage our thirst for meaning, for significance, for depth, but most of those sources of water are tainted by someone's self-interest or desire to sell us something.

Our souls truly thirst not for all of the status being sold by marketers to make us feel better about ourselves, but for the presence of God and a relationship with God. Knowing that I am loved by God, and saved by God out of God's mercy and grace bears out my significance. God is the meaning in this world. God is the well yielding only "living water."

Unfortunately I continue to go to that unhealthy river to find myself and my meaning in this world. And that water, while it eases my thirst momentarily, can ultimately only make me weaker instead of giving me strength. I need to connect to the only real source of refreshment: the presence of God.

Then I can stop drinking from that polluted river.

July

JULY 1

Pounding the rocks to dust

[The LORD] heard my cry. He lifted me out of the slimy pit . . . he set my feet on a rock and gave me a firm place to stand.
PSALM 40:1-2

I once read a tragic news story about young Zambian children who went each day to a quarry to break stones into dust. The dust was then sold to bring in money for food. One little boy said simply of his work, "It's a hard job. Sometimes I hurt myself."

It breaks my heart to think of a child having to pound rocks into dust day after day. Sadly, I also know too many adults who endure a spiritual version of that ordeal every day, trying to overcome mistakes or hurts of the past. For years they have worked in the quarry, trying to destroy rocks of guilt and fear and pain by their own power.

I spent years chipping away at the rocks, thinking I had to reduce them to dust myself before I could approach God. The truth, though, is that the destruction of those heavy burdens is not my "hard job," but God's. He will "lift me out of the pit" and remove those burdens if I will only let Him. God weeps when I hurt myself trying to do that work.

In His mercy, God makes the places once most frightening to me the scenes of His greatest acts of healing and forgiveness. Those rocks I could not budge become "a firm place to stand" and see clearly the power of God.

The LORD hears my cry when I am in the dark pit. He calls back to me, and to all hurting human hearts.

He's calling his children out of the quarry.

JULY 2

Temporary housing

Jesus answered, "If you want to be perfect, go, sell your possessions and give to the poor, and you will have treasure in heaven. Then come, follow me." When the young man heard this, he went away sad, because he had great wealth.

MATTHEW 19:21-22

I read that the trailers provided to hurricane victims were only designed to last two years. Maybe that design is an effort to save money. Or maybe it was a way of encouraging evacuees to seek something more permanent, to rebuild a new life rather than clinging to the old one.

I wonder if God uses that approach of "planned obsolescence." Perhaps He hopes that, when I will realize that this human shell and my precious material goods won't last forever, I will seek a more permanent place to live, with Him. Replying to a man asking about eternal life, Jesus said, ". . . go, sell your possessions and give to the poor, and you will have treasure in heaven. Then come, follow me."

Jesus' response saddened the man, "because he had great wealth." Indeed, we all "go away sad" when we realize that nothing of this world can last forever. And yet, beyond the aging temporary housing where we live, beyond the obsolescence of material things, waits the one permanent dwelling place: the God of all the universe. With open arms, God waits beyond it all: merciful, embracing, loving.

Eternal.

JULY 3

Fireworks

... Jesus called out with a loud voice, "Father, into your hands I commit my spirit." When he had said this, he breathed his last. The centurion, seeing what had happened, praised God and said, "Surely this was a righteous man."

LUKE 23:46-47

One year on the third of July—while living in the Northeast—I went for a drive along Long Island Sound. As I returned after dark, the sky along the coastline exploded with brilliant fireworks. Though I hate the noise and danger of fireworks on the ground, I love fireworks and their lights in the nighttime sky.

As we seek divinity in the human world, it is often difficult to distinguish the dangerous noise on the ground from the light in the sky. People want us to believe that God is harsh, unforgiving, so they clamor around in judgment and impatience. Many begin to think they know exactly what God wants, and they make much noise and cause much harm, ostensibly in God's name.

But true worship of God, in which the human soul says, "Father, into your hands I commit my spirit," embodies mercy, compassion, tolerance, trust. The faith that Christ showed on the cross, quiet trust no matter the circumstances, is the kind of faith that signals the presence of righteousness. And such trust is not about making dangerous earthbound noise on God's behalf.

It is about lighting up the sky with hope.

The freedom trail

"So do not be afraid of them . . . what is whispered in your ear, proclaim from the roofs. Do not be afraid of those who kill the body but cannot kill the soul. . . ."

MATTHEW 10:24-33

Recently I saw Boston's Freedom Trail, which highlights sites and events leading up to the American Revolution. I found it very poignant to stop and think, "In such ordinary places, independence started."

Events and places leading to spiritual independence are less visible, but even more life-changing. As the soul begins to turn toward God, seemingly everyday moments and sites take on significance. The day I stood up and did the right thing, or decided I would not take part in the company line, or chose to be myself instead of one of the crowd are all moments on my own freedom trail.

In the midst of moral choices, though, I seldom have the eyes to see such moments as liberating. I struggle to "proclaim from the rooftops" the secret that we need not truly be caught up in the ways of humans and the ways of this world. In the moment, I struggle to remember that nothing this world throws at me can "kill the soul."

The next time I make a good and moral choice—turning toward God in even the smallest way—I hope to recognize it as a step on the freedom trail. I hope to remember that I have done something to change not only my life, but a little part of the world.

In such ordinary places, independence starts.

JULY 5

Keeping out the looters

When an evil spirit comes out of a man, it . . . says, "I will return to the house I left." When it arrives, it finds the house swept clean and put in order. Then it goes and takes seven other spirits more wicked than itself, and they go in and live there. And the final condition of that man is worse than the first.

LUKE 11:24-26

Often, it seems, when a despot is overthrown, the newly freed territory becomes a prime target for looting. Perhaps the people held down by tyranny have no reference point for freedom, so they imitate the take-it-by-force mentality of the former ruler.

Spiritual freedom can also be heady and overwhelming. Sometimes I break one "bad habit" or way of thinking only to replace it with another. So Jesus' story about one evil spirit being replaced by seven other "spirits more wicked than itself" certainly resonates with me. If I feel self-congratulatory over making a change in my life, I'm very likely to fall victim to the next "evil spirit" or looter that comes along.

The only solution to the threat of replacing one "demon" with another is to fill that newly freed space with the active presence of God. When the tyrant is overcome, I have to seek God, living the life of God in an outward and visible way. I have to go to God constantly in prayer, thanking him for vanquishing the slavery I once knew and asking Him to fill me with his grace and presence. That space simply must be filled with something positive.

Otherwise the looters will have a field day.

JULY 6

The check

". . . This is the bread that came down from heaven . . . he who feeds on this bread will live forever."

JOHN 6:58

Not long ago, when I ate alone in a restaurant, the server left the check on the other side of the table, almost as if to imply that someone else would pay it. (Or maybe she thought it would ruin my appetite when I saw what the meal cost.)

I frequently practice avoidance behavior, though, pretending that the check on the other side of the table is for someone else, pretending that I don't know the consequences of my actions and my inaction. Even on my better days, I begin to operate in that conditional human way, thinking the right choices buy me God's favor in some cosmic transaction. I slide into believing that giving other people my love or withholding it will change their actions. I feed on a form of bread that will fill me in the moment but leave me empty in eternity.

Yet when I love someone not because of what that person can do for me, not to change that person's behavior, then I have found "the bread that came down from heaven," the bread that will allow me to live forever. The love of God is a gift, not a transaction. The love I extend to another human being should be a gift, not a transaction. It should be something I give freely, paying no attention to the check waiting on the other side of the table. Someone else has already paid it.

By loving me in all my unloveliness.

JULY 7

Grown-up toys

Do not put your trust in princes, in mortal men, who cannot save. . . . Blessed is he whose help is the God of Jacob, whose hope is in the LORD his God. . . .

PSALM 146:3, 5

In a department store I saw a toy cell phone, designed to look like a real phone except with huge numbers for little hands to hit more easily. I thought how tragic it is that all of us, as children, long for the trappings of the grown-up world, never realizing how much weight comes with those trappings.

Every day I try to give my worries to God, but like a child I cling to that need to be "more important," craving power so much that I take those worries right back. I want to be self-reliant, to appear strong to the world, to have the trappings of responsibility, but I forget how much weight comes with them.

When I "put my trust in princes, in mortal men, who cannot save," I forgo the peace that comes only from putting all of my anxieties and dreams into God's hands. I am blessed—truly, deeply, and irrevocably blessed—when I surrender myself entirely into God's tender care, when my "hope is in the LORD my God."

In my insecurity, I like to pretend that I can do it all myself, but I know from vast amounts of experience that days and moments of peace come only when I rely solely on God. So why even try to have all the grown-up toys and attendant worries when I could live as a child of God?

Why covet the weight of the world?

Through the fire

... now for a little while you may have had to suffer grief in all kinds of trials. These have come so that your faith—of greater worth than gold, which perishes even though refined by fire—may be proved genuine ... when Jesus Christ is revealed. Though you have not seen him, you love him; and even though you do not see him now, you believe in him and are filled with an inexpressible and glorious joy. ...

1 PETER 1:6-8

Years ago, a dear friend's house caught on fire; for insurance purposes, she had to look at the destruction and try to inventory what had been lost. But instead of focusing on what was lost, she focused on changes she could make as she rebuilt.

Many of us look at what remains in our lives and try to reconstruct what used to be there. We struggle to inventory those things that once seemed so precious, but which we now cannot even identify. And having been through the fire, we see what is "genuine" and joyous in this life. And with God, we may even see the joy that can come in rebuilding.

Every human being goes through the fire in one way or another. We endure loss. We make mistakes. We suffer because we put great value in the temporal. And yet, the eternal remains, in our "faith—of greater worth than gold."

Yes, in this transitory, human life, much, much has been lost. But hope endures because the Christ endures. "Though we have not seen him, we love him."

So we focus not on what is lost, but on the eternal joy of rebuilding.

JULY 9

What God has done to us

... one of them opened his sack ... and he saw his silver in the mouth of his sack. "My silver has been returned," he said to his brothers. . . . Their hearts sank and they turned to each other trembling and said, "What is this that God has done to us?"

GENESIS 42:27-28

Angry about the way my bank operated, I decided to move my account to another bank. I had all sorts of ammunition loaded up for when the teller asked me why I was closing it, but she didn't even ask. I was terribly disappointed that I didn't get to "speak my mind" to criticize the bank and strike back.

It was, for me, a case of wanting to use right (a.k.a. God) as a weapon. I wanted to make the point that I was doing the righteous thing, not simply because it was right, but so that someone would notice that I was doing the right thing.

When Joseph's brothers acted with deceit and malice, they expected to be punished, for righteousness to be used as a weapon against them. So when money they thought lost was returned, they asked, "What is this that God has done to us?" They deserved and expected punishment, and it didn't come.

Sometimes the mercy of God confounds my human heart, too. I know what I deserve, and I don't understand when He shows me mercy rather than punishing me. How am I supposed to live with a God like that, who won't be used as a weapon to beat me down, or to beat me up? What is this that God has done to us?

What is this that God has done *for* us?

All that moves

The poor will see and be glad. . . . Let heaven and earth praise him, the seas and all that move in them, for God will save Zion and rebuild the cities of Judah.

PSALM 69:32, 34-35

After one ugly little day at work I went to the beach to gaze out at Long Island Sound. From where I sat the water looked infinite. Somehow it made me feel better to see something that immense when the details of my small life felt so painful.

With a constant awareness of the vastness of the universe, and the simultaneous awareness of the immensity of its Creator and His grace, I am strangely more able to deal with petty human junk. When I'm hurt or angry, I know that this is not all there is to life, that I can let go of it in light of what lies out there in an ocean that extends beyond my sight.

All humans searching for God in all of time have felt the tension between infinity and finitude, between the transcendent God and the God mixed up in the details of our lives. We pray, "The poor will see you and be glad," and then "Let heaven and earth praise him, the seas and all that move in them."

I may be feeling "poor" today in my heart. But although I get trapped in my own little troubles, I can look out there and know that something greater awaits, beyond the sea and all that moves in it. I can do it because of the vastness of God.

And because of what He moves in me.

JULY 11

Mine

You foolish Galatians! Who has bewitched you, before whose eyes Jesus Christ was publicly portrayed as crucified? Let me ask you only this: Did you receive the Spirit by works of the law, or by hearing with faith?

GALATIANS 3:1-2

A place called Bodie, California got on the map in the 1870s when gold was discovered there, and wealth-seekers thronged to it. Bodie now bears the designation of "ghost town." People only go there now to "mine" the past, to see what life in those days looked like.

Today, though, we constantly seek meaning in having more in this world: more money, more status, more relationships, more material things. People rush to worldly success, a place that cannot sustain them spiritually or emotionally. All we can gain under our own power is transitory. We work harder and harder to get more things, and we wonder why we feel so empty at night.

The problem is that any pursuit of eternity or meaning through this temporal life is a search for gold that will eventually run out, and the place where we sought it will become a ghost town. Any "works of the law," or works of our own hands, will pass away; we cannot earn our salvation. To believe we can bring meaning to our own lives is to discount Christ's sacrifice on the cross. No matter how hard we work in this world, we cannot find eternity on our own. We find eternity only in the city of God.

Any city we build with our own hands will eventually become a ghost town.

JULY 12

Carrying a torch

[Jesus] went and lived in Capernaum . . . to fulfill what was said through the prophet Isaiah: ". . . the people living in darkness have seen a great light; on those living in the land of the shadow of death a light has dawned." From that time on Jesus began to preach, "Repent, for the kingdom of heaven is near."

MATTHEW 4:12-17

Criticism of China's human rights policies led to protests against the Olympic Games before they were to be held there. On at least one occasion, a protester had to be tackled and arrested to prevent his grabbing and extinguishing the Olympic torch.

Such tensions make me extremely uncomfortable. My non-confrontational self wants people to let such traditions go on rather than making them about seemingly insurmountable global issues. In the deeper part of me, though, the part connected to God, I know that such discomfort nearly always precedes growth and change.

I experience that same tension when I hear the word, "Repent." I'm a good person; I do the best I can. Why disrupt my life? Why not just play along and let the torch pass quietly? But the truth is that each time a human chooses comfort over holiness, the cosmos loses one more opportunity for the kingdom of God to break in. So, yes, that one familiar torch may get delayed or extinguished. The world may be very uncomfortable.

But in our discomfort, we will begin to see not one little torch, but the "great light" of God.

JULY 13

Finding the right key

The spiritual man makes judgments about all things, but he himself is not subject to any man's judgment. . . . But we have the mind of Christ.
1 CORINTHIANS 2:15, 16

In a lecture hall at school stood a beautiful grand piano, its keyboard cover locked most of the time. I know the cover was necessary to keep people from mishandling the piano, but it seemed wasteful to have such a beautiful instrument locked and held silent.

I often picture the human intellect as similarly "locked down," particularly with regard to the pursuit of God. Faith is championed among the religious, and intellect is often relegated to something worthless in seeking God, or even as an obstacle.

But why would God the Creator give humans an instrument as powerful and elegant as reason, and then lock the keyboard so that we cannot or should not use it? Why can't we question, using the reason God gave us, and still have faith in God? If I hesitate to use my intellect to ask questions about God, haven't I shown an absolute lack of faith in God's ability to withstand those questions?

I believe that we are designed to use our human reason in our spiritual discernment. We will never know the mind of the Lord fully, but I believe God gives us intellect as a tool for becoming a spiritual human, in pursuit of "having the mind of Christ." Otherwise, why would God give us such a gift?

Why give us the instrument to make beautiful music and then lock the keyboard?

Tomb of the unknown

Wisdom, like an inheritance, is a good thing . . . but the advantage of knowledge is this: that wisdom preserves the life of its possessor.
ECCLESIASTES 7:11-12

I find it strangely sad that DNA testing has been so effective in identifying remains of U.S. soldiers that it is unlikely that we will have a "tomb of the unknown soldier" for future conflicts. I always saw such a memorial as not only about unidentified soldiers who have fallen, but also about all of the people and ways of life and circumstances that fall victim, unnamed, in war.

It is one more place in which the advances of science have made us believe that all forms of important knowledge are accessible to us through the intellect. I am grateful that loved ones can have closure about their losses, but in our quest for human knowledge we're losing the wisdom to admit that some knowledge is beyond us.

Wisdom "which preserves the life of its possessor" requires our realization—our admission—of God's immensity, of God's mystery. If I believe that I understand everything about God, I am not pondering God at all, but some pared-down version of deity which I have created.

Our intellects want to convince us that all forms of knowledge are available to us. But our hearts and our souls, knowing better, can stand before the tomb of the unknown soldier and weep over all we have lost . . .

. . . and over all the "knowledge" we have gained.

JULY 15

God's echo

I myself am convinced, my brothers, that you yourselves are full of goodness, complete in knowledge and competent to instruct one another.
ROMANS 15:14

As I played some music I had long ago put on my computer, I realized that one hauntingly beautiful piece didn't sound familiar. Yet I knew that I must have heard it and loved it at one point, as I had added it to my "favorites." It was a deep and strangely moving echo from another time and place.

I very often feel that same sense of an echo within me, a voice that whispers, despite all surface evidence, that I am of God, made to be purely and completely with God. Before the human heart turned from Him, we were made first in His image; that incompleteness I so often feel is a longing to get back to where I am wholly and joyfully lost in Him. As Paul wrote, "I am convinced that you yourselves are full of goodness, complete in knowledge and competent to instruct one another." We have the capacity for good always in us. We simply bury it under our own selfishness and fear.

I am painfully aware of the way that I continually separate myself from God, of the ways I tarnish His image by failing to love others while calling myself a Christian. And yet, somewhere deep within me is that echo, like the music I heard last night, that once formed me and calls to me again. It turns out, in that context, that the music I heard is aptly named.

It's called *Going Home*.

JULY 16

The flow of good(s) and service(s)

[Jesus said] "Now this is eternal life: that they may know you, the only true God, and Jesus Christ, whom you have sent. I have brought you glory on earth by completing the work you gave me to do. . . I have revealed you to those whom you gave me out of the world."

JOHN 17:3-6

My internet service provider offers a brief list of news headlines every day, a list dominated often by headlines about economic news. It's a bit scary to me how preoccupied we Americans are with the health of the economy as measured by the flow of goods and services.

When Jesus described the characteristics of eternal life, economic gain didn't even make the list. Such issues, which indeed can feel paramount in a human life, cannot last in eternity. All that lasts is knowledge of God, which results not in our buying one another but in our tending one another. Jesus showed us, in His life, how to heal and lift up other human beings. In that compassionate work, He reveals God to us and we become God's, and part of eternity.

Of course, it's easy for me—someone with enough food and enough money—to say that the material things don't matter. But even I know that those things are temporal, not eternal. I also know that it does last when we exchange not services, but service, when we exchange not goods, but good.

Or, to put it more accurately, we exchange God.

JULY 17

All we ask or imagine

And I pray that you . . . may have power . . . to grasp how wide and long and high and deep is the love of Christ, and to know this love that surpasses knowledge—that you may be filled to the measure of all the fullness of God. Now to him who is able to do immeasurably more than all we ask or imagine . . . to him be glory in the church and in Christ Jesus. . . .

EPHESIANS 3:17-21

Archaeologists have discovered remains of a people who lived thousands of years ago and yet managed, in primitive canoes with no navigation equipment, to spread their culture across large expanses of the Pacific Ocean. They probably never imagined how far they could go, because they had no maps, no understanding of how vast the ocean could be and what might lie beyond the horizon.

I suspect that all mortals are in the same "boat" when it comes to daring to see what is beyond the imagination. We cannot imagine that a gentle life can fill us, particularly when the sea on which we operate thrives on turbulence and activity. But to live in God—and to allow God to live in me—carries me beyond anything I could "ask or imagine."

God allows me to leave all human competition and status behind and arrive at a place where love surpasses knowledge, where I can be "filled to the measure of all the fullness of God." How could I have asked or imagined such a world as this one I find in God, beyond the human horizon?

How could any of us imagine we could find this place in our simple little canoes?

JULY 18

The umbrella

[The LORD] rescued me from my powerful enemy, from my foes, who were too strong for me. . . . He brought me out into a spacious place; he rescued me because he delighted in me.

PSALM 18:17,19

One morning as I walked in the rain under my umbrella, I heard a runner approach from behind, and I stepped aside to let her pass more quickly. She seemed surprised at the courtesy, but I thought, "Why wouldn't I let her by? I'm the one with the umbrella."

As a person who trusts deeply in the goodness and redemption of God, I often feel like "the one with the umbrella" in the storm. I feel covered, protected, knowing that God "rescues me" from people and circumstances "too strong for me."

My human instinct, when encountering those who routinely hurt others, is to stand stubbornly in the way, keeping them out in the rain as long as possible. Why embrace or forgive a person who acts like that? Shouldn't life be as difficult as possible for someone who ignores God?

Yet God has "brought me out into a spacious place," a place where I can let my ego step aside and let the meaner and seemingly more powerful side of human nature pass me by. I know that God loves me no matter what this world does to me. The Creator of the universe has rescued me. He delights in me. I don't need to prove anything by forcing someone into the rain. I'm the one who knows about the love of God.

I'm the one with the umbrella.

The mingling of earth and sky

[Hagar] gave this name to the LORD who spoke to her: "You are the God who sees me," for she said, "I have now seen the One who sees me."
GENESIS 16:13

I used to be a bit anxious about air travel, but with more experience, that anxiety turned to wonder. Each time, as the plane gathers speed and then slips into the air, I find myself thinking how amazing and marvelous it is that earth can mingle so easily with sky.

I have that same appreciation for the mingling of the ordinary with the divine, when I realize that the God who creates the universe takes a personal interest in me. The difference in magnitude alone—of creature versus the Creator—makes that proposition unbelievable. When I add to it my own decisions to separate myself from God, I find it almost unbearably beautiful that God chooses to have a relationship with me.

Hagar experienced such amazement when she encountered God, through an angel, in the wilderness. Feeling alienated from her own life, she had gone into the desert, but the angel convinced her to return home. Incredulous, she named the Lord, "the God who sees me," saying, "I have now seen the One who sees me."

To know that I am allowed to see the God who sees me—in all my imperfection—is to see earth mingle with sky again. I find it amazing and marvelous, but despite that wonder, I have no problem believing in God.

I find it much more incredible that God believes in me.

JULY 20

Room to forgive

"However, the Most High does not live in houses made by men. As the prophet says: "'Heaven is my throne, and the earth is my footstool. What kind of house will you build for me? says the Lord. . . .'"

Acts 7:48-49

One apartment I moved into was considerably smaller than my previous place. In the old one, I had plenty of room to hide things, in spare rooms and closets, but in the new one, the space was so small I had to keep things in order.

Too often we humans choose to live in a small space spiritually, where the sins of others are judged and pronouncements made about the fate of the sinner. But standing in as God's proxy judge means I have to keep my own small space tidy. It also implies that being with God is the result of something humans do rather than a result of something God has done.

When I judge someone else's sins, I live in a small place that doesn't leave room for the grace of God. For "the Most High does not live in houses made by men," or in hearts made by men. He does not live in the narrow space of one human's judging another, but in the boundlessness of one human's forgiving another.

I get to decide the size of the place where I will live with God. Will I decide to live in the small place, where every little thing that's out of place looms large? Or will I live in the larger space, where we forgive one another and embrace one another? What will be my choice today?

What kind of house will I build for God today?

JULY 21

Throwing away the gift

Then Mary took . . . an expensive perfume; she poured it on Jesus' feet and wiped his feet with her hair. . . . But one of his disciples, Judas Iscariot . . . objected, "Why wasn't this perfume sold and the money given to the poor? It was worth a year's wages.". . . "Leave her alone," Jesus replied. "It was intended that she should save this perfume for the day of my burial. . . ."

JOHN 12:3-5, 7

I saw a young woman come into a restaurant with her small boy to get dinner to go. She let him put money into a prize machine, and he was delighted to get a miniature soccer ball. Then when he did something she didn't like, she angrily threw the ball into the trash and left with the boy, who cried loudly and plaintively for his toy.

I am thankful that God has not acted so mercilessly when I have wasted gifts in my life. I crave them as fervently as that little boy, and show little gratitude even when I get exactly what I covet. Though He hopes that I will use the gift in His service, He doesn't slam it into the trash when I disappoint Him.

Good gifts, though, become better when they're used as God intended them to be used. Like Judas, I constantly protest that gifts aren't more "practical," and I am gently reminded by God that those gifts were not designed for my benefit, but to serve Him and others. Still, if I receive a marvelous gift and do not use it as God intended, He doesn't throw it away.

I do.

JULY 22

The sleeping giant

I am in pain and distress; may your salvation, O God, protect me . . . .
Let heaven and earth praise him, the seas and all that move in them.
PSALM 69:29, 34

Near New Haven, Connecticut is a state park called "Sleeping Giant," so named because a ridge running through the park resembles a giant man lying on his back. Legend says that the giant was once an angry spirit, but is now subdued by a spell so that he poses no further threat.

I once thought of God as a threatening "sleeping giant," a being who had created the world but who then became vengeful or took no interest in the small concerns of human beings like me. I thought of God as the Creator, removed to another realm, and I could easily think such grand thoughts as, "Let heaven and earth praise him, the seas and all that move in them."

But what, I wondered, did that immense Creator—that sleeping giant—have to do with me? I looked at that mountain ridge for years, expecting that God would move in a gigantic and probably threatening way, or not at all.

Finally, though, I saw God not in the outline of a sleeping giant, but in the everyday acts of tenderness and compassion that other people offered me. When they held a hand, or dried a tear, or shouldered a burden with me, I didn't see ordinary human beings. I saw the God of heaven and earth offering me salvation from my "pain and distress." Sadly, I initially didn't think to look for an immense God to be expressed in ordinary acts of loving kindness.

In other words, when I couldn't see God, I was the one who was sleeping.

JULY 23

Motive

. . . whatever is true, whatever is noble, whatever is right, whatever is pure, whatever is lovely, whatever is admirable—if anything is excellent or praiseworthy—think about such things. Whatever you have . . . seen in me—put it into practice. And the God of peace will be with you.

PHILIPPIANS 4:8-9

In an old crime drama, a detective ruled out robbery as a motive in a murder case, saying, "You didn't find anything missing." While I understood the meaning, the phrase did strike me; how can you "find something missing"?

And yet, being motivated to search for God often happens that way. We have much in this world to occupy us, and yet none of it fills us. We begin to sense that there is more to human life than life on earth. We begin to believe that there is something above us, something that gives meaning. That "something" is not here, and even though we can't name it, we "find something missing."

Believing that what is above is more important than what we can find on our own fuels the search for God. Something larger than ourselves motivates not only our search, but our desire to love other people. We "think about such things" as "whatever is true . . . noble . . . right . . . pure," and we know that our mean experience here cannot be our destiny. The things of earth do not fill us, so, though we can't name them, we seek the things of heaven.

We ache because we find something missing.

JULY 24

Finding the equator

Balak said to Balaam, "What have you done to me? I brought you to curse my enemies, but you have done nothing but bless them!" He answered, "Must I not speak what the LORD puts in my mouth?"
NUMBERS 23: 11-12

One hot summer day I heard a woman lamenting unusually high temperatures here, saying, "It's hotter here than it is in Brazil." That statement wasn't quite as extreme as it sounded; since Brazil is below the equator, it's winter there when it's summer here.

We human beings love facile comparisons, but such sweeping statements seldom express real truth. To understand a person's priorities, for example, we need to know what stands at the center of that person's life. A season of cold for one may be a more temperate season for another.

Balak, a powerful military man, brought Balaam in to curse his enemies. Instead of cursing them, Balaam blessed the people, which infuriated Balak. He said, "What have you done to me? I brought you to curse my enemies, but you have done nothing but bless them!"

The earthly man inaccurately assessed the center of the God-seeking man's life. One saw intimacy with God as one more weapon to use against enemies, while the other saw the people as the beloved of God, not as an inconvenience to military power. Seeming weakness to human eyes can be strength to divine eyes. Winter and summer can be easily confused.

It all depends on that relationship to the equator.

JULY 25

To the high place

When the devil had finished all this tempting, he left [Jesus] until an opportune time.

LUKE 4:13

On a gorgeous afternoon I hiked up a mountain trail leading to a breathtaking overlook. I almost turned back in the middle of the climb because I was feeling fatigued and weak. Seeing the view from the top, though, made me grateful for having stayed the course. I hope that I can remember that view the next time I tire on the climb.

When life runs smoothly, I feel magnanimous, anxious to forgive and forget. But when the climb becomes a bit steeper, I become tired, fractious, unforgiving. My instinct is to return to the low place, where people elbow each other aside for position, where pain and indifference escalate because we want so desperately to "win." When insecurity or fatigue sneaks in, it becomes "an opportune time" for me to be tempted to remain in the lowlands instead of seeking higher ground.

Still, I know that I am made to live above this world, to see the view from the high place. I am meant to be with God, not scrabbling down below for more possessions, more prestige.

Of course, now that the work of that particular climb is over, it's easy to say that I will persist next time, that I will do whatever it takes to rise above the petty and transitory nature of human life on earth. But it wasn't easy; it cost every bit of my energy to make that climb.

And yet, I can't wait to go back.

JULY 26

Love never fails

Love . . . is not self-seeking, it is not easily angered, it keeps no record of wrongs. . . . It always protects, always trusts, always hopes, always perseveres. Love never fails.

1 CORINTHIANS 13:5-8

Increasing concern over global warming prompted huge corporations to advocate protection of the environment. Some suggested that such "concerns" were motivated by the firms' desire for positive publicity, leading to increased profits.

Sadly, even individual humans often simply cannot conceive of pure motives. We have become accustomed to using virtue or even a flawed idea of "love" to win something or precipitate something which will benefit us. We have seen too often how so-called love is used to manipulate us. We have seen too often how we ourselves have used so-called love to manipulate others. So like those corporations, we see love as something to trade, not something to pursue in pure form.

So it's no surprise that we cannot fathom the pure, unconditional love of God for us. We wonder what the catch is. We wonder what it will get for us if we try to love someone else in that way. But in God's sense of the word—agape—"Love is patient. . . is not self-seeking." Such love "always protects, always trusts, always hopes, always perseveres."

Our concept of love falls tragically short of what love can be in God's eyes, and in God's hands. In God, love remains perfect. So it "gains" us nothing to love.

And yet, it gains us everything.

JULY 27

All lost together

. . . a certain royal official whose son lay sick at Capernaum . . . heard that Jesus had arrived . . . [and] he went to him and begged him to come and heal his son, who was close to death.

JOHN 4:46-47

When I first moved to a new place, four friends from home were with me to help me get settled. We frequently got lost, but it wasn't frightening because we were all lost together. After they left, though, I discovered that it's not as much fun to be lost alone.

Sometimes I wonder if this whole culture we have built holds together because our human hearts can endure lostness if we're all lost together. Perhaps we obey this worldly system because to abandon it is unbearably frightening. We have to believe that the things of this world mean something. To consider that we have spent our lives pursuing something insignificant is beyond comprehension. Though lost in most of our pursuits, we at least have the comfort of knowing that we're all lost together.

The royal official who sought Jesus' help had realized that all of his success in this world meant nothing in the face of losing someone he loved. He knew he was lost, and that the world's rewarding his lostness couldn't cure his precious son. So he "begged Jesus to come and heal his son." The official knew suddenly how much it hurts to be lost.

Even if the whole world is lost along with you.

Prisoners taking prisoners

Not many of you were wise by human standards; not many were influential; not many were of noble birth. But . . . it is because of [God] that you are in Christ Jesus, who has become for us . . . our righteousness, holiness and redemption.

1 CORINTHIANS 1:26,30

In the movie *Elizabeth: The Golden Age*, the queen of England prepares her country for war with Spain, a war which seems hopeless. Taking all possible measures to bolster her nation's defenses, the queen instructs, "All prisoners are to be released. England is their country, too."

That sentiment seems to approach the idea of the grace of God. While each human is a "prisoner" of fear, selfishness, greed, or other tyrants, God seeks to release all. God knows, too, that those released from their bonds can become powerful allies for the freedom of others.

We are saved by God; we cannot save ourselves, even if we are "wise by human standards," or "influential," or "of noble birth." In fact, ideally, those of us who feel undeservedly saved by God—undeservedly released from prison—should offer mercy and forgiveness the most willingly. After all, for one flawed human to call for punishment against another flawed human being is not righteousness: it is self-righteousness.

It is one prisoner pretending to hold another prisoner captive.

JULY 29

Phone home

"Come, all you who are thirsty, come to the waters; and you who have no money, come, buy and eat!. . . Listen, listen to me, and eat what is good, and your soul will delight in the richest of fare. . . . Seek the LORD while he may be found; call on him while he is near."

ISAIAH 55:1-2,6

One day I got word that someone had been ill, someone I love but whom I rarely call. I immediately called to check on him, but I felt guilty that it took a potential crisis for me to be moved to communicate with him.

I continually fight a similar battle in my prayer life. I am quick to pray when crisis comes, or when I am fearful, but sometimes I neglect to pray when times are good. I come to God when I am physically or spiritually tired or thirsty. And yet, if I would only stay in better touch with God by praying to Him more often, "my soul will delight in the richest of fare." When I am prayerful, ordinary days become blessed, and difficult days become manageable.

Many people say that they first knew of the presence of God when they had become painfully aware of their own powerlessness in the face of this world's fortunes. Many of us, it seems, only bothered to "Seek the Lord where he may be found" when we find ourselves in places of pain, loss, fear.

But seeking God when He is near means seeking Him every day. God is always near. God is always waiting for us to call back.

He must be sad that we only call when there's a crisis.

JULY 30

Empty words

". . . you hypocrites! You clean the outside of the cup and dish, but inside they are full of greed and self-indulgence. . . . First clean the inside of the cup and dish, and then the outside also will be clean."
MATTHEW 23:25-26

Far too often in my speech, I use empty words such as "things," or "stuff," because I'm too lazy to find the right word. How sad to have such a rich language and yet speak so often in the poverty of empty words.

Impoverished speech doesn't only come from a lack of skill, though, but from fear of vulnerability. I often say to friends "Take care," or when they travel, I say, "Be careful" as if the FAA would let them fly the plane. I use empty words when I should say, "I love you," or "I will miss you."

My speech, full and rich in an academic paper or a letter to a potential employer, is often poor and cowardly in personal relationships. How can I act as if a grade or a job is more important than a relationship, where the very presence of God flows in the love between two people? In such choices, I have "cleaned the outside" of the cup and neglected the inside, which is tainted not only by "greed and self-indulgence," but by fear.

I am deeply blessed in that I love many people. I hope they know that even if the outside of the cup is inscribed with empty words, the inside overflows with the grace of God. I hope they know, well, you know . . .

I hope they take care . . .

JULY 31

From here (to eternity)

... the LORD alone will be exalted in that day, and the idols will totally disappear.

ISAIAH 2:17

I grew up in the Midwest, have spent my adult life in the Deep South, and then went back to school in New England. Since my speech carries traces of accent from all three places, people often say to me, "You're not from here, are you?"

Every human lives in two very different places—one eternal and one temporal—and it's difficult, through our speech to identify our "native" land. I speak in bits and pieces of God's kingdom; I even live there in rare moments when I am more concerned with loving than with status. Still, the way I speak remains confused, sometimes focused on worldly things, sometimes focused on rising about those concerns. The flawed human in pursuit of God never quite seems to fit in.

The coming of God into a human life can be frightening because it changes us completely. But when that change comes, "the LORD alone will be exalted in that day, and the idols will totally disappear." Peace comes when the idols disappear and the human heart can focus solely on loving its Creator.

I long for the day when I care so completely for my God and my neighbors that the idols disappear. I want to let go of the anxieties of this world, even though that stance may make me seem out of place, a stranger. On that day, I will have no apology, but will offer a simple explanation.

"You see, I'm not from here."

August

AUGUST 1

I'd sooner see God

Jesus then took the loaves, gave thanks, and distributed to those who were seated as much as they wanted. He did the same with the fish.
JOHN 6:11

A frequent flyer program advertised its benefits by saying it "turns 'see-you-soon' into 'see-you-sooner.'" Who wouldn't be attracted by something free that allows us to see those we love more often?

So wouldn't the ultimate promise be one which allows us to see God—the One we are made to love—more frequently? We have the capacity both to see God and to allow others to see God in our capacity for compassion and kindness. When one human helps another in God's name, both get to see God. The more often we care for each other, the more the image of God is made manifest in the world.

Jesus doesn't simply multiply earthly bread; He multiplies the bread of heaven, allowing us to participate in eternity. That miracle happens when we live in a Christ-like way, encouraging each other, nourishing each other, caring for each other. In such actions, the body of Christ—like the bread and fish in His hands—is multiplied.

Each time I choose to help someone or to love someone without condition or thought of reward, I multiply the sightings of the God of the universe. Surely I will see God at the end of this life, but wouldn't it be better to see God now, in this world?

Wouldn't it be better to turn "see-God-soon" into "see-God-sooner"?

AUGUST 2

Living the words

Evening, morning and noon I cry out in distress, and [the LORD] hears my voice. He ransoms me unharmed from the battle waged against me, even though many oppose me.

PSALM 55:17-18

One morning I saw a familiar bumper sticker which read, "Smile! God loves you," and it did make me smile. But I had to wonder how many other people see those words and grimace. How many people see their lives falling apart and ask, "And you say God *loves* me?"

All human beings long to know that "Evening, morning and noon I cry out in distress, and [the LORD] hears my voice." I personally would love to be able to smile when "many oppose me," thinking, "It's okay, God loves me."

Yet if God's favor and protection are not manifested in success or good health in this world, then how are they manifested? Where are the places, in a difficult day, when I can smile because I know that God smiles on me?

We can see and feel and maybe even return the smile of God in the small graces we give to one another in God's name. Parting with some of my money to help a stranger, or taking time to listen to a friend's venting, or accepting the hug of a stranger: these are moments in which God smiles.

I know that God loves me, and I frequently smile about it. But what about the next person I meet? Will the suggestion that "God loves you" bring a smile, or disbelief? Sometimes it does no good to simply say the words.

Sometimes we have to live the words.

AUGUST 3

The rain of God

"For who is greater, the one who is at the table or the one who serves? Is it not the one who is at the table? But I am among you as one who serves. You are those who have stood by me in my trials. And I confer on you a kingdom, just as my Father conferred one on me, so that you may eat and drink at my table in my kingdom. . . ."

LUKE 22:27-29

The weather sometimes feels so hot and humid it feels like I'm trying to breathe underwater. So when that unmistakable smell of rain is in the air, I become exhilarated. Rain and thunderstorms can sweep away the heat, making everything feel cleansed. I love the smell of rain.

I often think that the kingdom of God smells like rain, a promise that can wash away the oppression of living in this world. In God's care, we learn to love Him and each other. As we serve, God "confers on us a kingdom," one filled with mercy and forgiveness, one in which our decision to love frees us from the oppression of having to perform in the human kingdom.

Despite my human flaws, I am offered the freedom of the kingdom of God every single day. So when the air of this world feels so heavy that I can barely breathe, I can turn again to God and know that this world cannot hurt me, that God holds me in eternity. I love living my days with that promise of forgiveness, that promise of a mercy so powerful yet so gentle that it sweeps away the heaviness.

I love the smell of rain.

AUGUST 4

Everything in a box

One of you will say to me: "Then why does God still blame us? For who resists his will?" But who are you, O man, to talk back to God? "Shall what is formed say to him who formed it, 'Why did you make me like this?'" Does not the potter have the right to make out of the same lump of clay some pottery for noble purposes and some for common use?

ROMANS 9:19-21

My move to attend seminary was my first time to use a professional mover. Usually I just stick my stuff haphazardly into a rented truck, but this time, everything had to fit in a box. It's not my natural mode of operation, to fit everything into a structured container.

I especially loathe the "everything in a box" concept when it comes to the perception of God. Others seem anxious to make God fit into human intellect and human characteristics. Humans are more comfortable if we can explain God, avoiding any sense of mystery, putting Him into boxes that we can manage and control.

But I am "what is formed," and I have neither the right nor the inclination to ask God, "Why did you make me like this?" God is immense, and by refusing to put Him in a box, I embrace His immensity and His continuing creation of me and the rest of the world. If I say, even in my own unvoiced expectations, what I think God can and cannot do, I have put Him in a box for my benefit. For my part, I prefer God's imagination and God's power to mine. He is the One who made me.

Why not let Him move me?

August 5

Hunter-gatherers

When the people saw that Moses was so long in coming down from the mountain, they gathered around Aaron and said, "Come, make us gods who will go before us. . . . [Aaron made] an idol cast in the shape of a calf, fashioning it with a tool.

Exodus 32:1, 4

One archaeologist has suggested that agriculture developed over the "hunter-gatherer" culture not out of inspiration, but out of desperation. Increases in population and changes in climate meant that humans could no longer depend on the earth to produce enough food, so they had to find ways to force that production.

Religion can go in similar cycles. We find God, in the hunter-gatherer mode, and then we try to find ways that we can cultivate that presence of God in our lives. To some degree, we seek a deeper experience of God, but a part of us also wants to control God and the way that the presence of God comes to us.

The people of ancient Israel had experienced God's presence, mediated by Moses. God had assured them that He would be with them and protect them. But rather than seeing that promise as grace, the people began yearning to precipitate the presence of God at their initiative rather than at God's. The hunter-gatherers began trying to grow the presence of God among them; they turned from the grace of God to an idol, something they could make and control for themselves.

God comes to us as God wills, out of grace, not out of our demands or our initiative. God lives here, among us and within us. God will always feed us.

We need not grow our own gods.

From the valley

Because God wanted to make the unchanging nature of his purpose very clear to the heirs of what was promised, he confirmed it with an oath . . . so that . . . we who have fled to take hold of the hope offered to us may be greatly encouraged. We have this hope as an anchor for the soul, firm and secure. It enters the inner sanctuary behind the curtain, where Jesus, who went before us, has entered on our behalf.
HEBREWS 6:17-20

On my way from Connecticut to Mississippi, I would drive through several valleys, including the Shenandoah and Hudson River Valleys. For hundreds of miles, the views—with stunning mountains rising all around me—took my breath. How can anyone see such sights and not believe in God?

In my life, I found God initially not in the high places, but in the valleys. When I was at my lowest, because of lost loved ones and lost self, I began to look up. Finally, knowing that I was not in control, I saw the need for God. Then, when I found a curious, wordless comfort despite my loss, I began to see the presence of God. I found, in my valley, the mountain of God's "hope as an anchor for the soul, firm and secure" carried to me by Jesus.

Of course, I love being on the mountaintops, when everything seems to go well. Unfortunately, when I'm on top of the world, some important things and people can look mighty small. From the valley, though, I know the immensity and power of God.

How can anyone look up from that valley and not believe in God?

AUGUST 7

Low-resolution images

Love never ends. . . . For now we see in a mirror, dimly, but then we will see face to face. Now I know only in part; then I will know fully, even as I have been fully known.

1 CORINTHIANS 13:8-13

A photography magazine I once saw includes, in its guidelines for submission, a warning about sending "low-resolution versions" of photographs. The magazine will look at such submissions, but requires a high-resolution version for publication. It urges contributors to "ensure you are saving the best quality images possible."

Rarely in life will my human efforts to live in the image of God qualify as a "high-resolution version" of that image. Even the good I do can look unclear if I look closely at it; often good comes from motives which are not so good. On other occasions, I give my very best, only to see later that I made a poor judgment, and have—despite good motives—done something harmful to another.

The beauty and burden of being made in God's image, to do God's work, comes from this challenge of "resolution." I try to live for God, but I know that I can only love conditionally, that I cannot understand the kind of love God asks of me. I see "in a mirror dimly," and based on that look in the mirror, I do the best I can. It isn't the best quality image of God possible, but it is my gift of gratitude to the living God. And God accepts and honors such gifts . . .

. . . even if they are low-resolution images.

AUGUST 8

Need to (not) know

But just as you excel in everything—in faith, in speech, in knowledge, in complete earnestness and in your love for us—see that you also excel in this grace of giving.

2 CORINTHIANS 8:7

When I first moved from the laid-back South to the frenetic Northeast, I marveled at the familiarity with which the "natives" spoke of traffic, exit numbers, alternate routes. When I became more familiar with those same topics, I thought, "There are some skills I wish I didn't need."

Over years of being defensive, insecure, and fearful, I've cultivated other skills I'd prefer not to have. When I get my feelings hurt, my instinct is to use the offender's tools against him. I sharpen the perfect reply; of course, in using it, I sink right down in the mud with him.

The "grace of giving," though, can be learned in exactly the same way that the other tools were sharpened: through practice. I can practice hesitating a moment before striking back, learning to give and forgive instead of escalating the hurt. I can take a deep breath and remember that one moment of triumph is not worth the regret that will follow.

Yes, I get hurt, and certainly something in me holds satisfaction in thinking that I could hurt right back, and probably very skillfully. Once I would have thought it desirable to "excel in everything."

But there are some skills I wish I didn't have.

AUGUST 9

Like wildfire

Be merciful to me, LORD, for I am faint; O LORD, heal me, for my bones are in agony.

PSALM 6:2

The wildfires raging across one state moved so quickly that people barely had time to get out alive. One resident, speaking of the fearful arrival of the smoke and fire, said that it was suddenly so dark that "It looked like midnight in the middle of the afternoon."

To be honest, I haven't yet encountered the spiritual version of that scene, at least not personally. But now that God has come into my life, I know that a part of me will question Him—hard—when tragedy comes. I know that I will ask how it can suddenly look like midnight in the middle of the afternoon, how God can visit tragedy on me when I work hard to follow Him and obey Him.

But such questions return me to that familiar, ancient human place of thinking that something I do causes God to save me. Such assumptions leave the concept of the grace of God completely out of the picture. God came to me when I had done absolutely nothing to deserve Him. He stays with me when anyone else would walk away and write me off.

This world is so dark, requiring me to measure up and compete for and earn every scrap. But God remains "merciful to me when I am faint," despite all I do to fail Him. It may be midnight in this world now, but in all that scrabbling, clawing darkness shines the light of grace.

Almost like the middle of the afternoon.

This old thing

". . . I have spoken to you of earthly things and you do not believe; how then will you believe if I speak of heavenly things? . . ."

John 3:12

One item I moved with me was a very small cedar chest, one that a local furniture store gave each of us girls graduating from high school in 1973. After moving, I realized that I had kept that cedar chest only because it had been in my life so long. I didn't even like the thing.

Often in my life I label something essential only because it has been with me a long time. I have long clung, for example, to the idea that God could not love me because I am not worthy. It took years for me to realize that assumption was flawed, that God loves me absolutely despite my failing. Even now, knowing that concept of God isn't accurate, I continue to carry it because it's so familiar.

Nicodemus had long carried the treasured thought that his actions—observing the law—could bring him to God. Jesus tried to convince him to relinquish his mistaken definition of faithfulness, and his control. He had to let go of those cherished and flawed earthly perceptions and put his mind instead on "heavenly things."

I know the confusion Nicodemus felt. My instinct is to hang onto the idea that I can save myself, yet in my heart I long to trust in God's grace alone, to embrace the heavenly over the earthly.

It surely is hard, though, to let those old things go.

AUGUST 11

Can't buy me love

Therefore Jesus told them, ". . . The world cannot hate you, but it hates me because I testify that what it does is evil."

JOHN 7:7

Television commercials for a new product often include those familiar words designed to make me order the product immediately and probably at an inflated price. Those magic words are, "Not available in any store."

I only wish I had realized earlier in life how that phrase–"Not available in any store"–applies to everything of genuine significance. The forces of this temporal world would have us believe that everything important can be bought. But in truth, nothing I can obtain on my own holds significance in eternity. Only love—bestowed by God and shared with others through God—matters.

Jesus knew His message threatened those temporal forces; He said, "[The world] hates me because I testify that what it does is evil." He knew that His ministry would draw fire because it exposed the evil of the day's established order, religious and economic. Religious leaders had their positions to protect. Political leaders had their power structure to defend. The rich had their possessions to exalt.

Ultimately, though, all of this world's status symbols evaporate. After two thousand years, the men who pegged their hopes on religious power are gone. The rulers who oppressed the powerless are gone. The rich man and his material possessions are gone. Only Jesus remains.

But He is not available in any store.

Upstairs, downstairs

". . . May there be peace within your walls and security within your citadels." For the sake of my brothers and friends, I will say, "Peace be within you." For the sake of the house of the LORD our God, I will seek your prosperity.

PSALM 122:7-9

The people who lived in the apartment above me didn't seem to realize there was anyone below them. At all times of the day and night, I heard large bumps, pounding, and running steps. My instinct was to have the same lack of consideration in my place, but that would hurt the people below me, not the ones making the noise.

In truth, everything I do wrong intentionally does hurt the One above me, as my lashing back hurts God more than anyone else. I should seek for others around me to have less noise—to have "peace within their walls and security within their citadels"—not for their sake, but for "the sake of the house of the LORD our God."

The lesson still hasn't completely sunk in, but taking revenge and lashing back feels good only for an instant. It doesn't fix anything. It doesn't give a lasting peace, only a momentary and shallow victory. Instead, it infuses the soul with venom that poisons not just that one relationship, but all relationships. Why can't I remember this lesson—that little or no good comes from lashing back, from answering evil with evil?

Why can't I learn to stop making noise to protest noise?

AUGUST 13

Fall from space

First he said, "Sacrifices and offerings, burnt offerings and sin offerings you did not desire, nor were you pleased with them" (although the law required them to be made). Then he said, "Here I am, I have come to do your will."

HEBREWS 10:8-9

A government satellite in orbit went haywire and threatened to plummet back down to earth. Since the satellite would probably burn up reentering the atmosphere, though, it was not seen as a threat to hurt anyone.

It is a fairly regular occurrence for something I have elevated to centrality in my life to come crashing back down to earth. Though human creations may be able to reach the sky, they cannot stay there. So any earthly thing I raise up for worship is destined eventually to come plummeting back down to earth.

Much of the history of God's people has told of such objects falling out of the sky. We have tried—through sacrifices, the law, human relationships, material gain—to put something we can make on our own at the center of the universe. It never works, but we keep trying.

The debris with which we humans have littered the heavens can all be rendered unnecessary if we would learn to stop trying to placate other "gods" and say simply to the one true God, "Here I am, I have come to do your will." Idols made with human hands will always, always fall, and people will get hurt when their gods fall from the sky.

But God gets hurt when we put them there.

A safe place to stop

The hour has come for you to wake up from your slumber, because our salvation is nearer now than when we first believed.

ROMANS 13:11

One Saturday I drove home in a rainstorm so fierce that twice I had to go around trees that had fallen across my lane of the highway. I thought about stopping, but I was afraid it would be more dangerous to stop, because then a tree could fall on me.

I spent many years on the spiritual road with the same mindset. I knew that my priorities were not particularly meaningful, but I was afraid to stop for fear I would get hurt more severely. I knew that once I thought about what I was doing, I would find that the self-absorbed, busy life I led didn't hold much significance. Yet I couldn't afford to examine my life too closely; it felt more dangerous to stop than to continue down that road.

Eventually I had so many crises at once that I could no longer pretend my life was working. I sat by the side of the road, fearing I would get hurt there, but knowing I would get hurt if I continued on that road. Stopped in that scary place, I learned that, with God, I could stop playing this world's games in an effort to find significance. I could transcend the trouble and the enforced busyness and self-importance of this human place. "The hour had come for me to wake from my slumber." God's salvation was very near.

As near as my admission that I could not go on alone.

Paint it black

. . . Gamaliel . . . addressed them: ". . . Leave these men alone! Let them go! For if their purpose or activity is of human origin, it will fail. But if it is from God, you will not be able to stop these men; you will only find yourselves fighting against God."

Acts 5:38-39

In a TV show I once saw, a house was vandalized and the outside of the windows painted black. In the morning, the occupants overslept because light could not get in.

When it came to Christianity, I used to paint the windows black on the inside. I saw people acting in the name of God, yet being mean-spirited, unloving, unforgiving, and I fought hard to keep the light of God out of my life. I didn't realize at the time that it wasn't God I was warding off at all, but false representations of Him made by humans.

In the days of early Christianity, Gamaliel, a wise teacher, urged those wanting to victimize Christians that God can take care of Himself. He insisted that "activity of human origin . . . will fail" but that God working through humans will prevail. He was right; in my own life, false pictures of God fell away, and the light eventually shone through those who truly loved God.

Sadly, in my fight against false representations of God, I fought against God as well. Finally, gratefully, I learned the truth—that painting the windows black doesn't destroy the light.

It only keeps that light from reaching one dark and stubborn soul.

AUGUST 16

The desert

At once the Spirit sent him out into the desert, and he was in the desert forty days, being tempted by Satan. He was with the wild animals, and angels attended him.

MARK 1:12-13

A magazine photograph of Phoenix, Arizona, showed the city bordered by the stark browns of the desert. The caption said that the city required a great deal of water "to keep the desert at bay."

Though keeping the desert at bay sounds like a good idea, that effort may also hinder my ability to hear God in depth. Even for Jesus, time in the desert represented a time for his ministry to be clarified. There Satan tempted him with other callings which may have had value but which belonged to someone else. There Jesus could hear the priorities of God instead of the priorities of humans.

In times when I struggle and seem the most out of control—the times that feel like desert—I often hear God most clearly. My priorities are sifted out so that I remember that the things that most often preoccupy me have no real value in eternity. In the desert, the pressures of schedules and assignments and everyday anxieties fall away, and I see that nothing matters except my love of God and of other people.

God lives within me, so I will never be thirsty. I can afford to go into the desert to let go of the noise of my human life.

Perhaps the last thing I should try to do, then, is to keep the desert at bay.

August 17

Will I recognize Him?

As evening approached, there came a rich man from Arimathea, named Joseph, who had himself become a disciple of Jesus. Going to Pilate, he asked for Jesus' body, and Pilate ordered that it be given to him.

MATTHEW 27:57-58

Not long ago I read a magazine story in which a reporter tried to determine what had happened to a young girl from a war-torn country. The girl had appeared on the magazine's cover decades ago. As he searched for her, the reporter kept wondering, "What does she look like today?"

I often ask the same question about the face of Jesus. He did the unthinkable in His time, communing with people discounted by society, touching and embracing lepers, loving people in a way that others had not seen before. What does that face look like now? Will I recognize Him when I see Him?

Immediately after Jesus' death, others were able to see what He looked like through Joseph of Arimathea, a man who risked Roman wrath by claiming the body of Christ. It might not have been considered a courageous gesture in the world's eyes, as there were no battles or weapons involved, but it was courageous. The man stood up for what he knew to be right.

Joseph of Arimathea claimed the body of Christ. He was the body of Christ, living and breathing on earth. Obedience to God is embodied in the human being who does what is right, no matter what the world thinks of that decision.

That's what Christ looks like today.

Concrete desert

My salvation and my honor depend on God; he is my mighty rock, my refuge. Trust in him at all times, O people; pour out your hearts to him, for God is our refuge.

Psalm 62:7-8

In the middle of a city street, I saw one square piece of sod which apparently had fallen from a lawn care truck. It was all dried out and looked kind of forlorn, something supposed to live and grow but instead rudely deposited in the middle of a concrete desert.

In my prayer life I too often sit, disconnected from God, supposedly a growing, living thing but stuck in the middle of this world. My prayers take a form that is not about communion with God at all; I pray for things, for circumstances to go my way, for success in this world. I try to make possessions and accomplishments my refuge, something to set me apart from everyone else in the world, but that approach never, ever works.

As the psalmist says, "My salvation and my honor depend on God; he is my mighty rock, my refuge." Nothing in this world can save me from this world; God is my only salvation. But when my prayers focus on things instead of asking to understand and to have the heart of God, I am like that living thing with no potential for growth. I sit withering, disconnected from the source of growth, from nutrients, from living water.

The deepest part of me does not want things; the deepest part of me wants God. When my prayer is for Him alone, for Him to fill me so that I can live in peace and quiet strength, then I will be connected again to the source of all growth.

It sure beats being rudely deposited in the middle of a concrete desert.

AUGUST 19

Sneaking past the filters

Therefore, I urge you, brothers, in view of God's mercy, to offer your bodies as living sacrifices, holy and pleasing to God—this is your spiritual act of worship. Do not conform any longer to the pattern of this world, but be transformed by the renewing of your mind.

ROMANS 12:1-2

Frequently in the junk folder of my e-mail, I receive messages in which words are intentionally misspelled. I suspect the misspellings are designed to sneak spam e-mail past filters set up to catch and block those specific words.

I once put up elaborate filters for the word "God." I was so put off by superficial religious posturing that I wouldn't allow myself to think of God or to hear about Him. What I had characterized as God, of course, was nothing more than self-interest dressed up in a religious package.

I began to long for God, though, when I saw other people choosing to embrace me and others on His behalf, giving up their time, energy, and resources to help me. They "offered their bodies,"—and their lives—as "living sacrifices, holy and pleasing to God." Loving me and other human beings was their "spiritual act of worship," and worship spelled in that unexpected way slipped through all of my defensive filters. So God does not, as I once thought, equal church and the self-conscious, self-righteous display of piety.

God equals caring about and caring for the next human being I meet.

AUGUST 20

The need for speed

I have seen something else under the sun: The race is not to the swift or the battle to the strong, nor does food come to the wise or wealth to the brilliant or favor to the learned; but time and chance happen to them all.

ECCLESIASTES 9:11

I once saw a car decked out with NASCAR stickers and a bumper sticker saying, "There is no finish line." I suppose that race fans prefer to think that the race is always on, as they feel the "need for speed."

My need for speed decreases by the day, not because I'm old and boring and tired but because I no longer need to win anything to feel good about myself. And so the words from Ecclesiastes resonate with me, not out of despair, but out of hope. They tell me that when some ill befalls me, I needn't see it as punishment, just as I shouldn't let good fortune convince me of my virtue. "Time and chance happen to them all."

The real force in life, anyway, is not under the sun, but above it: the power of God's grace. And like earthly circumstances, heavenly grace "doesn't come to the wise or wealth to the brilliant or favor to the learned."

Grace comes to us not because of our actions, but because God is pure love. We don't have to earn grace or elbow someone else aside and win to get it. So while I agree with the bumper sticker that "There is no finish line," I take it one step further.

There isn't even a race.

August 21

The least of these

". . . For I was hungry and you gave me something to eat, I was thirsty and you gave me something to drink, I was a stranger and you invited me in, I needed clothes and you clothed me, I was sick and you looked after me, I was in prison and you came to visit me . . . whatever you did for one of the least of these brothers of mine, you did for me.'"

MATTHEW 25:35-37,40

Before moving, I donated many things to "charity," as I didn't want them to be wasted. Then I learned that some things I had offered were going to help a specific person set up a household. I even met that person. That knowledge gave me renewed energy about helping, because I was helping a real person, not just an organization.

Jesus tried to tell His hearers that following Him is about loving specific people, about opening our eyes and unstopping our ears to see the needs and hear the cries of other—very real—people. He even told his followers that, if their insular lifestyles wouldn't let them see the face of the poor, they could imagine His face there. He taught them that "whatever you did for the least of these brothers of mine, you did for me."

Anonymous helping can be more comfortable, because if I don't see a face, then I can stay in my safe place and forget that real people struggle while I have more than I could ever use. Without a doubt, it is harder to ignore need when that need has a face and a name.

Especially the face and the name of Jesus.

AUGUST 22

The mean old man

The LORD is my strength and my shield; my heart trusts in him, and I am helped. . . . Save your people and bless your inheritance; be their shepherd and carry them forever.

PSALM 28:7,9

As kids, my brother and I used to roam all over our neighbors' pastureland and woods. I remember one day that we hid from a neighbor because we had heard he was a mean old man and figured he would throw us off his land. Later, when I met him, I was shocked to find out that he wasn't mean at all; it was just a myth we had built up that had never been dispelled.

Like many people, I once thought of God as an old man in a bad mood, one who would seize any reason to throw me out and ban me from His presence. I hadn't met Him personally, but because of the way others had described Him, I hid from Him. As with my neighbor, I was shocked to find out that God is not a mean old man, but a forgiving, loving shepherd who picks me up no matter how far I fall and carries me into eternity.

I bear God's "inheritance," His legacy of light in a dark world, so He wants me to succeed. Instead of a cosmic policeman, "The LORD is my strength and my shield; my heart trusts in him, and I am helped." Every day I give thanks for learning that God is not law, but love, not an enforcer, but an embracer. I give thanks to—and for—the LORD, my strength and my shield.

Every day I give thanks that I finally met that "mean old man."

AUGUST 23

My own business

Since you died with Christ to the basic principles of this world, why . . . do you submit to its rules? . . . These are all destined to perish with use, because they are based on human commands and teachings. Such regulations indeed have an appearance of wisdom, with their self-imposed worship, their false humility and their harsh treatment of the body. . . .

COLOSSIANS 2:20, 22-23

A few years ago I went into business with a friend to publish a book. Later when she wanted to exit the business, it changed from partnership to sole proprietorship. The freeing part of the change was that, if I wanted to give away a book, I wouldn't "hurt" anyone but myself.

I often take comfort in convincing myself that a decision, especially a bad one, affects only the person making it. In God's eyes, though, any negative impact on one affects all of the body of Christ. We are on this earth to love God and love each other, so we're all in this together, like it or not.

It's easy to say that my actions are my business as long as they don't hurt anyone else. But if I am hurt, the body of Christ is hurt. Such rationalizations "are destined to perish with use, because they are based on human commands and teachings." No matter what the wisdom of the world says, separating myself and my decisions from others is simply not God's way. I am part of the body of Christ. I do not "own" myself. I belong to God.

God is my soul proprietor.

Prints of peace

The acts of the sinful nature are obvious . . . those who live like this will not inherit the kingdom of God. But the fruit of the Spirit is love, joy, peace, patience, kindness, goodness, faithfulness, gentleness and self-control.

GALATIANS 5:19, 21-23

Going through boxes of old photographs, I threw away hundreds of negatives I had saved for years. At first I wanted to look at each strip to see if I should save any, but it was too tedious looking at that tiny negative image and trying to figure out what the picture had been. I saved prints, but threw away all negatives.

For decades I didn't want to look at God at all because He was presented to me only in the negative, a light that saw only my mistakes. I was unable to understand how a force focusing on punishment could make life better. I grew very weary of hearing that I should change my life or else God was going to get me.

My life turned toward God when I stopped squinting at negatives and saw His spirit working in others. That picture of "love, joy, peace, patience, kindness, goodness, faithfulness, gentleness and self-control" was worth keeping. I still can't see the negative, figuring out how to live my life by hearing only what *not* to do. To live in peace, I have to see what God does want of me. So I am determined to hold in my heart only the true picture of what God looks like.

Who wants to look at a bunch of negatives?

AUGUST 25

The key enemy

Come near and rescue me; redeem me because of my foes. You know how I am scorned, disgraced and shamed; all my enemies are before you.

PSALM 69:18-19

News reports said that the elimination of a particular man had given the United States a great deal of leverage in besting a specific group of terrorists. Intelligence forces then had access to his computer records giving leaders' names, locations, movements, and other critical information. The fall of one key enemy, it was hoped, would lead to the fall of many others.

I have "key enemies" in my spiritual life that often don't look like enemies at all. Sometimes I withhold part of myself from God, out of fear of losing something precious to me or out of fear of exposing myself as weak and sinful.

But if I hold back portions of my life, unable to release them into God's keeping, then gifts become enemies. When I do give over one aspect of my life—small or great—completely into the hands of God, I feel that one potential enemy of the building of God's kingdom has fallen.

Someday I hope to be able to love God with all of my heart, and to genuinely consecrate to Him all of my gifts, my hopes, my fears, my anxieties. So my prayer this day is simple: "Dear Lord, all my enemies are before you. All my gifts are before you. They are yours." On that day, the key enemy, my ego, has fallen.

And the tide of the war has turned.

Music of the past

O my Comforter in sorrow, my heart is faint within me. Listen to the cry of my people from a land far away. "Is the LORD not in Zion?"
JEREMIAH 8:18-19

Sometimes I hear a song on the radio that immediately overjoys me. The joy comes from my associating that song with a wonderfully affirming and positive time in my life. So it isn't the music that lifts me, but the memory echoing in it of a distant time, a distant place.

Deep within me, too, runs a chord connecting to a distant past of unspeakable joy, a time when the human soul was still intimate with God. Even when I have faced loss in my life and I knew nothing of God, that deep chord of comfort sustained me. My heart and soul could hear some music of the past. I couldn't quite identify it or explain it, but it soothed me profoundly. It still does.

It seems that, even in times when it appeared as if God was absent, my heart knew His presence. The words that go with that music, perhaps, are, "O my Comforter in sorrow, my heart is faint within me. Listen to the cry of your child from a land far away."

Too often, I have gone to a land far away from God, a land which glorifies human self-reliance over dependence on God. But each time I learn that God has not left me at all; I have left God. Then, amid the noise and haste, the music resumes, bringing me back to that time and place of assurance, of peace. O my Comforter in sorrow, my Bringer of joy.

O, my God.

AUGUST 27

A good day

What good will it be for a man if he gains the whole world, yet forfeits his soul? Or what can a man give in exchange for his soul?
MATTHEW 16:26

In my dad's favorite movie—*Little Big Man*—an old Native American dramatically declares, "Today is a good day to die," and walks up the mountain to meet his death. He lies down, but instead of dying, he remains alive and gets caught in the rain. He walks back down the mountain to live among his people for many more years.

Such a progression might do all of us well in trying to live, in this world, the transcendent life offered by God. We could say to ourselves, "Today is a good day to die!" and give up all of our worldly concerns in an effort to allow God to embrace us fully. The moment I declare, "Today is a good day to die," and die to myself and my own ego is the moment God can give me the life He has dreamed for me.

Instead, I spend my time pursuing transitory things and relationships that I think will bring me happiness. Instead of listening to God, I listen to my own human desires and ideas of happiness. I might even "gain the whole world," but I lose the ability to transcend this life. I "forfeit my soul" in the sense that I cannot be filled with God if I am full of myself.

I can live in eternity on this day, in this place, if I allow my earthly concerns to die and make room for God. I can walk down the mountain and live as one of God's people for eternity. I'm beginning to think that maybe today is a good day to die to myself . . .

. . . and to begin to live fully in God.

Identity theft

And you will be called priests of the LORD, you will be named ministers of our God. You will feed on the wealth of nations, and in their riches you will boast. Instead of their shame my people will receive a double portion, and instead of disgrace they will rejoice in their inheritance. . . .

ISAIAH 61:6-7

Throwing away credit card statements, I take care to shred them in tiny pieces. I have heard enough stories of identity theft to make me very careful with papers I discard.

Unfortunately, like many people, I spent years being careless about protecting my spiritual identity, my authentic self. Disconnected from God, I allowed total strangers to steal my identity. Like most insecure humans, I routinely traded away my authentic self to gain others' approval.

True identity surfaced when I gave up on the idea of gaining human approval and sought only God's approval. I tore up all imagined indebtedness to humans. Once I knew that my real self could only be found in God, and not in human definitions, other people would never again have the opportunity to steal the person I am created to be.

When I am defined solely by God, I become whole—and holy—"a priest of the LORD," able to "feed on the wealth of nations." And it turns out that I have an inheritance, so I needn't be indebted to anyone in this world. I can throw out the bills; my identity remains safe.

Even better, the debtors have been paid.

AUGUST 29

Shake, rattle, and roll

". . . Remain in me, and I will remain in you. No branch can bear fruit by itself; it must remain in the vine. Neither can you bear fruit unless you remain in me."

JOHN 15:4

Months after Hurricane Katrina hit, I read about persons displaced from their homes by the storm and living in small trailers on the Gulf Coast. When heavy thunderstorms came, one man said of his trailer, "It rattles. It rolls. It's telling you to get out."

Periodically I have to go through such a shakeup with regard to the priorities in my life. I begin thinking that my full daybook is a measure of significance, that the busier I am, the more important I am. Then, when the storms of tragedy or crisis come—to me or to a friend—I see how shaky that set of priorities is. Such a measure of the meaning of life has no consistency, no eternal meaning. It rattles and it rolls.

The blessing is that my God is a forgiving God, welcoming me back each time I have wandered too far into those other priorities. He reminds me that to be detached from Him is death, that for my life to bear real fruit, I must remain with Him, and in Him. When the winds howl, I can rest safely in God.

When change comes in my life, God is changeless, my stable place of refuge. This life, this schedule that I think of as so important, really doesn't mean much in the long run. It's a dangerous way to define my essence. It's a shaky place to live. It rattles. It rolls.

It tells me to get out.

AUGUST 30

Simple

I love you, O LORD, my strength. The LORD is my rock, my fortress and my deliverer; my God is my rock, in whom I take refuge.

PSALM 18:1-2

Two expressions in our American idiom are meant to communicate that something is not particularly difficult. We say something is either "not rocket science" or "not brain surgery." (One friend, though, got in a hurry and said, "We're not talking about rocket surgery...")

As a human being living in the modern world, though, my instinct is to complicate issues, to take things that aren't exactly rocket science and make them complicated. I tend, for example, to complicate endlessly my relationship with God when it is not complicated at all. He wants me to put Him first, to say simply, "I love you, O LORD, my strength," and to build everything on Him as my "rock, my fortress, my deliverer... in whom I take refuge." Simple.

The catch is that the words "simple" and "easy" are not always synonymous. It is very simple to say I must put God first, but in a human mind and body and an endlessly complicated human world, it can be very difficult.

So when I become agitated about something of this world, I try to distill all priorities down into one: "I love you, O LORD, my strength." Admittedly, it can be very difficult to do, but it isn't complicated.

We're not talking rocket surgery here.

Hopefully

No one claimed that any of his possessions was his own, but they shared everything they had . . . Barnabas (which means Son of Encouragement), sold a field he owned and brought the money and put it at the apostles' feet.

ACTS 4:32, 35

I have long seen language purists wince when hearing the word "hopefully" in place of "It is hoped." The word "hopefully" should describe our attitude in waiting, not the thing we hope for. "We wait hopefully for Christ's return," not "Hopefully Christ will return."

For me, the idea of hope is not something to be thrown around lightly; it is the major change in my life since I began seeking God. I often despaired in those earlier days, seeing nothing but darkness, because my happiness was pegged on transitory things and relationships.

Now, though, I travel my day filled with hope. Like the earliest apostles, I begin to see that an inordinate attachment to material things doesn't fill me, but empties me. When my life is driven by how many things I can get and keep, I don't own those things at all. They own me. The hope that now fills me is a gift received from God through His people, and one I can give back to God through His people.

When we encourage each other to look for the eternal God instead of the transitory thing, we will see not the darkness of this world, but will find the light of Christ in every human face, every human encounter. We will live for Christ.

Hopefully.

# September

SEPTEMBER 1

If these stones could speak

Then the LORD answered Job out of the storm. He said: "... Where were you when I laid the earth's foundation? Tell me, if you understand."
JOB 38:4

I once read an article about the massive monument at Stonehenge, England. The writer declared that the "purposefully placed stones are fraught with meaning."

It seemed a bold statement. But whenever our human minds encounter something immense, with an apparent design, we naturally make the leap that greater meaning lies within that design. The earliest seekers of God saw first not a loving force, but a natural force, one bringing smoke from the mountain or lightning and thunder from the sky.

When Job questioned his fate before the Lord, he, too, assumed a grander design. Job assumed that behind the massive stones that had crashed his world to pieces lay a force of good, an explicable motive and design.

It's natural and appropriate for me to believe there is a grander design, but I also think I wander into hubris if I begin to believe that the grander design is mine to understand. As God said to Job's questions, "Where were you when I laid the earth's foundation? Tell me, if you understand."

The stones in our life do take shape because of God's design and God's meaning. But to honor God as God, I have to remember that I was not here when the earth's foundations were set down, and I will never be able to explain all of that lies beyond or above this life.

And yet, those stones must be "fraught with meaning," right?

SEPTEMBER 2

You are here

Now if there is no resurrection. . . why do we endanger ourselves every hour?. . . If the dead are not raised, "Let us eat and drink, for tomorrow we die."

1 CORINTHIANS 15:29-30, 32

When I first moved to the Northeast, I walked a great deal around an unfamiliar downtown area. I had a very good map, though, and was comforted to know that I could stop at any moment and re-orient myself by connecting a spot on the map to the spot where I was standing.

In my spirituality, I often wander around in unfamiliar theological territory, and I become a bit rattled by being in places I don't understand or recognize. Then I remember that the orientation point in all of Christianity is loving God and loving other people. If I focus on those two priorities, even when I and God's other children are particularly unlovable, then I know I have re-oriented myself to the presence of God. I can find my way anywhere from there.

For me, the ability to love in the face of ugliness all comes back to the resurrection. The resurrection means that God helps me endure this world, knowing that it is not the end-all and be-all. The resurrection means that earthly hurts are only transitory. The resurrection means that each time I love someone who is unlovely—in a sense "endangering myself" by being vulnerable—I have used the map to get back to the presence and power of God. And in that moment of loving, I have held onto a piece of eternity.

The peace of eternity.

SEPTEMBER 3

"God loves ou"

"I am not insane, most excellent Festus," Paul replied. "What I am saying is true and reasonable. . . ."

ACTS 26:25

Driving through a college town, I once saw a sign reading, "Welcome back students. God loves ou." Though the letter "Y" was missing, it was clear that the proprietors believed in the love of God for all.

But the message of Christianity isn't always so knowable for those who want that message to conform to strictly human reason. Paul, confronted by his accusers, insisted that, "What I am saying is true and reasonable." Yet even those of us who believe with all our hearts in the love of God cannot always make that belief of the heart square with the reason of the mind. I believe that "God loves ou," (and me) but I can't explain why He would, or why I believe.

It makes no sense because we use the human version of love—conditional, temporal, flawed—to try to understand the love of God. But God loves me perfectly, without expectation of what I might do for Him. I am God's creation, and God loves me, no matter what I've done.

So, despite my inability to make a logical argument to prove God's love, I know in my heart that He does, and that He sent a human being to this earth to show me how to love in that same, perfect way. I believe in God, and I can make the leap to "God loves ou." But that unconditional love can seem unreasonable in human terms.

So I continue to look for the missing "why."

SEPTEMBER 4

Resurrection

God has raised this Jesus to life, and we are all witnesses of the fact.
ACTS 2:32

As I waited in church one morning before services began, I heard one woman greet another. The second woman immediately blurted out excitedly, "I got a job!" Sitting there that Sunday, I felt that I had heard for myself the announcement of a minor resurrection.

Each day, each of us endures a variety of small deaths: either literal deaths or other, lesser blows like the loss of a job, the death of innocence, or a failure to meet expectations—our own or someone else's. And yet, as Christians, we know that our faith in God has conquered death, even literal death, and that same power conquers the smaller deaths we endure every day.

So a lost job, or a broken expectation or a disappointment holds no power over the heart which belongs to God. Although life can often be so hard that we cannot remember our faith in resurrection, we know that "God has raised this Jesus to life, and we are all witnesses of the fact." Each of us has endured something we thought must kill us, and yet we go on, with hope, in the arms of God.

A new job. A clear prognosis. An expected child. One more morning, dawning bright and clear on an empty tomb, despite the deaths we encountered the previous day. God raises the human heart to life—again and again and again. We are all witnesses of the fact of resurrection.

In fact, we are the resurrected.

SEPTEMBER 5

The mouth of the cannon

[Jesus] called a little child and had him stand among them. And he said: "I tell you the truth, unless you change and become like little children, you will never enter the kingdom of heaven...."

MATTHEW 18:2-3

The front page of an area newspaper once showed the most unnerving photograph. A 19-month-old child, visiting a Civil War military park with his parents, was shown peering into the mouth of a cannon, a stuffed toy on his back and a look of wonder on his face.

When Jesus asks us to "become like little children," I think He wants us to trust Him so much that we are not afraid to look straight into the mouth of this world's guns. My instinct, when faced with a cannon, is to try to find a bigger cannon of my own. But it's hard to have peace in my heart when I have helped fill the air with the smell of gunpowder.

So rather than shooting back, Christ asks me to live in peace, under His protection. Knowledge of the presence of God equips me to peer into someone else's weapon without fear. Even when I am attacked and wounded by humans, I can persevere, knowing that this world is temporary, that God's presence renders the weapons of this world harmless in eternity.

I am God's precious and beloved child. He holds me in His arms, this day and always. My childlike weakness, in surrender to His strength, protects me from harm.

Even if I'm looking straight into the barrel of the cannon.

Hammers and nails

My salvation and my honor depend on God. . . .

PSALM 62:7

One night I couldn't get an old song out of my head, one which says, "I'd rather be a hammer than a nail." How tragic it is not only that this world requires some of us to get pounded and some of us to do the pounding, but that the hammer looks at the nail and says, "There but for the grace of God am I."

But in some sense, the grace of God is found in greater supply where circumstances are more dire; grace is often much more obvious for the nail than for the hammer. The deepest spirituality is found not in seeing others' troubles and saying, "Thank God I'm not there," but in being present and saying, "Thank you God, for letting me be here with someone who needs you."

My indicator of grace is not good fortune, but the ability to rise above earthly circumstances, good and bad, to be in the presence of God. "My salvation and my honor depend on God," not on what I have or do here. If my life must be measured, I want to measure it only by the moments spent in the presence of God.

Would I prefer for my life to be easy, to be the hammer instead of the nail? Of course. But in that choice, I would also miss opportunities to know unquestionably the grace of God so often seen clearly in my own need, and in the needs of others. So would I rather be a hammer, or a nail?

It depends on which is needed to build the kingdom of God.

SEPTEMBER 7

Present tents

Though you have not seen him, you love him; and even though you do not see him now, you believe in him and are filled with an inexpressible and glorious joy, for you are receiving the goal of your faith, the salvation of your souls.

1 PETER 1:8-9

I read about a woman on the Gulf Coast who, months later, was still living in a tent as a result of Hurricane Katrina. She said, "I keep telling myself, one day, I will wake up and everything will be back in the place it was supposed to be."

In the most difficult days of my life, I, too, kept hoping to awaken from a bad dream to see things back where they were supposed to be. A time of change or transition is like living in a tent: I'm not in the new place yet, and I still long for the old place. Usually, though, such tents are the best possible places to draw close to God, because other support systems and all illusions of self-reliance are gone.

No matter how frightened I am, I try to remember, ". . . even though you do not see him now, you believe in him. . . ." Even as my body and mind endure trouble, my soul is saved from that trouble, because it is made not for this world at all, but for God's world. If I always cling to the way things used to be, I will never get a glimpse of other, fuller lives God may hold for me. So my main concern is not whether things are "back in the place they're supposed to be," but whether I am in the place I'm supposed to be.

Even if it's sitting in a tent, waiting for God.

SEPTEMBER 8

The opera singer

For I am afraid that when I come I may not find you as I want you to be, and you may not find me as you want me to be.
2 CORINTHIANS 12:20

A former neighbor upstairs was an aspiring opera singer. I would hear her playing the piano and practicing repetitive voice drills and scales. When she made mistakes, she tried again. I didn't mind the aural intrusion; I liked thinking that something that sounds like noise on one day would become great music another day.

Hearing the imperfect practice of the opera singer makes me wonder why I'm not more patient with other people in my life. I get frustrated when they don't understand me, or when they hurt me thoughtlessly. I get frustrated and angry with myself when I know I have let someone down or hurt them. "I am afraid that. . . I may not find you as I want you to be, and you may not find me as you want me to be." But we can only become all we are destined to be in God if we try our voices, make mistakes, and try again to get it right. Amid all that practice, someone has to put up with a lot of noise.

The mistakes, the repetition, and the sense of being invaded by the noise of another will always come before the great aria. All of our human mistakes are, in some form, part of the process of our growing into the image of God. My neighbor—geographic or spiritual—hopes to perform the perfect aria someday.

And if I can be patient with the noise now, I will be part of the music then.

SEPTEMBER 9

The road to Jerusalem

The LORD said to Satan, ". . . The LORD, who has chosen Jerusalem, rebuke you! Is not this man a burning stick snatched from the fire?"
ZECHARIAH 3:2

I once read of a traveler in unfamiliar territory who asked a local resident if the road on which they stood led to the place the traveler sought. The local man answered politely, "In my experience it has never gone there."

Such wisdom could have saved, and could still save, my tramping along dusty roads that have no hope of leading to the place I seek. I have traveled untold miles, for example, along the road of criticizing and deriding others so that I could feel smarter, more clever, more important. Of course, such roads have never gone to a place where I feel good about myself: expansive, loving, near to God.

The best route to that place seems to be helping others: doing something tangible to heal and strengthen the body of Christ on earth. My soul goes from small human size to expansive God-seeking size, and I become "a burning stick snatched from the fire." I am God's dwelling place, His holy Jerusalem in this world.

So when I turn away from myself and towards helping others, I find God and my best self all at once. Will I continue, in weak, unGodly moments, to run other people down to feel "bigger"? Almost certainly. But will that road ever, ever take me to Jerusalem, to the big place where God lives?

In my experience it has never gone there.

SEPTEMBER 10

The hill teaches

[The Lord] will guard the feet of his saints, but the wicked will be silenced in darkness. "It is not by strength that one prevails...."
1 SAMUEL 2:9

A book I read described streetcars of another time, saying that the cars were generally drawn by horses, but they had power available to them for the "upgrades." It took a moment for me to realize the word "upgrade" spoke of a hill or incline, not of the modern sense of an improvement.

Spiritually, though, the two senses of "upgrade" can go together. I don't learn much about God, or even about myself, when all goes well. I become no wiser, no more patient, when circumstances feel easy and comfortable. After an unpleasant or frightening experience, though, I often find that I have learned something that equips me, through God alone, to make it up the hill and go on.

When I think my strength will overcome the junk of this world, I wear myself out, then beat myself up over what I should have done better. On the other hand, when I admit that I'm powerless, that I truly have very little control over this world, I find peace in God. "It is not by strength" that I get through a day, but by admitting my weakness and inviting God in fully.

Upgrades are everywhere out there. God will "guard the feet of his saints," even when those feet are struggling up a hill. Meanwhile, I have learned that the hill teaches.

Some days I feel so weak. I must be experiencing an upgrade.

SEPTEMBER 11

The day the world changed

"My command is this: Love each other as I have loved you."
JOHN 15:12

Once I heard a man reminiscing about hearing on the radio that Pearl Harbor had been bombed by the Japanese. His father told him that day in 1941, "When you go to school tomorrow, it will be a different world."

We remember, with frightening clarity, such times as Pearl Harbor and September 11th, events that have made this planet into "a different world." In an instant, it seems, the climate changes from one of peace or at least complacency to one of fear.

Yet I remember, with equal clarity, the smallest acts of kindness in my own life. I remember a car mechanic from 1973, in a strange town, who worked late so that I could get safely home to my parents. I remember the day my best friend did my laundry so I could leave in time for my sister's funeral. Both experiences meant I was living, from that moment on, in "a different world."

God wants this world to change, not through momentous acts of war or terrorism, but through moments of compassion. God asks me, and every human being, to, "Love each other as I have loved you." We are to take care of each other, and the world begins to change when we do so. As seen from one set of human eyes, the world begins to change.

I remember the moment when my friend helped me, the day a stranger reached out to me in kindness. I remember.

That was the day it started to be a different world.

SEPTEMBER 12

Small things

In a large house there are utensils not only of gold and silver but also of wood and clay, some for special use, some for ordinary. All who cleanse themselves of the things I have mentioned will become special utensils, dedicated and useful to the owner of the house, ready for every good work.

2 TIMOTHY 2:20-21

I always thought I could've been a much better athlete if I had only been taller. "If only" are words that have held a lot of power over me

But if I had been taller, I would have invested more of my time and self-image in sports, not a wise choice. I wouldn't trade anything for the life I have now, and I probably would be somewhere very different if sports had become my way of life.

Besides, those words, "If only" prevent my seeing what is right before me. To say I could have had a better life "if only" is to deny the holiness of the life God has given me. To live in "if only" weighs me down and keeps me from finding eternity in the small moments of this ordinary but holy human life.

I suspect most people have lived in the "if only" place, thinking that other lives and other choices had more potential to find meaning. We all wish to be "utensils of silver and gold," forgetting that the utensils for ordinary use are every bit as holy. After all, the ultimate meaning—God—lives in this life I have. God has given me this life that I have. It isn't a matter of resignation, but of appreciation.

Wishing for a taller life implies that God cannot make the smaller life holy.

SEPTEMBER 13

The divine express

As Peter traveled about the country, he . . . said to [a paralytic], "Jesus Christ heals you. Get up and take care of your mat." Immediately Aeneas got up. All those who lived in Lydda and Sharon saw him and turned to the Lord.

ACTS 9:32, 34-35

When I took the train into New York to attend church at St. John the Divine, the trip began slowly, with local stops at every little town. Then the train became an express, moving very quickly until it reached Grand Central Station.

I enjoy so much about life that I am constantly hurrying through one place to get to another. I have lived on the assumption that riding the express train is always better than riding the local.

But in the last few years, I have come to believe that the kingdom of God is not only a destination, but also the journey itself. I believe that the potential for eternity is embedded within this life, not just waiting at the end.

Each time I stop to love or help someone on God's behalf, I become part of God's eternal work, God's eternal presence. Like Jesus and the early apostles, I have the opportunity daily to put aside my schedule and my agenda to help someone else. And when I do, God is present for both of us.

So the express ride to the kingdom of God has little in common with the train to New York. The fastest trip to the city skips the small places instead of stopping for every one.

But on the way to God, the more I stop, the faster I get there.

SEPTEMBER 14

Beginnings and endings

Very early in the morning, while it was still dark, Jesus got up, left the house and went off to a solitary place, where he prayed. Simon and his companions went to look for him, and when they found him, they exclaimed: "Everyone is looking for you!"

MARK 1:35-37

In one 24-hour on-call stint at the hospital, I held the hand of a young woman expecting a child, whom she had already named "Miracle," and I held the hand of an 81-year-old woman as she left this life.

When I read the words of Simon, who told Jesus, "Everyone is looking for you," I hear echoes of both families' experiences: one with new life beginning and the one remembering a long life. In both birth and death, God is present; the two doorways are equally holy.

Most people, I think, can imagine that God is present in those huge moments of birth and death, in those moments of loss and of miracle. It can be more difficult, at least for my tiny little mind, to see God in ordinary days. I can see Him better when, like Jesus, I take some time in a solitary place, when I seek God intentionally, in the quiet of my own heart.

I don't know why life begins and ends as it does. I don't know exactly how God is present, in birth and in death. I do trust, though, in my own heart, that God is here in those beginnings and those endings.

And God is present even in the smaller beginnings and endings that will come in this ordinary day.

SEPTEMBER 15

Found

"Or suppose a woman has ten silver coins and loses one. Does she not light a lamp, sweep the house and search carefully until she finds it? And when she finds it, she calls her friends and neighbors together and says, 'Rejoice with me; I have found my lost coin.' In the same way, I tell you, there is rejoicing in the presence of the angels of God over one sinner who repents."

LUKE 15:8-10

While watching television one day, I saw a message running along the bottom of the screen which said, "The Amber Alert has ended. The child has been found." It felt marvelous to know that at least one "Amber Alert" had the happy ending of a found child instead of a tragic ending of loss.

In spiritual terms, such endings are ever possible by the grace of God. I believe that God remains always ready to forgive, to embrace even a person who has repeatedly turned away from His offers of redemption. And I suspect that God rejoices every bit "over one sinner who repents" as much as parents celebrate the end of a lost child alert and the return of a loved one.

God has saved tens of millions, and God has offered salvation to every human being who has ever lived. Given those numbers, it would seem insignificant when one more person returns, and yet, "there is rejoicing in the presence of the angels of God." With every individual happy ending, for God and the company of heaven, there is much to celebrate.

After all, "The child has been found."

SEPTEMBER 16

Just sitting there

If I must boast, I will boast of the things that show my weakness.
2 CORINTHIANS 11:30

At work with some other chaplains, we often commiserated about our feelings of powerlessness. We lamented not knowing what to do in a situation and "just sitting there."

The more I see of the harsh world, though, the more I think that there is nothing insignificant about "sitting there" with someone else in pain or in fear. I often don't feel I have the courage to "just sit there." It is easier to take action, to pretend I can fix something in an unutterably sad situation.

Yet being present with another human being brings healing much more than some imagined prescription we might offer. In being simply present with others, I "boast of the things that show my weakness." When I admit my own powerlessness, I leave room for the grace of God to lift all of us above the pain.

The incarnation of Christ, for me, was the ultimate example of being present in the human condition. God could have provided some miracle at the last moment to prevent Christ's dying on the cross. But a god of miraculous deliverance from death would give me much less comfort than a God who chooses to be fully present in both life and death. So yes, I believe that God is present—incarnate—in those moments when we are just sitting there.

In fact, I think God is especially present in those moments.

SEPTEMBER 17

Gone too far

As for an idol, a craftsman casts it, and a goldsmith overlays it with gold and fashions silver chains for it. . . . [God] sits enthroned above the circle of the earth, and its people are like grasshoppers. He stretches out the heavens like a canopy, and spreads them out like a tent to live in. He brings princes to naught and reduces the rulers of this world to nothing.

ISAIAH 40:19-23

Whenever I get directions to an unfamiliar place, I prefer to know of a landmark which indicates that I have already missed my destination. I like for directions to say, "If you get to X, you've gone too far."

I would also prefer that directions from God would tell me exactly when it's time to turn around and retrace my steps. I probably need to turn around, for example, when my will conveniently coincides too often and too neatly with what I perceive to be God's will, when that inner voice I ascribe to God is actually my own voice. Rather than choosing something I want—an idol cast by human workmanship—I can find peace only in the one "who stretches out the heavens like a canopy. . . and reduces the rulers of the earth to nothing."

Following God requires me to put aside any idol that I can make for myself, or of myself, and to seek God's will even when it is frightening or difficult or "inconvenient." So when God's will frequently looks too much like my own will, I know I have probably gone too far.

It must be time to turn around.

SEPTEMBER 18

One in a million

". . . In the future, when your children ask you, 'What do these stones mean?' tell them that the flow of the Jordan was cut off before the ark of the covenant of the LORD. . . ."

JOSHUA 4:6-7

A New York Times headline declared, "Crime numbers keep dropping across city." Yet when I had a chance to venture into New York alone, I chose not to, mostly because I feared becoming a victim of crime. A crime rate that drops to one victim in a million is meaningless if I happen to be that one.

I believe that many people assume, in the same way, that grand talk of forgiveness and redemption is meaningless to them personally. They think, "Don't talk to me about the millions of people God has forgiven. He won't forgive me. He won't forgive this." Truths that are clear to those who know God's history are not as clear to others.

The "sign" erected in the Jordan River looked like a pile of rocks to those who didn't know the story. Like that sign, someone has to explain, to those who don't know God, that He longs to forgive, that forgiveness is not at all about what I have done, but about what God has done.

Someone has to say that it is not a matter of whether I will be offered forgiveness, but whether I will choose to take it. From the human point of view, the chances of being forgiven do seem remote. But why not seek forgiveness, even if it is a one-in-a-million shot?

I could be that one.

SEPTEMBER 19

From the great height

Help me, O LORD my God; save me in accordance with your love. Let them know that it is your hand, that you, O LORD, have done it.
PSALM 109:26-27

One day I saw, with a friend, "before and after Katrina" satellite views of the Mississippi Gulf Coast. In the image, houses looked small, and boats and cars weren't even discernible. My coworker said of the photo, "Makes you feel kinda small, doesn't it?"

I once had that same feeling of smallness, in the sense of insignificance, every time I thought of God. I couldn't imagine that God in His heaven, looking down from the great height, would have any interest in someone as small and unimportant as I am. I certainly couldn't fathom that He took a personal interest in me.

Now, though, I know better. I have seen circumstances which have convinced me that God is intimately involved in my life. I have felt healing in my heart over the hurts of a lifetime, and I know that God has "saved me in accordance with His love." I have seen turns of events that I don't believe could be anything less than the hand of God.

Others may think that such things "just happen," but I believe that God is at work, today, every day, not just in the world, but in my life, in me, in my heart. I believe that God sees me and you, and saves me and you, every single moment, even from the great height.

Makes you feel kinda big, doesn't it?

The narrowest places

Jesus replied, ". . . if the Son sets you free, you will be free indeed. . . . Yet you are ready to kill me, because you have no room for my word. . . ."
JOHN 8:36-37

One night at the grocery store I became irritated because every place I wanted to go was blocked by someone else's cart. Why do people always seem to choose the very narrowest place to stop, the only place where there's no room to go around?

God-seekers also often choose the narrowest place; I know that I usually seek out people who think as I do rather than seeking out those who might bump me out of complacency or teach me some new truth about the vast, living God. I love to stop in the narrow spots; they're much less scary than the wide-open spaces of loving all in God's name.

Jesus encountered, at every turn, people trying to block Him into the narrowest place, the place where they felt superior to those who "didn't get it." And yet a soul filled with God doesn't contract; it expands. God's presence allows me to confidently accept and love even those who disagree stridently with me because, as Jesus told His critics, "if the Son sets you free, you will be free indeed."

Sometimes, sadly, we don't want the freedom of expansive places, but crave the predictability and self-righteousness of the narrow ones. We sacrifice the truly liberating presence of Jesus in the interest of winning an argument.

And so we kill Him because we have no room for His Word.

SEPTEMBER 21

Fall

Where is the wise man? Where is the scholar? Where is the philosopher of this age? Has not God made foolish the wisdom of the world?
1 CORINTHIANS 1:20

In my autumns in the Northeast, I looked forward to the spectacular colors of changing leaves. I thought of those colors as being painted on—as an addition of color—when in fact the color results from a disappearance of chlorophyll and a paucity of light. So the brilliant color comes not from something being added, but from something being taken away.

Spectacular colors admired by humankind often come about not from an addition of something worthwhile, but out of disconnection from life and light. When I become complacent and self-satisfied, I stop growing spiritually. I may seem more successful on the outside, and wiser in this world, but inside I cannot be at peace if I rely only on myself.

Living for God can seem weak and boring to the human eye. If we forgive others who "deserve" our wrath, we'll never get anywhere in this world. On the other hand, if we fail to find compassion for others in their mistakes and aches, we forsake the image of God within us. When earthly values take precedence over heavenly ones, we may see more color, not from something being added, but from something being taken away. Forsaking the presence of God, we are exiled to the low places on earth.

Maybe that's why we call it "fall."

SEPTEMBER 22

Turning point

"This, then, is how you should pray: "'Our Father in heaven, hallowed be your name, your kingdom come, your will be done on earth as it is in heaven. . . .'"

MATTHEW 6:9-10

After a televised baseball game, one commentator asked another of the game, "What was the turning point?" The other man, rather than naming a point in time, named a person as the "turning point."

Isn't the turning point of Christianity—even of the world—also a person rather than a moment in time? For millennia, God has revealed Himself to humans. But even in the best of circumstances and the purest of hearts, the understanding of God was blurred by human fear, human pride, human desire. We have had millions of moments in which we felt the presence of God, but invariably our experience of God was diluted by our human understanding and our inadequate human words.

Then came the turning point: not a moment in time, but a person. In Christ, God's revelation became a human body speaking human language, yet still the perfect picture of God. "This is what I look like," God told us in Christ. A human being living in perfect love for God and human reveals God clearly, precisely. We no longer need to see God through imperfect filters.

In such a person, I suddenly know what it means to say, "Your kingdom come. . . on earth as it is in heaven." I see Jesus, a man living the life of perfect love, bringing the kingdom to me. I see a person.

I see the turning point.

SEPTEMBER 23

The hands that do His work

Nehemiah said, "Go and enjoy choice food and sweet drinks, and send some to those who have nothing prepared. . . . The joy of the LORD is your strength" . . . Then all the people went away to eat and drink, to send portions of food and to celebrate with great joy, because they now understood the words that had been made known to them.

NEHEMIAH 8:10, 12

Waiting in line behind a young family, I watched as a little girl, held in her father's arms, kept presenting her hands to him to kiss, one and then the other. Each time he did it, the little girl laughed, absolutely delighted that dad would play this game again and again.

Sometimes I get that same feeling when I do something tangible and down to earth to help another person. When I help someone else, knowing it is what God asks me to do, I feel that I have presented my hands and my work to Him. And He is perfectly willing to bless that work, to kiss my hands again and again, as long as His people are tended to.

The people of Nehemiah's time were told "The joy of the LORD is your strength," and they were urged to "send something to those who have nothing prepared." They finally understood what God asked of them, and they were allowed to present their hands to Him for their Father's tender kiss. God blesses what we do on another human's behalf, not only the work, but the hands that do the work.

He will never tire of kissing His child's hands.

Forgive us our debts

". . . I will give them an undivided heart and put a new spirit in them. . . . They will be my people, and I will be their God."

EZEKIEL 11:19-20

On television I heard an ad for a consumer debt management company. Incredibly, the ad stated, "Everyone wants you to be out of debt."

In my experience, almost the opposite is true; our economic system is fueled by debt, most of it incurred to make us look successful in the eyes of the world and in our own eyes. No, it seems to me that most of our society wants us to be indebted, if not financially then in terms of the power structure.

From the spiritual and emotional point of view, debt is also pervasive and destructive. If we try to earn our way to God, we cannot have "an undivided heart" and the new spirit God wants for us. Continually incurring debt—thinking that our being with God results from something we do rather than from God's grace—also subtly convinces us that others have to earn our love and compassion. The whole system crashes under the weight of debt and self-interest.

God, I believe, wants us to feel liberated from debt, to love unconditionally and extravagantly, not to parcel out compassion as we can afford to. Certainly we are indebted to God for everything that matters, but He doesn't even ask us to try to pay all we owe Him.

Maybe that's the origin of the term "grace period."

Ordnance

When a Samaritan woman came to draw water, Jesus said to her, "Will you give me a drink?" . . . The Samaritan woman said to him, "You are a Jew and I am a Samaritan woman. How can you ask me for a drink?" (For Jews do not associate with Samaritans.)

JOHN 4:7, 9

I once saw a military sticker on a car for something called "Ordnance Corps." It reminded me of how, years ago, I confused the word "ordnance," meaning weaponry, with "ordinance," meaning a law or regulation.

It seems a common tactic, too, in the Christian world—that confusion of ordnance with ordinance, weaponry with law. We desperately want to measure and exclude people according to the law, using it as a weapon to control, to separate us from them.

That tendency apparently isn't new; the Samaritan woman was surprised that a Jew would ask her for water, "For Jews do not associate with Samaritans." That "ordinance" may not have been a law, but it was certainly a guideline few challenged, one of many designed to separate the spiritual "haves" from the "have-nots."

Yet the presence of Jesus is not reserved for an elite few, for those who obey the ordinance or bow to the ordnance. Whenever the law got in the way of loving a human being, Jesus chose neither the weapon nor the law. Jesus chose, without exception, to love, and He asks me to do the same.

He asks me to leave the ordinance, and the ordnance, behind.

Running backward

Then Jesus said . . . "Everything [the Pharisees] do is done for men to see: . . . they love the place of honor. . . . [But] The greatest among you will be your servant. For whoever exalts himself will be humbled, and whoever humbles himself will be exalted."

MATTHEW 23:5-6, 11-12

At a park trail I saw the oddest sight, a man who appeared to be running toward me, but who was actually moving away from me. It took a moment for me to realize that he was running backward, occasionally glancing over his shoulder to make sure he didn't back into someone.

Often religion amounts more to running backwards than to making progress toward God. Sometimes I look at other people and compare their ways of seeking God to mine; I'm sorry to admit that I can feel pretty smug about my own spirituality. But the moment I take pride in spiritual practices is the moment I have started running backward, away from my God.

Jesus urged His followers to observe the law but cautioned them not to wear their religiosity like a badge. Of those who practice prideful, conspicuous piety, He cautioned that, in God's kingdom, "whoever exalts himself will be humbled, and whoever humbles himself will be exalted." Those who serve others with no regard for their own position or importance will appear, by this world's standards, to be running backward. But they will be the ones running forward.

Directly into the arms of God.

Homemade prisons

. . . O LORD; may your love and your truth always protect me. For troubles without number surround me; my sins have overtaken me, and I cannot see.

PSALM 40:11-12

A newspaper headline which read, "Woman, 29, dies in prison," caught my attention and made me deeply sad. What a shame, I thought, that such a young life should end in captivity, in despair. Apparently that woman lost sight, somewhere along the way, of what life is all about: living for God and loving other people.

But don't we all lose sight of that truth? In the eyes of this world I am free to do what I want, to spend my money and time as I choose. But when seen through the lens of eternity, I am imprisoned by materialism and fear. Forgetting that I am loved and beautiful in God's eyes, I collect things and people to convince myself I am loved and beautiful. At that point, "my sins have overtaken me, and I cannot see." I have forgotten (again) that the things and people I collect not only cannot save me, but hold me in captivity. I have forgotten that God's love and truth are all I need to live free.

Of course it is tragic that such a young person would die in prison. But in truth any life lived in prison—even prisons not made of concrete and steel—is lost. In fact, the life of captivity most of us lead may be even more tragic than the wasted life of that 29-year-old woman.

At least she didn't buy her own walls.

SEPTEMBER 28

The bearer of all things

In bitterness of soul Hannah wept much and . . . made a vow, saying, "O LORD Almighty, if you will only look upon your servant's misery and remember me, and not forget your servant but give her a son, then I will give him to the LORD for all the days of his life. . . ."

1 SAMUEL 1:10-11

One gorgeous afternoon, I saw a father walking with his young son, perhaps five years old. The father was carrying a large toy gun. I suspected that the son had insisted on taking the toy on their walk, but soon grew tired of carrying it and passed it along to dad.

I wonder if God often feels as if I treat Him the same way. Most of my prayers focus on what I want in this world, often on "toys" I perceive as critical to my happiness. Then, when those things I once wanted so badly become a burden instead of a joy, I pass them off to God.

Hannah once bargained with God, promising to use an earthly gift—a son she desperately wanted—in the service of God. "O LORD Almighty," she prayed, "if you will only look on your servant's misery and remember me. . . " Down the line, I suspect Hannah prayed to God again to help her manage that gift of a son.

But the incarnation of Christ should change the way I pray. Instead of praying for more toys, more worldly success, I should pray simply for God's presence in my earthly life. I should ask for the one gift that brings me peace: for my Father to walk with me.

Then, when life gets tough, He'll have nothing to carry but me.

SEPTEMBER 29

New life forms

Jesus then took the loaves, gave thanks, and distributed to those who were seated as much as they wanted.

JOHN 6:11

Two large lakes were discovered in Antarctica, buried under ice two miles deep. Since "exotic ecosystems" no longer present in our world may still thrive in those lakes, the discovery could provide keys to "new" life forms. In truth, though, they would be new to us, but actually very old.

Sometimes I feel that the image of God, the image in which I was created, remains buried under miles of ice in my soul. The greatest miracles in my life occur when some vestige of that image surfaces, when I stop posturing long enough for God to work in me, and through me.

I have no doubt that Jesus could feed thousands with a loaf of bread, but perhaps part of the miracle had to do with people, normally selfish and guarded, who shared their food. Perhaps His presence—especially His willingness to love unconditionally—"melted the ice" of defensiveness, selfishness, and fear until people were willing to help feed perfect—and imperfect—strangers.

If I could trust God completely and let the layers of ice melt away, maybe I could truly love people who hurt me instead of simply tolerating them in hopes of winning points in some cosmic game. Maybe I could truly forgive instead of holding onto wrongs like bargaining chips or markers of my own martyrdom. Maybe I would see life forms which are new to me.

But truly very old.

SEPTEMBER 30

Home

At that very time Jesus cured many who had diseases, sicknesses and evil spirits, and gave sight to many who were blind.

Luke 7:21

In a baseball playoff game one year, a team went 0 for 13 with runners in scoring position. They put plenty of runners on base, but they couldn't find a way to get them home.

Coming through when it counts is a highly valued attribute, particularly in our society. Yet in the truly important places—in the face of a frightening diagnosis, a hopeless personal situation, or economic ruin—I am so limited in my capacities that I feel I cannot come through for another person. So I shy away from those clutch situations, knowing I cannot feed all of the hungry, cure disease, or erase damage done by one human being to another. My flawed human measuring system tells me that, if I can't fix the problem, I have failed.

God, though, does not ask or expect me to fix anything. He simply asks me to be present with those who are hurting, to bring His healing presence to other people. God is the one who does the healing, the restoring, the bringing back to life.

All I can do in those critical situations is to offer another person the love of God. Although He may use my hands, my heart, my voice to bring healing, the work of restoration is His alone. Ultimately, only God comes through in the clutch.

Only God can bring us home.

October

OCTOBER 1

After the fall

"Let us acknowledge the LORD; let us press on to acknowledge him. As surely as the sun rises, he will appear; he will come to us like the winter rains, like the spring rains that water the earth."

HOSEA 6:3

Returning home one day, I enjoyed a delicious combination of sensory experiences. I saw trees in which leaves had already begun to change to bright oranges and yellows just as I caught the scent of freshly mown grass. I felt a great sense of anticipation, the bittersweet loss of one season and the embracing of another.

All of life holds such cycles, leaving behind one treasured season only to find gifts in the next one. In this world, as in the spiritual world, the change from one season to another involves both a dying and a being born. When I have failed miserably in one place, it usually means that God is about to refresh me in some new and unexpected way. "As surely as the sun rises, he will appear; he will come to us like the winter rains, like the spring rains that water the earth."

I hate to see summer go. But the autumn season will run its course, followed by winter rains and then "the spring rains that water the earth." Warm weather and the smell of freshly mown grass will return. In painful times, it's good to know that seasons will turn soon enough. Rebirth won't come immediately, but it will surely come.

God wouldn't give us a fall without a promise of new growth.

OCTOBER 2

Wasted space

Before I was afflicted I went astray, but now I obey your word. You are good, and what you do is good; teach me your decrees.

PSALM 119:67-68

On my way to work each morning, I used to pass an abandoned industrial building which must have been a half-mile long or more. It was no wonder it stood empty, as there couldn't be many companies that would need a building that size. Every time I saw the massive building, though, I thought "What a waste of space."

But over the years, I have allowed much space in my own heart and in my own spirit to be absolutely wasted. Instead of spending my energy on taking care of myself and others, I have allowed self-recrimination and regrets from the past to paralyze me. All of that space in me—space which could be filled with compassion, with tenderness, with the grace of God—overflows instead with the cobwebbed debris of the past.

It makes no sense, though, to focus so much energy on the past when "I went astray" if I truly believe that God is a God of mercy, of forgiveness. If I could fully accept God's forgiveness, then I could move on, healed and whole. I could see the goodness of God and allow Him to teach me that goodness if I could only discard the junk of the past and allow God to fill me in the present.

Sadly, when I cannot accept forgiveness myself, the junk stays put, preventing me from functioning fully in the present. What a waste of space!

Not to mention a waste of grace . . .

Pleas and thank you

So then, just as you received Christ Jesus as Lord, continue to live in him, rooted and built up in him, strengthened in the faith as you were taught, and overflowing with thankfulness.

COLOSSIANS 1:6-7

In a TV crime drama, a district attorney tried to cut a defendant a break on sentencing because of the circumstances of the case. Another attorney told him ruefully, "Sometimes the good you do doesn't do you any good."

That sentiment captures, for me, a major misconception about our morality and compassion in relation to seeking God. We mortals tend to think not of good for good's sake, but of cause and effect. We want to believe that our moral actions are the cause of God's favor, that our choices somehow bring us the grace of God. We slip into thinking of our actions as pleas for God's mercy, proof that we should be saved.

Instead, though, our loving and right actions are the effect, the response of a grateful human being aware of God's unspeakable gift of grace. That grateful response is manifested when, "just as you received Christ Jesus as Lord, continue to live in him. . . overflowing with thankfulness." In other words, our moral and loving actions are not "pleas" for mercy, but "thank-yous" for it. God has already saved us.

So our good doesn't have to "do us any good."

OCTOBER 4

Silent witness

What I tell you in the dark, speak in the daylight; what is whispered in your ear, proclaim from the roofs. Do not be afraid of those who kill the body but cannot kill the soul.

MATTHEW 10:27-28

Even after decades of conflict and destruction in Afghanistan, a number of 2000-year-old artifacts were preserved. That preservation was made possible by secrecy; as one man said, "If we had not hidden them, the treasures of Afghanistan would have been lost. Those who knew the truth kept silent."

Unfortunately we often use that same mindset in "protecting" the truth about God. We learn, in the solitude of our own human hearts, that only God can save us. We find that treasure, buried beneath mountains of worldly success and worldly insistence that we should control our own lives and save ourselves.

I believed for years that the world was right, that I should be more in control and more self-sufficient. Ultimately, though, I learned the real treasure of God, that the grace of God prevails when all else seems to be slipping away. For the longest time, I honored those who "could kill the body but cannot kill the soul."

I now know the truth, and I refuse to keep silent in some misguided effort to "protect" that treasure of truth. The truth is that this world—with all of its things and people—passes away, and only the grace of God remains. So it is that grace of God that we should treasure.

Those of us who know the truth simply cannot continue to keep silent.

OCTOBER 5

Grand opening

For I am about to fall, and my pain is ever with me. I confess my iniquity; I am troubled by my sin . . . O LORD, do not forsake me; be not far from me, O my God. Come quickly to help me, O Lord my Savior.
PSALM 38:17, 21-22

I saw a familiar convenience store with a big sign reading, "Grand Opening." The store had been open for years, but new management must have wanted to attract customers by implying that the place was new. Again.

Every day I can have a "grand opening," in which the old is swept away to make room for God's presence. I can continually start over if I embrace God's mercy and forgiveness. Even when—or perhaps especially when—I feel that "I am about to fall" because "I am troubled by my sin," God stands ready to clear the record and allow me another "grand opening."

Sometimes it's hard to believe that God will forgive me again, or at all. But to turn away from God's forgiveness because I cannot forgive my own sins amounts to putting myself arrogantly in God's place. Forgiveness and newness are available to me now, today, if I accept those gifts from God and give up the guilt and self-recrimination.

It doesn't matter how long I have known about God, or how many times I have disappointed God and myself by making mistakes. All that matters is that I ask God, "Come quickly to help me, O Lord my Savior." If I do that today, everything can start anew. We can have a grand opening.

Again.

OCTOBER 6

The God rush

He who speaks on his own does so to gain honor for himself, but he who works for the honor of the one who sent him is a man of truth; there is nothing false about him. Has not Moses given you the law? Yet not one of you keeps the law. Why are you trying to kill me?"

JOHN 7:18-19

One documentary about the California gold rush said that, amid the gold frenzy, the best way to make good money was not looking for gold, but selling tools and other materials to the ones looking for the gold. Some things never change.

Most of us still look for some sort of gold, some sense of meaning or vitality in life, and many others try to find meaning by selling something to us. When Jesus spoke of people who were trying to kill Him, he spoke literally. People in our time don't literally seek to kill Jesus, but they are perfectly willing to let Him die of neglect while we pursue the other values peddled by this culture.

It is frightening to speak up when injustice is being advertised as success, or when authenticity is sacrificed for status. It takes courage to suggest that life may be about more than winning and buying. Forgiveness and compassion bring the accusation of weakness. People who emphasize God and other humans above success are labeled unambitious. The irony is that all of our buying and selling and searching isn't a search for gold at all, but a search for God.

And the only tool we need to find Him is the willingness to look.

OCTOBER 7

Busting out

The chief priests and the teachers of the law heard this and began looking for a way to kill him, for they feared him, because the whole crowd was amazed at his teaching.

MARK 11:18

Often I used to travel a route which passes a prison, and along the road were signs which said, "Correctional facility: No stopping next two miles." At first I thought the sign was strictly about my safety, but someone told me it also allows authorities to be aware of vehicles which might be stopping to help prisoners escape.

Systems designed to keep people in line have to be vigilant about those who threaten to free others of the system. In human history, the prime example of a threat to the status quo was Jesus, a man who taught that loving people was more important than controlling them or judging them. In fact, when the authorities of Jesus' time heard the message of radical love He put forth, they "began looking for a way to kill him."

Some stories—like this one—will endure as long as humans exist. The systems which thrive on keeping people imprisoned—economies, governmental systems, societal pecking orders—continue to send the same message that was sent about the man Jesus thousands of years ago. Those messages tell us we should never slow down. We should never offer help in this fast and competitive world. We can't be stopping continually on our way to 'progress.'

Someone might get out of prison.

OCTOBER 8

The home team

The idols speak deceit, diviners see visions that lie; they tell dreams that are false, they give comfort in vain.

ZECHARIAH 10:2

One Sunday evening in a restaurant I watched part of a football game. Everyone else there cheered for the home team, but I secretly cheered for the other side, a team I have followed since childhood. I felt very uncomfortable about celebrating my team's success or lamenting the other team's, as those sentiments definitely went against the crowd.

I often fight a battle within myself over which "team" to support in this world. I know that material things and earthly status hold no real meaning. I know that only God matters. And yet, cheering for God rather than the material way definitely goes against the crowd.

I can rationalize most of the guilt away, but the fact remains that I worship the "idols [which] speak deceit." I allow myself to believe that the right thing, person, or accomplishment will bring meaning to my life. My heart wants to speak of God and the eternal love of God, yet I seek the idols that "give comfort in vain." I listen to dreams that lie. Often I abandon God's "side" because it isn't popular in this place to cheer against the home team.

I can't believe my own lack of courage. Why do I sit here, desperately wanting to side with the kingdom of God, yet so often siding with the material kingdom? I know better.

Why don't I *do* better?

OCTOBER 9

Today

. . . the whole crowd of disciples began joyfully to praise God in loud voices for all the miracles they had seen: "Blessed is the king who comes in the name of the Lord! Peace in heaven and glory in the highest!"
LUKE 19:37-38

One car company ran TV ads which de-emphasized the need to "act now" to take advantage of sales. That company instead emphasized the long-term benefits of owning one of its cars.

I would love to see Christianity's reputation move, to some degree, in the opposite direction. Spirituality is often sold as changing the end of life—the ultimate long-term investment—but less often on the immediate change that spirituality can bring to the quality of life. I heard about "peace in heaven and glory in the highest," but most days I needed peace on earth, peace in my own little human heart.

I have found, though, that honoring God through my actions today doesn't only bring rewards in the long term, but also in the short term. At the end of the day, I beat myself up less. I drag around less of the baggage of resentment. I worry less. I laugh more.

So I would hope that we Christians would eventually learn to sell both the long-term and short-term benefits of this vehicle of faith. My day will be better and more peace-bringing, to me and others, if I live a godly life day to day. So God won't only save me in the long run; God will save me today.

But only if I act now.

OCTOBER 10

The charge

[The heavens and the earth] will perish, but you remain; they will all wear out like a garment. Like clothing you will change them and they will be discarded. But you remain the same, and your years will never end.

PSALM 102 :26-27

In the movie *Seven Years in Tibet*, an Austrian mountain-climber is arrested by British soldiers simply for being on the "wrong side" of World War II. As he returns from a failed ascent and the soldiers tell him he is under arrest, he demands, "What's the charge? Failure to summit?"

Is concern over the "failure to summit" the main charge we Christians level at one another? I certainly love to pick apart others' routes to God. But am I truly concerned that such people have "failed to summit,"—that their experience of God is not as deep as it could be? Or do I simply covet a bigger merit badge for piety?

All human thought on God, though, is irrelevant in the presence of God Himself. The matters of heaven and earth "like clothing will be changed and discarded," but God "will remain the same, and His years will never end." Ultimately, the soul missing the experience of God is not the one I criticize, but my own. When I denigrate another human being, I fail to love, and I step from the immediate presence of God. Forfeiting my chance to be with Him, I am the one guilty of the irrevocable charge.

Failure to summit.

OCTOBER 11

Unlit candles

If you have any encouragement from being united with Christ, if any comfort from his love, if any fellowship with the Spirit, if any tenderness and compassion, then make my joy complete by being like-minded. . . . Do nothing out of selfish ambition or vain conceit. . . .

PHILIPPIANS 2:1-3

A friend who works in risk management was asked if employees in our agency were allowed to have candles in their offices. His response, in keeping with safety codes, was that candles were fine as long as no one lit them.

How many spiritual candles have I collected that I'm afraid to light? God gives me gifts of His peace, His presence in my life, and yet I don't use them to light the darkness. I supposedly seek the mind of Christ, but I mostly like showing it to people who appeal to me, who build me up. I find it terribly difficult to love those "other" people.

Yet the place where light is most needed is not in the bright corners of my life, for the people I like, for the parts of me that I like. The light is most needed when I encounter someone I don't want to care for, or care about, someone I believe has nothing to offer me. If I only tend to those people who make me feel good, then I basically act out of "selfish ambition or vain conceit." There's nothing Christ-like about loving only those who are lovable, or only those who have the good taste to love me.

Unlit candles will never dispel the darkness.

God's pocket

. . . we will tell the next generation the praiseworthy deeds of the LORD, his power, and the wonders he has done. . . . Then they would put their trust in God. . . .

PSALM 78:4, 7

One day I saw a little girl with perhaps her very first pair of sunglasses. Fascinated with them, she kept putting them on, taking them off, then turning them over and over in her hands. Finally, she decided to put them in a very safe place: her dad's jacket pocket.

All that is most precious to me is safer in God's keeping than in my own hands. Gifts in my life—people, relationships, talents, joys—have no lasting significance in my hands, but they become meaningful and holy when I slip them into God's pocket. Even negative experiences become sacred when I give them to God. Loss opens doors of compassion for others who have lost. Hurt reminds me to define myself only through God, and not through the opinions of others. Mistakes bring humility and a greater likelihood of forgiving the next time I am wronged.

All children of God need to remember "the wonders He has done," to teach their children to trust God so that the true meaning of life echoes down through the generations. The lesson I want to pass on is that nothing means much if I cling too tightly to it, but that every cherished experience and person in my life becomes holy when I let go. It's okay; they'll be safe now.

They're in my Father's pocket.

OCTOBER 13

Out of the way

"What is this you are doing?" they asked. "Are you rebelling against the king?" I answered them by saying, "The God of heaven will give us success. We his servants will start rebuilding. . . ."

NEHEMIAH 2:19-20

An old commercial showed people taking appliances—presumably still working—and destroying them to make way for newer, fancier appliances. The ads suggested, "The only thing standing between you and your new refrigerator is your old refrigerator."

Much of life today is about getting rid of the old to make way for the newer, the more expensive. Although I, like others, have allowed marketers to program me that way, I know I am wasteful and extravagant to discard the old if it works perfectly well.

In the spiritual life, it is an advantage to throw out the old ways to make room for a new way. In antiquity, people were incredulous at the idea of throwing out the old way of life to choose instead the Godly way. Nehemiah, when asked, "Are you rebelling against the king?" was confident that the new way—the way of God—would protect him. Those tied to the old ways were stunned by the thought.

Then, and now, finding God requires tossing out former priorities and engaging a new set of priorities. In this case, maybe we should toss out the old, even if we think it's still working.

Perhaps the only thing standing between me and my new life is my old life.

No accounting for grace

"The workers who were hired about the eleventh hour came and each received a denarius. So when those came who were hired first, they expected to receive more. But each one of them also received a denarius [and] began to grumble against the landowner . . . [who said] 'Don't I have the right to do what I want with my own money?'"

MATTHEW 20:9-10, 15

At my local grocery store, the automatic door used to be a bit oversensitive. If anyone got within ten feet, the door opened and stayed open, seemingly a very inefficient way of running things.

Seeing the door open to God felt almost that same way to me. After years of indifference—even periods of antagonism—toward God, that door opened the minute I got near it. I had spent years in a seemingly endless succession of experiences that I thought would fill me but which left me increasingly empty. I thought only, "There must be more than this," and the door opened before me.

It certainly doesn't seem fair, by human standards of justice, that I have the same access to God as the person who has faithfully sought God and sought to please God for an entire lifetime. But like the landowner who chose to pay latecomers as much as early arrivals, God is the source of grace, the controller of grace. No, letting someone like me—with all my mistakes—draw near to God doesn't seem like a very efficient way to run things.

Thank God we humans aren't in charge of parceling out the grace.

OCTOBER 15

The new old

[Jesus] said to them, "Therefore every teacher of the law who has been instructed about the kingdom of heaven is like the owner of a house who brings out of his storeroom new treasures as well as old."

MATTHEW 13:52

A local retirement community ran an ad campaign in which a daughter is surprised at the amenities offered when her mother moves into the community. Mother says to daughter, "Welcome to the 'new old,' dear." It's a phrase running rampant in our society these days. In age, 60 is the "new 40." A young friend told me that, in terms of going out socially, "Wednesday is the new Friday."

In the kingdom of God, the "old" holds as much value as the new. Jesus said that one teaching the law "is like the owner of a house who brings out of his storeroom new treasures as well as old." Many wanted—and still want—to throw out any concept of law in building God's kingdom. But the law was put there for a purpose: to help mold each person into a dwelling place for God.

In the spiritual life, the old stance toward law is subsumed by the stance of loving God and others—friends and enemies alike. The old law becomes the framework for a new way of life where God not only dwells among us, but in us. The old law becomes a new way of living. And the new way of living takes us back to our creation in the image of God. Old becomes new, and new becomes old.

It's the same old (new) story.

OCTOBER 16

Wanted: Dead and alive

"The LORD brings death and makes alive; he brings down to the grave and raises up. The LORD sends poverty and wealth; he humbles and he exalts. He raises the poor from the dust and lifts the needy from the ash heap. . . ."

1 SAMUEL 2:6-8

In a favorite action movie—*The Fugitive*—a federal marshal continues to search for an escaped prisoner who, to all appearances, must have drowned. The marshal's assistant says of the escapee, "He's dead!" and the marshal replies, "That ought to make him easy to catch."

Being "easy to catch" can be a matter of life and death, at least spiritually. The words, "The LORD brings death and makes alive" don't simply describe the inevitability of life and death, but also describe the way that many of us experienced being "made alive." We die in some small or large way: losing something or someone we love, losing control, losing what we once thought to be our very selves. The LORD brings those deaths, and in return He offers life that transcends place and time.

So like the escaped prisoner in *The Fugitive*, I might look, in my most lost and most powerless moment, as if I might have died. In fact, though, that moment when I hit bottom in human terms is the moment that God can enter me fully and make me alive in exactly the way He created me to be. Yes, at that moment, I may have looked and felt dead.

That made me easy to catch.

On the side of the law

"You have heard that it was said, 'Eye for eye, and tooth for tooth.' But I tell you, Do not resist an evil person. If someone strikes you on the right cheek, turn to him the other also. And if someone wants to sue you and take your tunic, let him have your cloak as well."

MATTHEW 5:38-40

When a traffic light turned green one day, my moment of hesitation before entering the intersection prevented an accident, because another driver ran the light. The law would have been on my side, but law didn't matter. Someone could have gotten killed.

Jesus has tried for over two millennia to teach us stubborn humans the irrelevance of law when that law allows someone to get hurt. People of Jesus' time quoted the "eye for an eye" law—one which was simply a de-escalation of previous laws of vengeance—but He admonished them to do better. Love of God and neighbor calls for forgiveness and generosity where the law prescribes punishment or vengeance. Christ's death on the cross elevated loving over legalism.

So questions of "Who is at fault?" and "Who deserves punishment?" hold much less value in the kingdom of God than they do in the human kingdom. Law gives us structure and reference points, but Jesus was clear that love supersedes law every single time. If we focus only on the law—on punishment and reward—with no love for others, someone could get killed.

In fact, Someone did.

OCTOBER 18

The best of love

I want you to know, brothers and sisters, that the gospel that was proclaimed by me is not of human origin. . . .

GALATIANS 1:11

I once had a cassette music tape which split a song, "The Best of My Love," between the two sides of the tape. The music would fade out as one side of the tape ended, then the song would finish when the tape changed sides. To this day, I expect that song always to fade out and break in the middle.

Human minds also expect expressions of love to be divided. When someone says, "I love you," we often find ourselves waiting for the rest of the statement. Because we are accustomed to the limitations of human love, we expect, after hearing, "I love you" to hear a "because" or a demand.

But the love of God cannot be understood using measures of human love or described in human terms; the gospel is not "of human origin." God's love is absolute, unconditional. It is not justified by our earning it, and God doesn't give it to push us to do something.

Human ears have become sadly accustomed to the incompleteness and conditionality of earthly love. Human hearts have been broken and manipulated so often by expressions of love that we fully expect to hear a song divided by an "if" or a "so." We struggle to believe that the music will not fade this time. We are scarred by human love.

We are scared to believe that God would let us hear, and join in singing, the entire song.

OCTOBER 19

Finding change

Though you have not seen him, you love him; and even though you do not see him now, you believe in him and are filled with an inexpressible and glorious joy, for you are receiving the goal of your faith, the salvation of your souls.

1 PETER 1:8-9

A friend told me that, when he was a boy, he and his dad would go for walks in a nearby park. Father would urge son to look closely along the path in hopes of finding lost coins. Only years later did the son realize that his father had "seeded" that path with change to keep his son occupied and attentive.

Often when "looking down," especially when I'm feeling frightened or down on myself, I find treasure along the path. I find new faith in people when they come through to help or comfort me. I find new strength in myself, strength I never would have seen in better times.

Finding such currency along the way gives me "an inexpressible and glorious joy," because I know God is here, along this path, seeding the way with those lessons of hope. So moment to moment, though I can't see God, I know His salvation.

Sometimes this path my Father and I walk seems rocky and difficult, and sometimes I find it hard to put one foot in front of the other. But just then, something glimmering along the way catches my eye. God shows me a shiny lesson of hope to bring light to my soul.

And suddenly I cannot wait to continue down the path to see what else my Father and I might find.

God's Symmetry

For everything God created is good, and nothing is to be rejected if it is received with thanksgiving. . . .

1 TIMOTHY 4:4

When I'm in the woods, I love to see trees that are crooked, or that have grown or adjusted in a certain way because of rocks or other features of the terrain. I very rarely see "perfect" trees, growing straight and true, as the most beautiful.

Yet something in our human nature urges us to see symmetry and sameness as signs of perfection. We think of regularity of features as closer to perfection, and adaptations are perceived as imperfections. I'm afraid we even think of symmetry in people as beautiful, as we're often more comfortable with the people who think most like the crowd.

Does God always favor symmetry? If "everything that God created is good," does God think of crooked trees as "less good" than straight, unmarred ones? Does God think of people who think differently or live differently as mistakes, something that should've been culled from the production line?

I think the less symmetrical manifestations of God's creation are not only not mistakes, but are among God's most beautiful creations. To embrace asymmetry in creation, and in self, is a step toward living fully in God's grace. So those trees that adapt to their environments and growing conditions may be among the least symmetrical of God's creations, but God created them.

And they are good.

A smaller plate

Taking the five loaves and the two fish and looking up to heaven, he gave thanks and broke the loaves. . . . They all ate and were satisfied. . . . The number of those who ate was about five thousand men, besides women and children.

MATTHEW 14:18, 20-21

At one point, I started eating my meals off smaller plates. When I used large dinner plates, I found myself eating more than I really wanted, because I felt the need for the plate to be full. In this little experiment, I found that I was consuming much more food than I needed because it was there on that big plate.

Sometimes we become satisfied because we have more, and other times we become satisfied because we want less. When I stop thinking I can make myself happy by acquiring more and more things, my "plate" becomes smaller and I realize I wasn't hungry for those things in the first place. Hungry for something eternal, I found no satisfaction in gorging myself on things that cannot last.

I have no doubt that Jesus was capable of "multiplying" the available food to feed thousands. I don't doubt that a miracle happened with those five thousand people. But they could have been "satisfied" for two different reasons. Jesus could have given them more food, or He could have made them want less. In other words, there's more than one way to "have everything you want." One way is to have everything.

The other way is to want less.

OCTOBER 22

The uncashed check

"Ask and it will be given to you; seek and you will find; knock and the door will be opened to you. For everyone who asks receives; he who seeks finds; and to him who knocks, the door will be opened."

MARK 7:7-8

Once I worked in a fundraising office where, to our surprise, we found an uncashed check for more than $10,000 in a donor's file. Though the bank accepted it without problem, it was unnerving to think that gift had been offered but might have been of no benefit to anyone.

How many "uncashed checks" are there among us Christians, people so aware of the concept of humility that we neglect to claim and use the gifts God has given us? The Gospel tells me to "Ask and it will be given to you." But what happens if a gift given to me goes unclaimed or unused? Which is the greater sin: failure to have humility, or allowing a gift given to me by God to be wasted because I don't want to appear proud or greedy in claiming it?

This line is, for me, a fine line to walk. God has given me gifts, just as He has given gifts to other people. If I pretend my gifts don't exist, haven't I wasted them, and, at least in part, wasted the precious life given to me by God?

All of that asking and knocking and seeking goes to waste if the gifts found in those endeavors are not used. There's no point of knocking if you have no intention of going through the door.

An uncashed check does no good, and disrespects the one who wrote it.

OCTOBER 23

The mechanic

Why do you boast of evil, you mighty man?. . . You love evil rather than good, falsehood rather than speaking the truth. . . . Surely God will bring you down to everlasting ruin. . . .

PSALM 52:1, 3, 5

Some days I wish I could be an auto mechanic instead of studying about God. Fixing a car requires great skill, but it seems nice and manageable. The job requires analyzing, determining the problem, and fixing it so the car runs.

Sometimes I foolishly wish that thinking about God could be as straightforward as fixing something that is broken. The human who acts with love toward God and toward others should be loved by God. Of the one who "boasts of evil," we could then say, "surely God will bring him down to everlasting ruin."

Honestly, though, I only wish for that cause-and-effect process to be in place for others—not for me. I wish others—when they sin—would get what's coming to them. When I sin, I pray that I will not get what I deserve. When I love evil rather than good, I don't want a mechanic to come in and fix the problem, bringing me to the deserved "everlasting ruin."

So maybe I don't, after all, want things to be so simple. When I don't operate as the Maker designed me, I don't want to be discarded or punished. I want to be embraced and so grateful for that embrace that I turn to God again, that I begin to live for God as I was designed.

Then, with God's grace, a machine once broken becomes whole again.

OCTOBER 24

Play

Then Judas Iscariot, one of the Twelve, went to the chief priests to betray Jesus to them. They were delighted to hear this and promised to give him money.

MARK 14:10-11

I continually see signs on cars proclaiming a little league all-star's name, number, and team. Children's sports—once designed for fun—seem to have become more of a training ground for potential greatness. It all makes me wonder: doesn't anyone just get to play anymore?

But I don't let myself play, either. Too often, I demean my own worth because of my failure to perform some earthly task. I sometimes lose the ability to trust in anyone but myself and my own capabilities. Then, if I'm not an all-star, I see no value in playing, and I lose my ability to believe in the simple grace of God.

Like most others, I have always known and deplored Judas' betraying Jesus for money. And yet, when I think that my worth is determined by my performance, I, too, have betrayed Jesus. I have said that His sacrifice was not enough to save me, and that I have to work hard to perform and save myself.

I want to trust God alone, to let go of my need to win my own salvation. It sounds simple, but it is very difficult in our competitive world. But can't we reach down into our own depths and reclaim the image of Christ within us? Can't we stop trying to perform and start living again, in God's embrace, with the innocence of a child?

Doesn't anyone get to play anymore?

OCTOBER 25

The heart knows

Though you have not seen [Jesus Christ], you love him; and even though you do not see him now, you believe in him and are filled with an inexpressible and glorious joy, for you are receiving the goal of your faith, the salvation of your souls.

1 PETER 1:8-9

When, in one hurricane season, enough storms occur that the available names are all used up, the next choice is using Greek letters to name storms: alpha, beta, gamma. But what else do you do when you run out of names?

I often find myself "running out of names" when I speak or write of God. Like many others, I use such human words as "awesome," "powerful," and "incredible"—ones so overused in our world that their meaning has been cheapened for us. But I don't know what else to say to describe how God changed my life.

I cannot literally see Jesus Christ. I cannot literally hear God. I speak in these human ways—of seeing and hearing Him—because my heart knows things that it cannot know in any way other than the presence of divinity. The heart knows what intellect and language can neither understand nor communicate. I will never understand how, when I seemed to have lost everything, I found peace and "an inexpressible and glorious joy." The only possible answer is God, a God who must be awesome, powerful, incredible. Such descriptions are woefully inadequate to tell of a God who has saved my life.

But what else do you do when you run out of words?

OCTOBER 26

Prisons

Suddenly an angel of the Lord appeared and . . . struck Peter on the side and woke him up. "Quick, get up!" he said, and the chains fell off Peter's wrists. . . . Peter followed him out of the prison, but he had no idea that what the angel was doing was really happening; he thought he was seeing a vision.

ACTS 12:7, 9

One weekend, in the hospital emergency room, I saw several patients hurt as a result of violence—one shot and one stabbed—and another man injured when he tried something too risky on a dirt bike. I was surprisingly unshaken by the bloody scenes, and later I wondered if I thought, in some part of me, that they had brought their injuries on themselves.

Yet though most of us contribute to our own suffering, we all equally need healing. I live in certain kinds of bondage—to materialism, to self-doubt, to unforgiveness—but that doesn't mean God will not help me and heal me. The others I saw in the emergency room live in prisons of force, of intimidation, perhaps of hopelessness. The walls of their prisons may look different, but all of us are equally in prison, equally in pain.

The hope, in a world run by man yet filled with God, is that we trust, as Peter did, the angel who comes to release us. Then, perhaps we can walk out of the pain, following the messenger and the message of God. Otherwise we are doomed to be in pain.

Otherwise we will continue to claw at prison walls, trying to release ourselves.

OCTOBER 27

Range of motion

Coming to his hometown, [Jesus] began teaching the people in their synagogue, and they were amazed. "Where did this man get this wisdom and these miraculous powers?" they asked. "Isn't this the carpenter's son?..." And they took offense at him.

MATTHEW 13:54-55, 57

When I'm stressed, I have minor problems with shoulder tightness and pain. Stretching exercises the doctor prescribed cause me some discomfort, but give my shoulder greater range of motion.

Failing to stretch spiritually can quickly cause a loss of range, too, a complacency which whispers that all I need in life is already within reach. My instinct is to avoid all pain, but if I avoid the pain of stretching, I fail to grow in God. My world becomes smaller and smaller. I experience less and less. I feel less and less. I see God less and less.

Others get nervous, though, when we grow and change. People who knew Jesus as a boy were amazed at the "wisdom and miraculous powers" He possessed as a man. Rather than being gratified at His growth, "they took offense at him." Perhaps they preferred a meek carpenter's boy who could be controlled. Or perhaps, seeing His spirituality, they were reminded of the smallness and complacency of their own souls.

Yes, pain—both within ourselves and in our relationships—will often accompany the stretching of our bodies, our minds, our souls.

But it's the price we have to pay for a full range of (e)motion.

OCTOBER 28

The God-made light

Do not hide your face from your servant; answer me quickly, for I am in trouble.

PSALM 69:17

One night a beautiful gold moon emerged through bubbly dark clouds, a gorgeous sight. At first, though, the glare of a streetlight prevented my seeing that moon. I had to stop in a certain place and shade my eyes from the harsh streetlight to see the beautiful sight at all.

I often let the glare of this world prevent my seeing the heavens. I get busy, and I forget to spend time simply being with God. Or I demand His action on my schedule, saying to Him, "Do not hide your face from your servant; answer me quickly, for I am in trouble."

When I am in trouble, my first instinct is always to ask desperately for God to fix that trouble in the way I think is best, which often turns out to be not the best at all. I don't want to wait on God's answers, but for Him to jump to my demands, to meet my deadlines. The manmade glare shines so relentlessly in my eyes that I cannot see my God, who, in truth, has never left my side.

"Answer me quickly, God who created me, who created the universe. Operate on my schedule, not on your own." It does sound a bit arrogant, doesn't it? Once more, I let the harsh glare of the light of this world prevent my seeing the light of God. It's time to stop, right here, to shade my eyes against the glare of the manmade light.

And to stand in the God-made light.

OCTOBER 29

Inevitable crash

And I saw that all labor and all achievement spring from man's envy of his neighbor. This too is meaningless, a chasing after the wind . . . here is the conclusion of the matter: Fear God and keep his commandments, for this is the whole duty of man.

ECCLESIASTES 4:4, 12:13

A leading business magazine once said that financial markets have always been unstable, and that, "[The markets] have imploded every decade or so." And yet, our competitive society and our human need to control hold sway over us, keeping us participating enthusiastically despite our knowledge that such pursuits cannot last.

So even those most involved in the business world admit that financial markets are shaky in any long term. We all see financial markets and financial success as something that will inevitably experience a downturn. In other words, "all labor and achievement spring from man's envy of his neighbor," and those pursuits turn out to be "meaningless, a chasing after the wind."

The only motives that can sustain us and allow us to participate in eternity are motives which come from a fear of God and from adhering to the commandment to love God and neighbor. We are asked to "Fear God and keep his commandments, for this is the whole duty of man."

Only the love of God remains when all of the worldly things pass away. Only the fear of God can motivate us to do something that will last. Anything else we value will inevitably implode.

And it will take our very selves with it.

OCTOBER 30

The bridge

I urge, then, first of all, that requests, prayers, intercession and thanksgiving be made for everyone—for kings and all those in authority, that we may live peaceful and quiet lives in all godliness and holiness.

1 TIMOTHY 2:1-6

I often cross bridges over rivers separating one state from another. In the middle of the bridge, a sign declares that I have suddenly entered another state. I always wondered how you could divide a river—living and flowing—with an arbitrary, static line on a bridge.

People constantly build bridges between heaven and earth, trying to find meaning, trying to find something lasting. But even the most faithful humans tend to draw a line on the bridge, to say everything on one side belongs to the sacred and everything on the other side belongs to the secular.

But we can't divide the holy from the common—in either places or in persons—any more than we can divide a river by drawing a line. The prayer is for everyone at all times, not just "kings and those in authority," to "live peaceful and quiet lives in all godliness and holiness."

We spend our lives on that bridge linking common and holy. We are holy in a convenience store when we help a neighbor. We can be secular sitting in the church if we're judging one another or seeking power over one another. Our God is a living God, and our God lives in this world with us.

You can't divide a river by drawing a line on the bridge.

OCTOBER 31

No fear

The righteous will see and fear; they will laugh at him, saying, "Here now is the man who did not make God his stronghold but trusted in his great wealth and grew strong by destroying others!" But I am like an olive tree flourishing in the house of God; I trust in God's unfailing love for ever and ever.

PSALM 52:6-8

This time of year, I get very weary of ghosts and goblins and scary movies and songs about witchy and evil women. The air is filled with the anticipation of fear. To many, apparently, this controlled version of fear is fun.

I once lived in a fear that was not fun, in an uncontrolled fear generated not by ghosts and goblins and scary music outside, but by my own insecurities inside. I needed for others to look small so that I could feel more confident; in a mild sense, I could only "grow strong by destroying others."

Now, though, I live only in "fear" of God, knowing that only He holds real power over me. I now worry less about what others think of me. I know in my heart, even when scary music plays inside, that God loves me and will always embrace me in His mercy and tenderness.

Instead of living in fear of having every little failure knock me down, I am now more often "like an olive tree flourishing in the house of God." His presence has banished the gnawing fear that I will be alone. The ghosts have disappeared.

From the inside out.

November

NOVEMBER 1

I see heaven open

Jesus said, ". . . You shall see greater things than that . . . I tell you the truth, you shall see heaven open, and the angels of God ascending and descending on the Son of Man."

JOHN 1:51

Almost every day, I receive mail addressed to the person who used to live at my place, and I dutifully write, "No longer at this address." It seems to take awhile for the system to get used to a new person at this address.

My psyche has spent several years trying to get used to the new occupant inside my heart. It often seems so much easier to revert to that old person, to be continually angry and fearful, to think first of myself instead of my God. While easier, it is certainly not the way of peace.

I'm learning gradually that those desires to go back to the place I used to live are some of my best opportunities to find God. Every occasion for fear or doubt or anger is also an occasion where God can enter my life with power.

Each time I want to become that old person who used to live here, to strike out at someone or to withdraw inside myself in fear, God is waiting for me to invite Him in. If I will look, there I can see "heaven open, and the angels of God ascending and descending on the Son of Man."

Jesus, the Word of God incarnate and the energy of God within me, patiently teaches me that a new creation can live at an old address. So when I think of going back, I need only remember those peace-giving, life-giving words.

That person is no longer at this address.

NOVEMBER 2

The rest of my life

We will not all sleep, but we will all be changed— in a flash, in the twinkling of an eye, at the last trumpet. For the trumpet will sound, the dead will be raised imperishable, and we will be changed. For the perishable must clothe itself with the imperishable, and the mortal with immortality.

1 CORINTHIANS 15:51-53

A local mattress company's advertising slogan urged the customer to patronize that company "for the rest of your life." The ad reminded me that the word "rest" can mean either the "remainder," or it can mean sleep, repose, restoration.

Unfortunately, many of us confuse the two, and we allow ourselves rest only in remainders of time, as an afterthought when everything else is finally checked off the list. The Christian way urges us to find rest in God, not as an afterthought, but as the first priority. To rest completely, though, we're asked to die to ourselves, to our own egos, so that "the perishable can clothe itself with the imperishable, and the mortal with immortality."

Our fear of physical death, though, keeps us from investigating this kind of "dying." We cling to this life, though it drains us. We worry so about disappearing that we do not allow ourselves to rest in God. If I can learn to put God first, though, peace will reign in my heart instead of the chaos that so often reigns there now.

And thanks be to God, I will enjoy the *rest* of my life.

NOVEMBER 3

The identity game

When men tell you to consult mediums and spiritists, who whisper and mutter, should not a people inquire of their God? Why consult the dead on behalf of the living?

ISAIAH 8:19

On an old TV game show, contestants tried to match strangers with their identities; which one was the bounty-hunter, wrestler, shark attack victim, belly-dancer?

It's a game that nearly every human has played with regard to God. Depending on circumstances, we pray for God to be doctor, Santa Claus, employment counselor, maybe even bounty-hunter. We ask the eternal and transcendent God to fix the things and people of this world. But that isn't aligning our will with God's; it is trying to mold God's will to ours. It is nothing more than "consulting mediums and spiritists, who whisper and mutter."

I have concluded that the goal of prayer is not to turn God into what I need, but to find a place where physical healing, jobs, material goods, and petty human desires no longer matter. I want to find the place where I can, with God, rise above the things I have so often "prayed for" to a place of eternity that transcends this world now.

Had I learned to play this identity game better, I would have seen God much earlier, and much more often. It turns out that He looks like compassion, forgiveness, tenderness. No wonder I missed seeing Him for so long.

I was led to believe He'd look more like a bounty-hunter.

NOVEMBER 4

What problems does your fuel cause?

All of us also lived among them at one time, gratifying the cravings of our sinful nature and following its desires and thoughts. Like the rest, we were by nature objects of wrath.

EPHESIANS 2:3

I heard a news story about alternate fuel sources for cars. One man emphasized the need to assess fully the effects that a new fuel will have on the environment. He suggested that we continually ask of new developments, "What problems does your fuel cause?"

Spiritually, emotionally, physically, materially, we all use different "fuels" to empower us. It's easy to get so wrapped up in our own progress that we don't see the impact of our actions on others. Possessing things is not dangerous, but taking pride in possessing them, especially taking pride in possessing something because someone else doesn't have it, pollutes the air around us.

When someone else has to be diminished in order for me to feel successful, my fuel makes it hard for the next person to breathe. I have turned, in a socially acceptable or even exalted way, to "gratifying the cravings of my sinful nature." That willingness to hurt or deprive others for my own gain makes me an "object of wrath."

Like the inventors of new fuels, I need to be more mindful of what my "progress" does to those around me. It's a critical question for every human seeking God to ask.

What problems does your fuel cause?

NOVEMBER 5

Complete

> *... Samuel said [to Saul], "You have not kept the command the LORD your God gave you; if you had, he would have established your kingdom over Israel for all time. But now your kingdom will not endure; the LORD has sought out a man after his own heart and appointed him leader of his people. . . ."*
>
> 1 SAMUEL 13:13-14

A phrase in English that has always interested me is the expression "once and for all" as synonymous with "forever." It has a marvelous finality to say that something is taken care of "once and for all."

Unfortunately, my approach to God has never had that permanent seal, as I commit myself to Him in a tentative and incomplete way. I say that I want all of my life in God's hands, yet I hold back memories that hurt too much to face or failures too disappointing to voice. So I give myself to God in fits and starts, and often find myself repeating the process of turning toward Him instead of giving myself to Him once and for all.

Saul paid the price of halfhearted obedience to God. He did not give himself completely to God in obedience, and as a result his kingdom would go to "a man after [God's] own heart." As a result, Saul didn't enjoy the eternal freedom that He could have found in God.

God doesn't want part of me: my time, or my gifts, or my works. God doesn't want anything so incomplete and halfhearted. God wants me to commit myself to Him just as He has committed Himself to me through His Son.

Once. And for all.

NOVEMBER 6

High definition

But Jesus said again, ". . . It is easier for a camel to go through the eye of a needle than for a rich man to enter the kingdom of God." The disciples . . . said . . . "Who then can be saved?" Jesus looked at them and said, "With man this is impossible, but not with God; all things are possible with God."

MARK 10:24-27

A woman I saw interviewed on TV described elaborate makeup services she provided to TV personalities. Apparently, with the extreme clarity of high-definition technology, old makeup techniques are not good enough; every blemish becomes visible like never before.

The high-definition lens is the one turned on each of us when we truly seek God. In that clearer light, we see what we have let define us, perhaps the valuing of earthly wealth or the accomplishments it represents. Under that more accurate lens, we have to relinquish self-definition. We have to trust that God will replace our pictures of ourselves with something that will last in the high-definition lens of eternity.

The moment I realize that I am not simply the sum of my earthly accomplishments, I am capable of being filled with God. When I let go of all I try to use to define myself and let God define me instead, then I become part of eternity. It sounds impossible. In fact, it is impossible for me, but with God, all things are possible.

Even letting go of all things.

November 7

Without love

If I . . . can fathom all mysteries and all knowledge . . . but have not love, I am nothing. If I give all I possess to the poor and surrender my body to the flames, but have not love, I gain nothing.

1 Corinthians 13:2-3

Ads about fibromyalgia, a mysterious ailment which causes pain in joints, muscles, and bones, showed one person suffering from the pain. She said, "Sometimes I need a hug, but I know it's going to hurt."

Often an awareness of love, which should cause great joy, can also cause great pain. When I remember that I am deeply loved by God, seemingly insignificant choices become important. A minor dishonesty causes great pain to the God who loves and animates me. Bad decisions about my self-care sadden God, who loves me and wants to see me healthy and happy. Hating myself for my own failures grieves God, the God of mercy and forgiveness, the lover of all souls.

And yet, I will take the pain that comes with the awareness of God's love for me. For without love, "I am nothing," no matter how strong my faith or my altruism or my mind may be. I have learned that, of themselves, gifts of words or intellect or charitable works cannot save me. Only knowledge of the love of God can save me. In short, I need to be loved.

And sometimes, knowing I am loved is going to hurt.

Healthy hearts

. . . we have peace with God through our Lord . . . we also rejoice in our sufferings, because we know that suffering produces perseverance; perseverance, character; and character, hope. And hope does not disappoint us, because God has poured out his love into our hearts by the Holy Spirit. . . .

ROMANS 5:1,3-5

Once I saw a TV commercial for a medicine described as "preventing one in three heart attacks." The claim sounded strange; it seemed impossible to me that someone could count and claim credit for something that didn't happen.

And yet, a large part of the Christian life involves not just what does happen, but what doesn't. When we say that we "rejoice in our sufferings," for example, we aren't enjoying suffering, but enduring suffering instead of defending ourselves and hurting someone else. Often my life is better because of something I didn't do.

When I have peace in God, then certain encounters stop happening in my life: confrontations, arguments, gossip, vengeance. Paradoxically, swallowing harsh words rather than speaking them acts as preventive medicine, giving me perseverance and character. If every person who is hurt chooses to hurt back, we have no hope for a better world. But every time a person who is hurt forgives, the world is made better, not just by what happens between two people, but by what doesn't happen.

And two out of two hearts grow stronger.

NOVEMBER 9

Giving and selling

"Teacher," they said, "we want you to do for us whatever we ask." "What do you want me to do for you?" he asked. They replied, "Let one of us sit at your right and the other at your left in your glory."
MARK 10:35-37

When I travel and use wireless internet, it always irritates me that the hotel directs me not to my home page, but to their home page. I guess I shouldn't be surprised, as this world is all about selling, not about giving.

Trying to be a Christian in today's society means a continual battle between the concepts of selling and giving. Society says we're weak if we give away something we could sell, while Christ says givers prevail over sellers. The battle is so confusing and so omnipresent that we even bring the standards of the world into our spiritual lives, as when the disciples saw their close relationship with Jesus as a status symbol rather than as a responsibility and a gift.

My instinct, confused by a lifetime lived to human standards, is to use even my life of faith to win or to set me above others. So it isn't easy, trying to be a member of the kingdom of God while living in modern human society. It isn't easy, but the rewards of doing it are instant. When I show humility, compassion, and generosity to another human being, I may not get "promoted" or make a profit, but I instantly step into the presence of God.

I step into that mysterious and joyful world where giving beats selling, every single time.

NOVEMBER 10

The grace of what didn't happen

Be at rest once more, O my soul, for the LORD has been good to you. For you, O LORD, have delivered my soul from death, my eyes from tears, my feet from stumbling, that I may walk before the LORD in the land of the living.

PSALM 116:7-9

One day I found out that the car I'd been driving for over a year had neither a spare tire nor the "tire repair kit" now issued with that model. I shuddered to think what might have happened if I'd had a flat tire and no way to get the car to a repair shop.

I'm beginning to think that the grace of God comes into play as much in what doesn't happen as in what does happen. I spent many years indifferent to God, and if I had been faced squarely with my own mortality in that time, I wouldn't have had anywhere to go with my fear. I was given grace in what didn't happen.

I believe God embraces even those of us who have been indifferent to Him, that He allows our souls to "be at rest once more," and that, even in my neglect, God "delivers my soul from death, my eyes from tears, my feet from stumbling." God is not only in the joys of my life, but in the tears unshed and the foolish steps not taken.

It can be sobering to think what could have happened along that road, with nowhere to go in a crisis. I could have been left sitting there—alone and frightened—but by the grace of God, that didn't happen. I got safely home.

And now that I'm home, I thank God for what didn't happen.

NOVEMBER 11

The mystery door

Then Jesus said to his disciples, "I tell you the truth, it is hard for a rich man to enter the kingdom of heaven." . . . When the disciples heard this, they were greatly astonished and asked, "Who then can be saved?" Jesus looked at them and said, "With man this is impossible, but with God all things are possible."

MATTHEW 19:23, 26

In a building I used to visit was a door with the strangest sign; it read, "Authorized personnel only. This is not an entrance or an exit. Please do not attempt to open." It drove me crazy; I'd have given anything to see what was behind that door.

We humans do not tolerate mystery well—even the most trivial mystery. We always believe that we can figure out anything, given enough time. Mysteries are meant to be solved. If doors aren't for entering or exiting, and we can't open them, why have those doors? If God didn't want us to ask and learn and know, why would He equip us with such brain power and creativity in the first place?

Modern-day Christians, like Jesus' followers, constantly want reassurance, some sense of certainty that we are on the trail of finding all there is to know about God. Jesus didn't feel the need to explain in detail to the disciples; He told them simply, ". . . with God, all things are possible." But rather than letting God be God, we want to know God as we know the things of this world.

We'd give almost anything to find out what's behind that door.

Darkness and light

Even in darkness light dawns for the upright, for the gracious and compassionate and righteous man. Good will come to him who is generous and lends freely...

Psalm 112:4-5

Years ago I saw a Broadway play called *Art*, a comedy about a man who spends big bucks for a canvas bearing only white paint. He spends most of the play trying to explain how something with no lines or shapes—with nothing but white space—could be art.

Great art, including the art of the Creator, is possible only when both light and dark are present. I never knew how the presence of God could change a life—and bring light to that life—until I encountered the deepest darkness. I never understood how dark my heart and its motives could be until I was freed by the light of God's mercy and forgiveness. Before I knew about that light, I couldn't bear to look at the dark.

I struggle with the thought that God might create evil and sin. I find comfort, though, in knowing that at least God can use the darkness to draw the image of divinity on earth. And God's saints, living in God's light, bear the clear image of God when they act against the dark backdrop of loss, fear, and even evil. "Good will come to him," and God will come to him, "who is generous" to others, particularly in times of darkness.

And God's great art appears, painted in darkness and light on a human canvas.

NOVEMBER 13

Please ask for more

They say, "God has forsaken him; pursue him and seize him, for no one will rescue him." Be not far from me, O God; come quickly, O my God, to help me.

PSALM 71:11-12

In the grocery store checkout line I saw an empty chewing gum display. On the bottom of the empty box were these words: "Is this box empty? Please ask for more." The smart-aleck in me thought, "Why would I want more empty boxes?"

Much of our world today believes that our faith is an empty box, that we Christians put more emphasis on the packaging of our faith than on the essence. They see us arguing with each other and stressing out over external issues, and they assume that we seek not God's glory but our own. They see that God is just one more thing in a to-do list or a weekly planner. Nothing about the noise we make supposedly in defense of God draws them one inch closer to exploring for themselves. "They say, 'God has forsaken him; pursue him and seize him, for no one will rescue him.' "

Many of the stances taken in the name of God are not about God at all, but about one person's wanting to win or to be elevated over another. But God is not an empty box. He is faithful, deep and wide, authentic—whether those of us who claim to seek Him are, in the moment, or not. God has not forsaken me. God will rescue me.

So when the packaging leaves me feeling empty, I go straight to the essence, to the Source. I ask for more. More God.

Not more boxes.

NOVEMBER 14

Proportional response

You love righteousness and hate wickedness; therefore God, your God, has set you above your companions by anointing you with the oil of joy.
PSALM 45:7

In a movie called *The American President*, U.S. interests are attacked by another country, and the President's cabinet advises him that a proposed retaliatory strike is a "proportional response." About to give the order to have people on the other side of the world killed, the President says grimly, "Someday someone's going to have to explain to me the virtue of a proportional response."

"Proportional response" seems to be the best I can do on many days. When people attack me, I attack back. When they get angry, I jump right into anger with them. When they love me, I love back. Proportional response.

God, however, does not seem to be in the business of proportional response. Though I love Him conditionally, He loves me unconditionally. And when I attack or doubt or abandon or neglect Him, He loves me rather than attacking or doubting or abandoning or neglecting me back. I often miss the mark on righteousness. I often let forms of wickedness live in my heart. And yet, even when I am so disappointed in myself that I can barely look in the mirror, God—my God—loves me and "anoints me with the oil of joy."

I hope no one ever convinces Him of the virtue of a proportional response.

NOVEMBER 15

Moving pictures

Those who passed by hurled insults at [Jesus], shaking their heads and saying, "So! You who are going to destroy the temple and build it in three days, come down from the cross and save yourself!"

MARK 15:29-30

One night, after watching a football game on TV, I went online and saw, from that game, a still photo of the quarterback throwing a pass. It was a good photo, but no still photo can convey the flow of a football game the way moving pictures can.

God's people have always tried to freeze God into a still photo, one moment in which we think we have glimpsed Him. I often catch myself believing that God can only do what God has done before, taking away His status as continuing Creator of the world. Or I freeze God's image into a small human frame, assuming that I know and can understand the limits of His powers.

The people who crucified Jesus and mocked His apparent powerlessness took a still photo of moving images. They thought that temples to God can only be made of stones, not of the spirit and heart and soul. They thought that the only way to win over the world is by avoiding physical death one more day, when everlasting life actually comes when we die to ourselves and to this world. We humans just don't get it, that God moves, lives, creates in the now.

We're still trying to take a still photo of the most moving picture in history.

NOVEMBER 16

Skating on the surface

... if you have been trapped by what you said, ensnared by the words of your mouth, then do this, my son, to free yourself. ... Go and humble yourself; press your plea with your neighbor!

PROVERBS 6:2-3

On Olympic figure skating, an "expert commentator" said of a skater under the most enormous pressure of her life, "She is known for having moments of brilliance followed by extreme sloppiness." Well, aren't we all?

Occasionally my human spirit musters the grace to help another human spirit with no thought of gain. But much of the time, even when I do the right thing, I am performing for God the judge, hoping He will notice my brilliance. In fact, the moment I revel in my own brilliance is the moment I slide back into sloppiness. As a performer, I spend much of my time and energy trying to rationalize why I did or said some wrong thing when I could simply admit the mistake and move back into positive places, with God and myself.

It seems so simple to hear, "if you have been trapped by what you said. . . then go and humble yourself." It's simple to hear, yet incredibly hard to do for someone who is always performing. Someday I hope to stop performing and start loving and living for God, for no score, no credit, but simply because God loves me. Right now, I'm stuck with the same pronouncement given the Olympic skater that night.

Moments of brilliance, followed by sloppiness.

November 17

Above and below

No, in all these things we are more than conquerors through him who loved us. For I am convinced that neither death nor life, neither angels nor demons, neither the present nor the future, nor any powers, neither height nor depth, nor anything else in all creation, will be able to separate us from the love of God that is in Christ Jesus our Lord.

Romans 8:37-39

Several years ago I saw a sign for a contracting company named, "Heavenly Floors." At first it seemed a paradox, to think of the heavens above in relation to floors below. I would be more comfortable with a company named "Heavenly Ceilings."

And yet, the same paradox exists in the life of a Christian believer in this world. Trust in God is not simply an ethereal, impractical-in-the-moment concern. Trust in God "above" serves as the firmest foundation for life on earth. Because my belief in God supports me on earth, "neither death nor life, neither angels nor demons, neither the present nor the future, nor any powers, neither height nor depth, nor anything else in all creation, will be able to separate us from the love of God that is in Christ Jesus our Lord."

If this day does not go particularly well—due to work or school or health or relationships—my heart can still rise to be with God, because nothing of this world can separate me from God. Paradoxically, the same God in heaven above serves as the rock-solid foundation beneath my feet.

I guess you might call that a "heavenly floor."

NOVEMBER 18

Are you sure?

You were taught, with regard to your former way of life, to put off your old self . . . and to put on the new self, created to be like God in true righteousness and holiness. . . . Be kind and compassionate to one another, forgiving each other, just as in Christ God forgave you.

EPHESIANS 4:22-23, 32

Ready to donate a very old computer to charity, I turned the machine on and typed in the old "format" command to wipe clean the hard drive. The machine kept asking me, "Are you sure? Y/N." Although I knew it needed to be done, I struggled to respond, "Y" for "Yes," knowing that everything on that computer would be lost to me irrevocably.

It's always difficult for me to detach completely from old attitudes, ways, relationships. As a follower of Christ, I want to "put off my old self" completely, but I have trouble responding, "Yes," when asked, "Are you sure?"

Can't I just get a new self that's basically righteous and holy, and yet cling to these nasty little pet resentments? Can't I be less compassionate, less forgiving, when the ungodly are involved? Isn't there some answer between "yes" and "no"?

Dear Lord, I am weak and polytheistic, letting those little gods of resentment, lack of forgiveness, and malice live on with you in my heart. Given my lack of courage and conviction, are you sure that you want to forgive me, to embrace me, even to use me as your tool to build a new kingdom on earth? Are you sure?

Y.

NOVEMBER 19

Annex

Several days later Felix . . . sent for Paul and listened to him as he spoke about faith in Christ Jesus. As Paul discoursed on righteousness, self-control and the judgment to come, Felix was afraid and said, "That's enough for now! You may leave. When I find it convenient, I will send for you."

ACTS 24:24-25

A city near my home wanted to annex into its control a new and growing area near the interstate highway, an area filled with businesses and potential sales tax revenues. When the city tried to exclude a lower-income residential area between downtown and the desired area, an outcry went up at the idea of annexing beneficial neighborhoods while conveniently excluding areas of no "use."

It's human nature to fear annexing the discomfiting and uncomfortable parts—of humanity, of ourselves, of the message. Felix, hearing the message Paul brought "about faith in Christ Jesus," wanted only the comfortable parts of that message, so he told Paul, "That's enough for now! You may leave. When I find it convenient, I will send for you."

The human heart in pursuit of God includes uncomfortable territory. When I bring myself to God, I bring all of me, the places of dark as well as the places of light. And God in His mercy does not choose to annex only the parts of me which will benefit Him. He does not say those words Felix used.

"When I find it convenient, I will send for you."

NOVEMBER 20

A heart for God

The LORD God ... commanded the man, "You are free to eat from any tree in the garden; but you must not eat from the tree of the knowledge of good and evil, for when you eat of it you will surely die."

GENESIS 2:16

A former college classmate appeared on national news one morning speaking of her research into repairing hearts and even "growing" human hearts. I was stunned at the ability of the human mind to analyze empirical data and come up with such solutions.

Such stories, though, do carry danger in that they convince us further that all knowledge is knowledge within the eventual reach of and domain of humans. If we can figure out how to grow a new human heart, isn't it just a matter of time until we know all about God, about God's motives and ways?

But knowledge of God is God's domain alone, not something we can determine in some cosmic laboratory given enough time. We know of God only when and only because God chooses to reveal Himself to us. We don't know God because our research has finally paid off, but because God, in His infinite grace and mercy, chooses to let us know Him in a moment of revelation.

Human frustration at living in this world is not our punishment for eating from the tree of knowledge. The ultimate knowledge we can possess is that God is God, and we are not. Yes, it is true that we may figure out a way to grow a new physical heart.

But to have a heart for God is a gift from God alone.

NOVEMBER 21

Kindling

". . . as I was on the road, I saw a light from heaven, brighter than the sun, blazing around me and my companions. . . I heard a voice saying to me in Aramaic, 'Saul, Saul, why do you persecute me?' . . . Then I asked, 'Who are you, Lord?' 'I am Jesus, whom you are persecuting,' the Lord replied."

ACTS 26:13-15

As I drove north one weekend, I saw many places already beginning to sell firewood and bundles of "kindling." Winter nights could get awfully cold for those who had bought only large chunks of wood and no smaller pieces to use in starting fires.

Only rarely do people catch fire for God in dramatic fashion, as Paul did on his road. For most humans, the fire has to start smaller: tiny flames enkindling rather than fire "blazing around me." Then, later, we begin to realize the warmth and light that acknowledging the presence of God can bring to a life.

People who think they have no interest in God can often find that interest kindled by others' small acts of compassion, forgiveness, or tenderness. Left to purely human instincts, would we care about each other, or for each other? If the answer is no, then some force greater than humanity is at work, a force often seen first not in blazes, but in more modest fires. Who knows when the smallest act of caring for others might start a fire for God?

Perhaps it's no accident that the word "kindling" starts with "kind."

You can go home again

For you were once darkness, but now you are light in the Lord. Live as children of light (for the fruit of the light consists in all goodness, righteousness and truth) and find out what pleases the Lord.

EPHESIANS 5:8-10

At one point, the news was filled with the story of two missing children returned home: one after four days and the other after four years. With the child gone for four years, outsiders questioned why, if he had freedom to come and go, he didn't return home or contact someone for help. His family, on the other hand, was simply grateful that their child is home.

When I have been spiritually lost, I have certainly had ample opportunity to return home. But when I show up on God's doorstep, He doesn't remind me of my mistakes in getting lost or staying lost. He simply wants me home. In fact, He welcomes me home.

Parts of some days, I live as a child of the light, and other parts of those same days, I choose the darkness. But every time I leave the darkness for the light, I "find out what pleases the Lord." He is pleased by my being with Him, and by my being good and righteous as a result of living in His presence. He is pleased by my return, no matter how long I have been gone, no matter how many times I passed up the opportunity to return.

Four days or four years. In captivity or free to return. The details don't matter much.

All that matters is that the child has come home.

NOVEMBER 23

The chorus

"May those who love you be secure. May there be peace within your walls...."

PSALM 122:6-7

An interesting TV ad that used to run showed large groups of people, all of them singing in unison, "I'm not like everybody else."

I have sung that song, wanting to fit it, yet protesting that I'm really not like the others. In the past, when my ambitions and desires didn't match what the world expected of me, I changed my ambitions. I spent years knowing that "I'm not like everybody else," but longing to fit in. I lived according to others' wishes and wondered why I felt such disquiet in my heart.

In years of trying to pour myself into someone else's mold, I found no peace within me. Even when it appeared that I was doing well by the world's standards, I knew that those were not the standards to use in measuring my life at all. I simply didn't realize that I needn't perform for anyone; those who truly love me don't need for me to be anything but at peace.

Ultimately I began to let go of worldly ambition, becoming more concerned with doing good than with looking good. Of course, seeking God's kingdom right in the middle of man's won't look successful to worldly eyes, but it is the only way to have peace within me. After all, I'm not like everybody else. Everybody say it with me.

"I'm not like everybody else."

Limping well

. . . Jesus asked [the man who had been blind], "Do you see anything?" He looked up and said, "I see people; they look like trees walking around." Once more Jesus put his hands on the man's eyes. Then his eyes were opened, his sight was restored, and he saw everything clearly.

MARK 8:23-25

A grade school classmate of mine had to be on crutches all the time. He was amazing, though, and even played kickball with us. He would swing on his crutches and send the ball flying, then move around the bases incredibly fast.

The human ability to adapt to adversity can be incredible, and yet that same adaptability can itself be crippling. The blind man whom Jesus healed probably would have been thrilled even with partial healing. It was a miracle for a man who had never seen to be able suddenly to see shapes, people who "look like trees walking around." But Jesus did not leave him partially healed; He touched the man again until the man "saw everything clearly."

When crutches or blindness are all we know, though, seeking healing means changing the way we define ourselves, a frightening experience. But just because we're able to live with infirmities doesn't mean we shouldn't seek to live without them. Jesus doesn't want to teach us to do well on crutches, or to limp well.

Jesus wants us to be healthy and whole, so that we can walk, and run, and perhaps even to fly.

NOVEMBER 25

Random acts

"But you are a forgiving God, gracious and compassionate, slow to anger and abounding in love. Therefore you did not desert them, even when they cast for themselves an image of a calf and said, 'This is your god, who brought you up out of Egypt,' or when they committed awful blasphemies."

NEHEMIAH 9:17-18

Once I read of police trying to deal with the inexplicable shooting of a local store owner. A police spokesman said in an interview about the incident, "Hopefully this was a random act of violence." It saddened me to think that we need to hope for random violence rather than violence directed specifically at us or those we love.

I often find myself wondering if—even hoping that—negative forces in life are random acts of loss or hurt. I know I have done plenty in my life to deserve God's punishment, and I continue to miss the mark even though I'd like to think I value my relationship with God above all. I continually return to false, self-made gods. I routinely forget God and step on others in my anxiety to feel important and successful.

And yet, at the foundation of the world, I believe, is a God of great mercy, a God who forgives, who is "gracious and compassionate, slow to anger and abounding in love." My life feels deep and rich and joyous; I never look back over my shoulder in fear of God's wrath.

So hopefully this grace I feel is not a random act of mercy.

NOVEMBER 26

Change the world

There [Jesus] was transfigured before them. His face shone like the sun, and his clothes became as white as the light. Just then there appeared before them Moses and Elijah, talking with Jesus. Peter said to Jesus, "Lord, it is good for us to be here. If you wish, I will put up three shelters—one for you, one for Moses and one for Elijah."

MATTHEW 17:2-4

The movie *Amazing Grace* tells about a man who helped end the slave trade in the British Empire. In the movie, the man feels called by God to be a preacher, but a friend thinks he should remain in politics instead. The friend asks, "Do you intend to use your beautiful voice to praise God, or to change the world?"

God doesn't "call" people into only overtly religious acts, but also into small acts of kindness, compassion, and courage. But even the people who knew Jesus wanted to separate religion from deeply held, transformative spirituality. Peter, having seen the miracle of Christ's transfiguration before him, thought immediately of capturing the moment in a religious shrine rather than letting the experience transform him.

Yet the presence of God is supposed to direct not only the big, dramatic "calls," but the seemingly small and insignificant moments when we have opportunities to care for one another. So the question remains: Will I use my voice to praise God, or to change the world?

Yes, I will.

NOVEMBER 27

Return and enter

I hold this against you: You have forsaken your first love. Remember the height from which you have fallen!

REVELATION 2:4-5

When I first started using computers after decades of typewriters, I would occasionally get confused until I remembered that the "Return" key was also the "Enter" key. It just didn't make sense to me to equate "Return" with "Enter."

Yet in the deepest, most important matter in the world—the union of human with God—I believe that returning and entering are exactly the same. At the time of human creation, we were made in God's image, a fact easy to forget when we see the depths to which human behavior can fall. Sometimes we lower our expectations of ourselves, failing to remember "the height from which we have fallen." But to "return" and recognize that I am made in God's image is to "enter" the kingdom of God—here, today.

Every human heart is flawed and prone to pursuing other "gods," to forgetting God and having "forsaken our first love." But focusing only on our sin and separation from God prevents our return and our entering the arms of God. Our own regret and guilt keep us away from the One we are made to love.

As a human being, I am not only made by God, but I am made for God and in God's image. To "forsake my first love" and forget that fact keeps me from returning. It keeps me from entering the kingdom fully.

It is, in fact, all one key. "Return" equals "Enter."

NOVEMBER 28

Grounded

And I pray that you, being rooted and established in love, may have power, together with all the saints, to grasp how wide and long and high and deep is the love of Christ, and to know this love that surpasses knowledge. . . .

EPHESIANS 3:17-19

On a long walk in the country, I was startled by some birds which flew suddenly up out of the long grass. I hated scaring them, but their fear of me allowed them to do what they are made to do, to soar in the sky instead of hiding in the grass.

My need for safety often keeps me on the ground when I should be flying. Are other people really so very certain of what God wants, of who God is? My heart and my mind always hold questions, doubts, fears, and to quell them or pretend they're not there forces me to remain on the ground when I want to be flying. Why would God give me such a gift as intellect if using it would keep me from soaring with Him?

But with one key piece of knowledge—of the love of God—I can express all questions and doubts right out loud without damaging my relationship with God. If I am "rooted and established in love," I will have the power "together with all the saints, to grasp how wide and long and high and deep is the love of Christ, and to know this love that surpasses knowledge . . . "

If I know how to love God and let Him love me, I needn't let the questions and doubts keep me on the ground; I can let them fly.

And they can help me fly.

Filling the glass

Then Peter began to speak: "I now realize how true it is that God does not show favoritism but accepts men from every nation who fear him and do what is right. You know the message God sent to the people of Israel, telling the good news of peace through Jesus Christ, who is Lord of all."

ACTS 10:34-36

Frequently I hear people describe the outlook of another person by saying that person "sees the glass as half-full" or "sees the glass as half-empty." Optimists see "full" and pessimists see "empty."

Personally, I think the glass is completely full; it just happens to be half-full of liquid and half-full of air, both commodities that we must have to live. Even what we perceive as "missing"—space we view as empty—can hold something essential to our humanity and our pursuit of God.

So when I see a person with loss in this life, yet who still feels blessed, I assume the rest of the glass is filled with something I cannot see or touch. The good news is that "God does not show favoritism but accepts men from every nation who fear him and do what is right." God hasn't rejected those experiencing loss. It's just that half of the glass holds earthly blessings, and the seemingly empty half holds something we cannot see.

When I had losses in my life, I thought my heart must be at least half empty. What I didn't know is that it was being filled with something—or someone—I just couldn't see.

I'm convinced the glass is completely full.

Holier and Thou

My soul is consumed with longing for your laws at all times. You rebuke the arrogant, who are cursed and who stray from your commands.
PSALM 119:20-21

As a chaplain, I once visited an elderly lady who sometimes got confused, and we talked about spirituality and priorities in life. She said, "Some people want to be holier than thou, but you can't be both. You can either be holier, or you can be thou."

At first I thought of the words as simple confusion, but then they began to work on me. Sometimes I embrace religion so tightly—and in a sense so competitively—that I squeeze God right out of it. I set myself up as "holier than thou," proclaiming that "My soul is consumed with longing for God's law at all times," and ironically urging God to "rebuke the arrogant." Desperate to point out how much deeper my spirituality is than someone else's, I completely forget about the grace of God. I attempt to use the tools of humanity to measure the essence of divinity.

We live on this earth as strangers because we are made to be with God. I foolishly apply a competitive earthly mentality even to the pursuit of God. In trying to demonstrate superior piety, I lose authenticity, and vulnerability, and the whole concept of forgiveness. I wish I could remember not to let religion get in the way of God, and that I don't need to be "holier" than someone else.

I only need to be with "Thou."

December

December 1

God with us

"The virgin will be with child and will give birth to a son, and they will call him Immanuel"—which means, "God with us."

MATTHEW 1:23

As persons contemplating marriage have tried to avoid using one last name over the other, or of hyphenating the last names together, some have chosen to create a new last name instead. So neither last name takes precedence, and the newly married couple embraces a new name in their new life together.

I have begun to think of the name "Immanuel," described by the angel who came to Mary before Jesus' birth, as that same "new" kind of name. In Jesus comes a new life, one in which the human life is infused with and energized by divinity. Only in the coming of Christ do we find such a coming-together of human and divine. Only in the coming of Christ do we realize the power and peace that fill us when we take not only our own name or God's name but a new name: "God with us."

This time of year, we anticipate the advent of new life, but it's easy to forget that Jesus' coming changes not only "the world," but each of our individual human hearts. Too often I discount courses of action because I think of them as impossible. After all, how could God possibly work through someone like me? How could someone of my gifts ever make a difference in this chaotic and mean world?

It can happen only when I embrace that new name offered by God in love: "God with us."

Immanuel.

DECEMBER 2

Away

. . . my cry came before [God]. . . . The earth trembled and quaked, and the foundations of the mountains shook. . . . He brought me out into a spacious place; he rescued me because he delighted in me. The LORD has dealt with me according to my righteousness. . . .

PSALM 18: 6-7, 19-20

In a shop one day, I saw a sign that said, "Don't throw anything away. There is no away." The shop lives up to the sign; it sells secondhand goods of every shape and value.

Each of us, if "dealt with according to our righteousness," would have been thrown away for not having lived up to the image of God in which we are created. If the God of heaven worked as the other "gods" in our lives do, we would have been discarded for failure to placate them and "perform."

Despite the psalmist's claim of righteousness, not one of us deserves the grace of God, yet every one of us has access to that grace. This God of the heavens, capable of causing the earth to "tremble and quake" remains somehow a God of tenderness who "rescues me because he delights in me."

We needn't trek up the mountain to placate this God; we can call to him in distress and invite him, in a very personal way, into our human lives. In his power, he could have discarded us as useless, but in his grace he rescues us. I am so thankful that this God of the mountain stoops to embrace me, that he doesn't choose to throw me away.

For our loving, merciful God, there is no away.

DECEMBER 3

Never again

The LORD... said in his heart: "Never again will I curse the ground because of man, even though every inclination of his heart is evil from childhood. And never again will I destroy all living creatures, as I have done."

GENESIS 8:21

One state health care system decided to remove all pharmaceutical company promotional items from its hospitals. Research had shown that even the cheapest gifts could change a doctor's prescribing decisions.

How sad it is that a prescription drug decision could be based on a free pen or notepad. But all manner of human decisions—from a toothpaste brand to the next President—are, to some degree, influenced by marketing. We want a 15-second sound byte about how to live in eternity. We make snap judgments and then pray for God to get us out of trouble.

But whether our mistakes are made in haste or after great deliberation, we can count on God's grace and forgiveness. After sending the flood to destroy the earth, God even looked back and decided on a different course the next time. "The LORD... said in his heart: 'Never again...'"

I find hope in knowing that God understands the words, "Never again," as I continually neglect to consult God when making decisions. I pay the price of regrets and pray for God to save me from myself. I routinely turn away from eternity out of laziness or selfishness. At least, that's what I have done in the past.

But never again . . .

DECEMBER 4

Winning and loosing

"I tell you the truth, whatever you bind on earth will be bound in heaven, and whatever you loose on earth will be loosed in heaven."
MATTHEW 18:18

Once I had to prepare to make two trips by air, one to the Midwest and one to the Deep South. I originally was going to fly in one trip, until I realized that I would need completely different kinds of clothes in the two places. I couldn't bear the thought of packing and carrying all that extra baggage.

And yet, I seem perfectly willing to carry all sorts of baggage in eternity. When I fail to forgive someone's perceived injury to me, my stubbornness seldom hurts that person. Instead, I take on extra baggage, and I make one more person inaccessible to me.

When Jesus said that "whatever you loose on earth will be loosed in heaven," perhaps He was suggesting that we lighten the baggage we carry. He does seem to be giving me some sort of power. But maybe instead of power over the other person's forgiveness, God gives me power to lighten my own load.

Failures to forgive poison my attitude toward people and events of the past, and sometimes even toward people and events now who resemble them. The inability to forgive other people doesn't "bind" them nearly as much as it binds me, so maybe it's time to acknowledge my old grudges and let them go. After all, I have a long, long way to go with God.

And I cannot bear the thought of carrying all that extra baggage.

DECEMBER 5

Saving breath

... he too shared in their humanity so that by his death he might ... free those who all their lives were held in slavery by their fear of death.... For this reason he had to be made like his brothers in every way, in order that he might become a merciful and faithful high priest in service to God....

HEBREWS 2:14-15, 17

I heard a woman in a restaurant lecturing her teenage son as he rested his head on the table. Exasperated, his mother said, "If you're not going to listen, I won't waste my breath."

Though he may have welcomed that prospect, he did straighten up and seem to listen. I would not be surprised, in a moment of wishing disguised as prayer, to hear those words from God: "If you're not going to listen, I won't waste my breath." I usually talk too much and listen too little, and yet He continues to love me, to communicate with me, to have mercy on my complacent, weak, and wayward soul.

God does "waste" His breath on me, breathing forgiveness into my heart even when I am too frightened or too angry at myself to accept it. He breathes peace into me where I hold those awful fears of being alone or of failing those I love. He breathes freedom into me, liberating me from the slavery of this world by focusing on His transcendence, moment to moment to moment.

I am eternally grateful for God's patience, eternally grateful that He chooses to waste His breath on me. I don't want God to "save His breath."

I want God's breath to save me.

DECEMBER 6

The reality of snow

My purpose is that they may be encouraged in heart and united in love, so that they may have the full riches of complete understanding....
COLOSSIANS 2:2

Once when living in the South and missing the snow, I kept watching one scene of a movie repeatedly to enjoy a snow scene: big, soft flakes falling quietly on a city. I love the snow; I think it is beautiful.

Well, it may be beautiful in the ideal, but the everyday reality of snow is not nearly as appealing. Real snow makes roads dangerous, gets into cars' wheel wells in big, ugly chunks, and gets piled up in sooty, grey mounds beside the street. The ideal and the reality widely diverge.

Who can argue, for example, with such elegant words as these? "My purpose is that they may be encouraged in heart and united in love, so that they may have the full riches of complete understanding, in order that they may know the mystery of God...." But the reality of those words sometimes isn't beautiful or inspiring. For me to be "united in love" with others, I have to stop whittling them down. "Encouraging in heart" and offering someone else the "full riches of complete understanding" require putting a busy day on hold to listen for a change.

Only by accepting the ugly, inconvenient part of the picture along with the elegant words can I live the life of loving God, and loving on God's behalf. I think God's command to "love one another" is a beautiful thing.

At least it looks great on TV.

DECEMBER 7

Emergency call

Be joyful always; pray continually; give thanks in all circumstances, for this is God's will for you in Christ Jesus.
1 THESSALONIANS 5:16-18

Social service agencies collect discarded cell phones to give to persons in need. Since all cell phones—whether they have paid service or not—are required to have access to 911 assistance, even a phone with no paid service allows someone in need to call for help.

Our opportunity to commune with God in prayer is a similar emergency measure. Prayer remains accessible to all persons, regardless of past mistakes or circumstances. That emergency connection, as close as my own willingness to seek God, saves my life. I can "pray continually," not only in a church or in a "spiritual" situation, but always in my heart.

The knowledge of that ever-present opportunity to open my heart to God allows me much joy in this life. I can "give thanks in all circumstances" because I know that God is present for me. I know that the life and death of Christ allow me to transcend this world, even when I have done nothing to deserve or "earn" that transcendence.

We don't have to continue to pay the bill in order to have immediate access to God. All we have to do is to remember that we are saved by God's mercy and grace, not through our own efforts. That knowledge allows me peace. That knowledge brings me joy. That knowledge brings me to "God's will for me in Christ Jesus."

That knowledge lets me "give thanks in all circumstances."

"The day of small things"

Then the word of the LORD came to me: "The hands of Zerubbabel have laid the foundation of this temple; his hands will also complete it. Then you will know that the LORD Almighty has sent me to you. Who despises the day of small things?"

ZECHARIAH 4:8-10

Increasingly, I see TV ads about people who give insanely large gifts—like cars—as Christmas presents. The ads focus more attention on the cleverness of the giver than on the gift or the one who receives it.

While we like dramatic gifts and moments, God treasures the smaller sacrifices we are willing to make in His name. It's difficult, day to day, to love other people, to withhold judgment or anger which seem justified, to think of others first, to remember God's generosity to us when worldly things go awry. All are "small gifts," but such gifts remake bits of the world in God's image.

Zechariah's vision included worry that the restoration of God's temple wasn't happening fast enough. But God, knowing the value of proceeding with small steps rather than staying gridlocked and overwhelmed by the enormity of the task, asked, "Who despises the day of small things?"

I cannot afford to buy anyone a car for Christmas this year. But I can make the world better by loving, forgiving, embracing, dignifying, healing. They may seem to be small things.

But such small things begin to restore the place where God lives.

December 9

Getting there from here

> ... *the waves broke over the boat, so that it was nearly swamped. Jesus was in the stern, sleeping on a cushion.* ... *[Jesus] got up, rebuked the wind and said to the waves, "Quiet! Be still!" Then the wind died down and it was completely calm. He said to his disciples, "Why are you so afraid? Do you still have no faith?"*
>
> MARK 4:37, 39, 41

I had an appointment downtown one day, but wasn't sure if I could get there because of heavy snow. A friend suggested that, even if I could get there, I should call ahead, in case the staff in the office couldn't make it.

I do tend to focus on whether I can "get there," without regard to what others may be able to do. Particularly when someone has hurt me or caused chaos in my life, I have trouble getting there in terms of forgiveness. In fact, often both sides feel wronged and feel the apology should come to them.

In such cases, though, calm can come even if both parties feel we can't get there from here. When I have been hurt and can't fathom forgiveness, I can pray to Jesus to forgive the person for me. I hope others are praying the same about me.

Faith in God allows us not to accomplish all things on our own, but to realize we don't have to. When the storm moves in and the waves are breaking over the boat, I don't have to find the calm. It doesn't matter if I can get there, or if the other person can get there.

Jesus can get there, even when no one else can.

DECEMBER 10

Answers and questions

Like newborn babies, crave pure spiritual milk, so that by it you may grow up in your salvation, now that you have tasted that the Lord is good.

1 PETER 2:2-3

I once saw a contestant on a quiz show who described a knowledge game she played with her family. In it, one person would read the contents of an encyclopedia entry and the others would try to name the entry. They determined the questions from the answers instead of the other way around.

When I first sought God, I got answers first, then questions. As anxiety began to dissipate and peace crept into my heart, I had the trust and faith in God to start asking questions. Having "tasted that the Lord is good," I began to hunger for more solid food—a deeper relationship with Him—asking the difficult questions. What does it mean, God? How can this be? Why did things have to happen this painful and frightening way?

At first glance it would seem an odd game to play: having answers before questions. But it is also probably the only way I could find peace in God. I can have confidence in His power and His caring for me, asking the questions instead of letting them fester in my heart. I am convinced that our powerful, merciful, loving God can handle the questions.

And I am convinced that He does not think less of me for asking them.

DECEMBER 11

The price is right

[Jesus] said, "Go away. The girl is not dead but asleep." But they laughed at him . . . he went in and took the girl by the hand, and she got up.

MATTHEW 9:24-25

As gas prices soared, I saw a gas station whose large sign indicated that gasoline was $1.009 a gallon. The place appeared to be open, but apparently the price was not accurate. If so, everyone would have been lining up to get in.

When I first started exploring a relationship with God, I held that same skeptical attitude, an attitude which kept me from even approaching God. I kept hearing about grace, and about the unconditional love of God, and I thought, "There's a mistake. Nothing so valuable can be so easy to get." If it were, everyone would be lining up to get it.

Even in Jesus' time, the phrase, "too good to be true" must have come up constantly. A powerful man whose daughter was believed dead asked, in desperation, for help. Others there laughed when Jesus said, "The girl is not dead but asleep." Yet even where human reason said there was no hope, the grace and power of God brought a human being back to life. I once thought it was too good to be true, but now I see it happen every day.

The love of God for a flawed and often faithless human being does seem too good to be true. If having the peace and presence offered by God were so easy to obtain—like cheap fuel at a deserted station—then everyone would be lining up to get it, wouldn't they? It can't be as simple as turning to God and asking for help.

Can it?

DECEMBER 12

Tastes like numbers

Jesus answered them, ". . . Do not work for the food that perishes, but for the food that endures for eternal life, which the Son of Man will give you."

JOHN 6:26-7

One morning I overheard an exchange between a mother and her young child. He had apparently tried a new food, and when she asked him how it tasted, he said, "It tastes like numbers."

The child's mixture of the concepts of taste and arithmetic symbols forced me to think in a way to which I'm not accustomed. Perhaps that strangeness of understanding is what Jesus was trying to convey when He spoke in parables, as when He said, "Do not work for food that perishes, but for the food that endures for eternal life."

Part of the reason we cannot understand God is our insistence on putting the divine into human terms, the transcendent into the empirical. The place where we are with God is a place so far beyond human understanding that our senses, sensibilities, and reason can never take us there. The place where we are with God is different, a place we can understand with our hearts but which we cannot describe with our words or know with our minds.

It may even taste like numbers.

DECEMBER 13

Last wish

My command is this: Love each other as I have loved you. Greater love has no one than this, that he lay down his life for his friends. . . .
JOHN 15:12-13

Too often in my e-mail account I get weird messages, usually from overseas, asking for financial help. (Sometimes they even call me "dear friend" in the subject line.) One I received recently said, "Fulfill the last wish of a dying man." I deleted it unopened.

If I had such a request in person, of course, I would react differently. If I knew a real, present person's death was imminent, and that I could do something meaningful in the waning moments of that person's life, I would help if humanly possible.

I don't know if Jesus foresaw His own death, but He must have known that a man with His teachings and His priorities couldn't last long in this greedy, power-driven world. So when He asked His followers, "Love one another as I have loved you," His words held the weight of "the last wish of a dying man." And if humanly possible, I want to fulfill that wish for Him.

Well, in theory I do, anyway. I know of some people I'll see today who are difficult to love, and fulfilling Christ's wish will be tough. So I will have to "lay down my life" for them, one moment at a time, putting aside my pettiness long enough to love in God's name, and in Jesus' memory. But I do love God. I want to do as His Son asked me. I want to fulfill the wish, not just of a "dying man."

But of a living One.

DECEMBER 14

Singing lessons

I keep asking that the God of our Lord Jesus Christ . . . may give you the Spirit of wisdom and revelation, so that you may know him better. I pray also that the eyes of your heart may be enlightened in order that you may know the hope to which he has called you, the riches of his glorious inheritance in the saints. . . .

EPHESIANS 1:17-18

In church one Sunday a friend sat with her grandbaby on her lap and sang directly to the child during hymns. The baby gazed lovingly at her grandmother, a bright smile and absolute delight on her face. Later, the grandmother told me, "I'm teaching her to sing."

God, like that grandparent, wants to teach me to sing: to delight in Him and to delight in other people. He holds me, sharing His music of compassion and forgiveness with me so that I can share those gifts with others. He wants me to look, with the "eyes of my heart enlightened," as that baby looked at her grandmother. He wants me to see, with those eyes of delight, "the hope to which he has called me" and "the riches of his glorious inheritance."

I cannot learn the music of joy if I focus on the highs and lows of this world. I can only learn it by focusing completely on God, by looking at Him so that He can teach me to transcend this life on earth and embrace life with Him. So when I seem removed from this world, inattentive to the noise of earth, it's because God is teaching me to hear the music of heaven.

My Father is teaching me to sing.

December 15

One perfect gift

"May those who love you be secure. May there be peace within your walls and security within your citadels." For the sake of my brothers and friends, I will say, "Peace be within you."

PSALM 122:6-8

I find this time of year maddening, particularly because I watch a lot of TV. There I see all the ads for the "perfect gift" not just for my friends and family, but for everyone. How can one gift be perfect for so many people whom the sellers don't even know?

Yet the one gift that is needed by all, fits all, and is welcomed by all, is the gift of peace. As the holidays begin, I find myself thinking that I want some space, some time of not having to be anywhere. I want to know that I've communicated to the people in my life how much they mean to me. I want to avoid participating in the craziness of holiday buying without being made to feel as if that attitude is un-American.

Now, as the holiday buying and selling season gets into full swing, I find myself wishing for not more, but less. I want to be less emotionally needy, less materialistic, less agitated, less competitive. "For the sake of my brothers [and sisters] and friends," I want each of us to seek peace: deep, abiding, personal peace. In other words, my Christmas list holds only one item: peace within the human heart. So amid the shopping and celebrating crush, may "Peace be within you."

Trust me. It's the perfect holyday gift.

DECEMBER 16

Passport

". . . whoever hears my word and believes him who sent me has eternal life and will not be condemned; he has crossed over from death to life."

JOHN 5:24

At one point, I spent hours looking for my passport, picturing it in a certain color of folder. It turned out, though, that the document wasn't in a folder at all, but in a box. So my own misconceptions about what I was looking for kept me from finding it.

When first seeking God, I also made assumptions about how God would look and act. I expected to find God in condemnation, and I wasn't even sure I wanted to find Him. So I missed countless opportunities to see God in loving kindness, in compassion, in forgiveness. My own misconceptions had me looking in the wrong places.

But "God did not send his Son into the world to condemn the world, but to save the world through him." I began to find God when I stopped looking for that preconceived package of condemnation, instead looking for God in loving gestures, in compassion, in strangers who took time to comfort me.

When I stopped picturing God as condemnation, I finally "crossed over from death into life." I gradually began de-emphasizing transitory things and relationships and began looking instead for the love of God, pure and simple and operative in the lives of His people. My preconceived ideas gone, I finally found that passport.

And I crossed the border from death into life.

DECEMBER 17

More or less

> *"In the beginning you laid the foundations of the earth, and the heavens are the work of your hands. They will perish.... But you remain the same, and your years will never end."*
>
> PSALM 102:25-27

At one time I heard a weight loss product ad on the radio claiming to be a "no risk" offer. If the first month's worth of product doesn't work, the company will send a complimentary second month's supply. Somehow getting twice as much of something that doesn't work doesn't sound helpful.

The logic sounds foolish—to follow up something ineffective with more of the same—but that logic is alive and well in the world today. If working doesn't bring us satisfaction, we work harder. If buying things doesn't make us happy, we buy more and bigger things. If power doesn't ring the bell, we seek more power over more people. If being maniacally busy doesn't make us feel important, we take on more activity.

It's a case of "more is less," in that we can only find fulfillment in God, and we can only hear the voice of God if we still the other noise in our lives. Those things we add more of will not last; "The foundations of the earth, and the heavens . . . will perish." But God "remains the same," and God's "years will never end." So jettisoning manic schedules, power-seeking and materialism doesn't empty us; it allows us to be filled, to see and hear God, the eternal. It isn't more or less true.

It's true that less is more.

DECEMBER 18

Whether to laugh or cry

And all the people gave a great shout of praise to the LORD, because the foundation of the house of the LORD was laid. But many . . . who had seen the former temple, wept aloud when they saw the foundation of this temple being laid, while many others shouted for joy. No one could distinguish the sound of the shouts of joy from the sound of weeping. . . .

EZRA 3:11-13

In seminary, on a long midterm exam, while I regretted not knowing certain questions on the test, I also was gratified at how much I did know. So when I left the room, I wasn't sure whether to laugh or cry.

A life seeking God often holds such ambivalence. When the foundations of the temple were laid, some celebrated and some lamented. Many shouted with joy, knowing that the dwelling place of God was to be rebuilt, but those who knew the temple's former glory wept. "No one could distinguish the sound of the shouts of joy from the sound of weeping."

Made in the image of God, we could weep all day if we focused on how far we have fallen away from that image. And yet, we still somehow know how to love. We know how to care about and for each other. We know that God is near us, within us.

When I think of my life with God, sometimes I can't distinguish the sound of the shouts of joy from the sound of weeping. O, my LORD, I have fallen so far. And yet, O, my LORD, you love me—and teach me to love. I know so little. I know so much.

I'm not sure whether to laugh or cry.

PRACTICALLY HOLY

DECEMBER 19

Unexpected gifts

> *. . . declares the LORD, ". . . I will bring [them] into the fire; I will refine them like silver and test them like gold. They will call on my name and I will answer them; I will say, 'They are my people,' and they will say, 'The LORD is our God.'"*
>
> ZECHARIAH 13:9

An office supply store used to run ads showing bewildered people seeking gifts for people they barely knew. They were advised to find help in the store's "Department of Unexpected Gifts."

Although I didn't go there on purpose, the department of unexpected gifts has helped me repeatedly in the last eight years or so. At one time, I had placed all of my hopes in transitory things and relationships. All at once, those possessions and experiences I thought I needed to survive went away. Those were the worst of times. But in retrospect, I know that they were also the best of times, because until then, I could convince myself that I was in control. I had no need to seek God.

Now, from a safe distance, I can see that those impossible times and devastating losses turned me toward God in a way that success and superficial happiness could not have done. Now I see that those horrible experiences refined me, like precious metal in a fire. Only in abject despair could I learn about the hope of the future offered by God. Only amid tragic loss did I learn about the grace of God.

I found it in the department of unexpected gifts.

DECEMBER 20

Wears God?

> ... I want to know Christ and the power of his resurrection and the fellowship of sharing in his sufferings, becoming like him in his death, and so, somehow, to attain to the resurrection from the dead.
>
> PHILIPPIANS 3:10-11

One Christmastime when I flew home for break, the late arrival of one flight caused me to miss the next flight by two minutes. I came very close to losing my equilibrium with a rude ticket agent, but I stopped short because I was wearing a "divinity school" sweatshirt. I wouldn't want to dishonor my seminary that way.

As a Christian and a human being made in God's very image, I need such awareness. Every single morning when I arise, I wear that image of God. While it's easy and often justifiable in a human sense to lose my temper with others, it does not honor the image that I wear every day.

Paul recognized that being in God's image, and being saved by God's grace, allows us to rise above the hurts and frustrations of this world. He knew that "dying" to the things of this world and, "becoming like [Christ] in his death," allowed him resurrection in Christ that very day.

Some major frustration almost certainly waits right around the corner. If I think only in human terms, I'm going to want to lose my temper. But I wear the image of the divine; I don't need to stoop to the earthly.

I wouldn't want to dishonor my God that way.

December 21

The gift of God

Therefore my people will go into exile for lack of understanding; their men of rank will die of hunger and their masses will be parched with thirst. Therefore the grave enlarges its appetite and opens its mouth without limit. . . .

ISAIAH 5:13-14

At this time of year I see countless old-time movies on TV about the "true meaning" of Christmas. Ironically, those movies are punctuated by countless commercials trying to sell me something, usually expensive jewelry or a car in the driveway bearing a huge red bow.

Like many people, I repeatedly try to assuage the longing I feel with the things of this earth. Yet those pursuits, rather than filling me, leave me feeling increasingly empty. Inanimate objects can never be the source of life; they can never quench deep hunger and thirst. In other words, the more material goods I consume, the more "the grave enlarges its appetite and opens its mouth without limit."

I struggle to remember that love is not measured by the cost of the car in the driveway or the gift in the jewelry box. Love springs from the coming of God into a human heart, a process made possible by the coming of Christ into the human world. And the best gift is passing that presence on to another person in the form of compassion or forgiveness. By taking care of someone else, I can give the gift of God.

And if I do it every day, I can beat the Christmas rush.

December 22

Prepared for the Lord

But the angel said to him: "Do not be afraid, Zechariah. . . . Your wife Elizabeth will bear you a son, and you are to give him the name John . . . he will go on before the Lord . . . to turn the hearts of the fathers to their children and the disobedient to the wisdom of the righteous— to make ready a people prepared for the Lord."

LUKE 1:13-17

One weekend before Christmas I turned off the TV when I was told that I would see, back-to-back, "Rudolph the Reindeer" and "Frosty the Snowman." I get frustrated by the plethora of such seemingly superficial and plastic "holiday specials."

And while I am quick to criticize others for making the season so commercial and secular, I know in my heart that I also lose sight of the holiness of Christmas. I catch myself wondering, like everyone else, how I will "get everything done in time." But in truth these days before Christmas should speak of a peace settling into my heart, not a frantic mad dash to beat the clock. The anointed one—the Christ—is coming to save me.

The one task before me is to listen to and obey God so that, like John the Baptist, I can "make ready a people prepared for the Lord." Or a person prepared for the Lord. Though I consider myself a strong Christian, in the chaos of this season I, too, struggle a bit to remember what is important. It's not Rudolph the Reindeer or Frosty the Snowman. It is Jesus.

It is the Christ.

DECEMBER 23

Noise reduction

"The poor and needy search for water, but there is none. . . . But I the LORD will answer them. . . . I will make rivers flow on barren heights, and springs within the valleys. I will turn the desert into pools of water, and the parched ground into springs."

ISAIAH 41:17-18

A friend once gave me a "sleep machine" to help mitigate the sounds of noisy neighbors. The machine, which makes a continual low-level sound, doesn't drown out the noise. I just don't hear it anymore.

I have come to believe that prayer works the same way: not drowning out the noise of this world, but showing me that the noise need not win. I have come to this conclusion by seeing prayerful people and their demeanor, amid sadness and pain that would lay most of us low. I cannot attribute the peace of such people to anything but an acute awareness of the presence and power of God, an awareness also known as prayer.

Without prayer, all of us are the "poor and needy [who] search for water, but there is none." Every noise within earshot shakes us or otherwise enters the consciousness. The human heart remains at the mercy of loss, hurt, fear, and anger, and those conditions dictate the progress of a day and a life.

When I stay in touch with God in honest prayer, though, the major and minor crises no longer dominate the day. Instead, the undertone of the day is one of peace. Deserts of loss become pools of water where God is present. It isn't that the noise of the world is gone.

I just don't hear it anymore.

DECEMBER 24

Unknown becomes known

> [Paul] said: "Men of Athens! I see that in every way you are very religious. . . . I even found an altar with this inscription: TO AN UNKNOWN GOD. Now what you worship as something unknown I am going to proclaim to you."
>
> ACTS 17:22-23

When my nephews were small, my parents and I always helped my sister put together the boys' gifts on Christmas Eve. They, of course, believed that the gifts were brought by Santa, and we almost blew that mystery when we accidentally showed them photographs, after Christmas, of our secret Christmas Eve assembly operation.

It's natural for human beings to embrace mystery in some form in order to bring meaning to the world. Such mystery may take the form of Santa Claus, or a superstition, or a vague prayer to an unidentified deity. The truth, though, is that we humans are made by God, for God, in the image of God, and a longing for something above us is a very part of our makeup.

It is my job, as a Christian who has witnessed and been gratified by the mercy of God, to proclaim to others the identity of this "unknown god" so many people seek. The One who saves us, who brings the gifts, who gives us life, is not just "something" above us or a manmade being to whom we address our wishes and hopes. The One who saves us is the one true God. My life, lived in peace amid the chaos, can be an image that tells others the true meaning of this season. My hope and prayer is that someone will look at this picture and finally understand the truth.

Then they will know who brought us those gifts in the dead of night.

Home for Christmas

The true light that gives light to every man was coming into the world. He was in the world, and though the world was made through him, the world did not recognize him.

JOHN 1:9-10

I used to hear the song "I'll Be Home for Christmas" and wonder about the words, "presents *on* the tree." The older tradition, though, was not to place gifts *under* the tree, but to hang them on the tree.

For the longest time, I had that same sense that I was misunderstanding the crux of Christianity, Jesus' death on the cross. I must be hearing it wrong, I used to think. How is it possible to reconcile the idea of "God is love" with the death of a perfectly obedient human being on a cross?

But the death of Jesus on the cross is the ultimate gift of the God of love, as it teaches us that the love of God always triumphs. Christ chose to be perfectly obedient even to the point of death. Jesus trusted that the love of God trumps anything this world can do to us.

The essence of Christmas is Christ, and the essence of Christ is trust in God's ability to win over the worst of this world. Surviving in this difficult place requires us to hope that the darkness will not win. Sadly, we too often forget that essence of Christmas; for "though the world was made through him, the world did not recognize him."

So I guess I did hear it right, both in the song and in the core of Christianity. "Presence on the tree" holds the essence of this holy season.

And that presence means we can all be home for Christmas.

DECEMBER 26

What you want

Remain in me, and I will remain in you. No branch can bear fruit by itself; it must remain in the vine.... I chose you and appointed you to go and bear fruit—fruit that will last. Then the Father will give you whatever you ask in my name.

JOHN 15:4,16

Right after Christmas, one retailer's ads urged consumers to use gift cards and "Redeem yourself. Get something *you* want." Enough of thinking of others, already!

My little human heart finds a lot of appeal in the thought of getting what I want instead of worrying about what God or anyone else wants. But the deeper, eternal part of me—the part connected directly to God like a branch to a vine—knows that selfishness doesn't work for long. It bears fruit, but not "fruit that will last." To know something eternal, and to have something eternal, requires me to be in tune with God's will for me.

The great irony that I have discovered, and continue to discover, is that God wants me to be the best possible me. He doesn't want to shape me into something that doesn't suit me; in fact, God wants to enhance and optimize my unique gifts and passions.

The truth is that I cannot "redeem myself" at all, much less by thinking only of myself. God wants me to get something I want, although it may be something that, in my superficiality and selfishness, I never realized I wanted. So in making me more joyful, God doesn't only change what I *get*.

He changes what I *want*.

DECEMBER 27

The tree in the road

. . . fix your thoughts on Jesus . . . [who] has been found worthy of greater honor than Moses, just as the builder of a house has greater honor than the house itself. . . . And we are [God's] house, if we hold on to our courage and the hope of which we boast.

HEBREWS 3:1, 3, 6

One day after Christmas, traffic snarled on a quiet residential street, as a Christmas tree blocked one lane. It had been blown from the curbside by howling winds that day.

I am always strangely relieved the holidays are over, and I feel guilty about that relief. It seems that, like having a Christmas tree blocking the road, we have to stop everything else, then hurry around to get everything done. Christmas is supposed to be joyful, holy, filled with hope, but most years I find it frenetic and wearing. It's easy to forget that the season marks the coming of the Christ, that we should "fix our thoughts on Jesus," about his making us into a house where God dwells.

And yet, the tree in the road may symbolize an even more important problem. Becoming dwelling places for God will cause some disruption, some disquiet in our lives. It isn't all about joy and light; it's also a life that asks us to "hold on to our courage" and realize that life lived for God isn't always easy and convenient. So maybe we hurry through the holidays partly out of our human fear of change. For a person wanting only to live a complacent life, Christmas isn't just *on* the way.

It's *in* the way.

DECEMBER 28

Uncertainty

Come now, you who say, "Today or tomorrow we will go to such and such a town and spend a year there, doing business and making money." Yet you do not even know what tomorrow will bring. What is your life? For you are a mist that appears for a little while and then vanishes. Instead you ought to say, "If the Lord wishes, we will live and do this or that."

JAMES 4:13-15

I once read an article about "futurologists" who make predictions about how the world will look in ten or twenty years. Noting how embarrassing it can be for those predictions to miss the mark badly, the article said of predicting the future, "Uncertainty looks smarter than ever before."

But uncertainty doesn't sit well with most of us humans, at least on the surface. We crave certainty, which is a fine approach for checkbook balances or medical diagnoses but a short-sighted approach with regard to God. I would love to know for certain what God wants me to do, and part of me wants to know for certain who God is.

Clearly it's impossible to predict the future, or to know exactly the mind of God. I need to remember that I "do not even know what tomorrow will bring." So rather than trying to predict the future, I should say instead, "If the Lord wishes" I will "live and do this or that." Besides, the natural progression of having certainty about the ways of God would be that God is no bigger than I am. I certainly don't care for that idea.

So suddenly uncertainty looks smarter than ever before.

DECEMBER 29

Seen and not herd

The LORD is my shepherd, I shall not be in want. He makes me lie down in green pastures, he leads me beside quiet waters, he restores my soul. He guides me in paths of righteousness for his name's sake.

PSALM 23:1-3

Does anyone else feel vaguely relieved when the Christmas rush is over? It feels mildly blasphemous, in light of the important role Christmas plays in American culture, to be relieved. But at this point I'm usually ready for some regular days instead of frenzied "holidays" that wear me out. I feel like a sheep being herded from one sale to the next, from one party to the next, from one obligation to the next.

But in the care of the Lord, the good shepherd, we are not simply part of the flock being driven by the forces and marketers of our culture. We are individuals, seen clearly by God, beloved of God. Each of us can take a deep breath and remember that, despite the chaos of the season, we celebrate in this time of the year (and always) the presence and protection of God.

God has entered not just the "holidays," but the ordinary days. In God, this "sheep" can "lie down in green pastures," enjoy "quiet waters," and be restored. No matter how much I have spent, or how spent I feel, I shall not be in want, because God is here.

Christmas has come and gone, and it's appropriate to breathe a sigh of relief at getting past the frenzy. But we can enjoy the deepest restoration and peace. The holiday has come and gone.

But the Reason for the holiday has come and decided to stay.

DECEMBER 30

Transformers

Not a blacksmith could be found in the whole land of Israel, because the Philistines had said, "Otherwise the Hebrews will make swords or spears!" So all Israel went down to the Philistines to have their plowshares, mattocks, axes and sickles sharpened.

1 SAMUEL 13:19-20

Wanting to learn more about the remake of the movie *Transformers*, I went to the film's website. Immediately, though, I had to choose a route into the website; my two choices were "Protect" and "Destroy."

The choice of paths is seldom so stark, but every day I make decisions about whether I will protect or destroy. Like every human, I have gifts, and I can use those gifts to build others or to bring them down. I can protect, or I can destroy.

In ancient times, the Philistines prevented the people of Israel from having blacksmiths because "Otherwise the Hebrews will make swords or spears!" But the human mind can be incredibly creative, so the oppressed people simply sharpened their farm and work tools into weapons. What had been designed to create and protect was altered so that it could destroy.

Somewhere today I will have an opportunity to make that decision, at least in a small way: to protect or destroy. If I choose to build up, the world will become a slightly better place. If I choose to knock down, the world will become a slightly harsher place. Will I use my tools, or sharpen them?

Will I protect, or will I destroy?

The God particle

And the peace of God, which transcends all understanding, will guard your hearts and your minds in Christ Jesus.

PHILIPPIANS 4:7

A recent magazine article spoke of the search for the "God particle," defined by the seekers as the smallest building block of the universe. The scientists doing the research want to find "what the universe is made of," or "a model of reality that snaps together neatly."

I also seek the "God particle," but my search does not take place in the realm of physics. I seek the core truth, the one bit of knowledge that allows me to rest easy, to know that the calamities of this world will not ultimately win. Like all human beings, I would love to be able to understand and to explain why things happen as they do.

But ultimately my search for understanding is a search for peace, not for quantifiable human knowledge. I can find that peace in Christ Jesus, the one human being in history who faithfully insisted that love always, always wins. Rather than save himself, he trusted God, and because he showed that God's love does indeed win out, I can live in peace.

I seek to understand and explain the ways of God not so that I will be smarter, but so that I will be more at peace with myself, the universe, and with God. So if someone offers me all knowledge, or simply all peace, there is no contest. I want peace, which will guard both my heart and my mind.

For "the peace of God transcends all understanding."

Index

A
abundant life 14, 174
action 51, 100, 129, 134, 168, 207, 243, 253, 281, 300, 333
anger 44, 48, 62, 120, 162, 330, 343, 354, 369, 384
anxiety 41, 79, 152, 192, 354, 371

B
baggage 41, 165, 306, 365
Bible 77, 363
blessings 34, 262, 358
blindness 45, 112, 132, 353
body of Christ 35, 50, 69, 234, 250, 256, 274
bondage 323
burdens 30, 64, 79, 130, 165, 202, 223, 293

C
change 12, 29, 30, 64, 80, 101, 121, 145, 153, 180, 206, 209, 213, 232, 262, 272, 276, 298, 306, 324, 341, 362, 387, 388
choices 37, 75, 100, 115, 135, 205, 207, 221, 271, 300, 336
Christ as model 45, 182, 234, 287, 362
Christ to the world 35, 50, 62, 65, 67, 117, 188, 385
Christian life 35, 37, 39, 55, 69, 75, 82, 100, 156, 161, 198, 267, 331, 337, 338, 346, 385
church 16, 188
comfort zones 37, 47, 52, 61, 101, 132, 153, 160, 191, 213, 254. 275, 305, 324, 348
compassion 23, 28, 34, 44, 45, 51, 55, 74, 92, 100, 119, 144, 154, 217, 223, 234, 276, 286, 289, 303, 350, 354, 382
complacency 191, 285, 286, 324, 366, 388
connections 187, 368
constancy 49
control 70, 84, 111, 124, 181, 237, 238, 239, 249, 275, 301, 304, 313, 326, 380
courage 60, 75, 110, 168, 250, 281, 303, 305, 347, 388
creation 14, 185, 237, 317, 356
crisis 230, 262, 339
culture 76, 83, 88, 132, 138, 173, 187, 198, 218, 228, 238, 303, 340

D
death 41, 75, 96, 104, 124, 163, 262, 269, 279, 281, 313, 331, 339, 344, 374, 377, 381, 386
demons 206, 260, 330, 332
desires 19
despair 62, 106, 130, 155, 179, 253, 264, 292, 380
direction 111, 282
doctrine 104
doubt 159, 162, 323, 330, 343, 357

E
ego 58, 68, 97, 148, 157, 194, 219, 258, 260, 331
emptiness 47, 66, 111, 177, 207, 212, 264, 311, 378, 382
eternal life 96, 203, 217, 373
everyday life 140, 141
evil 71, 77, 112, 142, 183, 206, 244, 320, 341
expectations 14, 151, 237, 268, 269, 356

F
failure 13, 26, 30, 269, 321, 328, 334, 336
faith 18, 51, 55, 103, 174, 204, 209, 214, 269, 342, 370, 371, 392
fear 24, 28, 92, 142, 153, 229, 231, 247, 258, 276, 287, 292, 328, 330, 331, 339, 366, 388

INDEX

focus 99, 110, 112, 126, 163, 225, 232, 267, 314, 370
forgiveness 81, 138, 150, 165, 189, 202, 229, 236, 283, 299, 302, 314, 359, 365, 370, 377
freedom 196, 205, 206, 229, 236, 285, 351, 366
free will 81

G
gifts 14, 18, 67, 94, 131, 174, 191, 222, 258, 309, 319, 362, 363, 369, 380, 385, 387, 391
God first 152, 177, 263, 331
God in this world 159
God's love 23, 54, 268, 292, 315, 336, 392
God's sacrifice 193, 212, 321
God's will 36, 60, 131, 142, 178, 181, 282, 332, 387
grace 12, 16, 27, 31, 34, 71, 74, 81, 116, 151, 154, 162, 187, 188, 190, 229, 238, 242, 253, 271, 281, 289, 299, 301, 311, 320, 339, 355
gratitude 18, 21, 67, 71, 125, 222, 240
grief 122, 126, 130, 170
growth 101, 111, 213, 251, 298, 324
grudges 365
guidance 152

H
healing 63, 80, 162, 189, 191, 281, 295, 323, 353
heaven 41, 109, 127, 135, 139, 203, 224, 287, 327, 330, 346
holiness 34, 213, 277
hope 12, 42, 49, 53, 62, 81, 91, 125, 142, 149, 159, 164, 179, 204, 209, 239, 253, 264, 316, 364, 372, 375, 380
humanity 358, 359
hunger for God 48, 66, 154, 382
hypocrisy 16

I
idols 22, 29, 116, 225, 232, 238, 246, 282, 305

image of God 69, 84, 97, 135, 141, 149, 151, 198, 234, 240, 273, 286, 295, 312, 341, 379, 381, 385
immensity of God 98, 211, 215, 237, 239
intellect 64, 87, 214, 215, 322, 357

J
joy 125, 131, 156, 209, 259, 288, 316, 368, 379
judgmentalism 83, 91
justice 13, 23, 164, 311

K
kingdom of God 46, 65, 124, 127, 194, 196, 213, 236, 271, 278, 305, 312, 314, 356
knowing God 195
knowledge 36, 87, 173, 193, 215, 349, 357, 368, 371, 392

L
law 42, 52, 74, 107, 243, 255, 290, 312, 314
lessons 104, 111, 245, 309, 316
limitations 53, 315
listening 147, 260
living for God 41, 52, 96, 163, 286, 292, 345
loneliness 152
loss 75, 76, 96, 117, 151, 165, 170, 239, 259, 279, 309, 358, 380, 384
love your neighbor 37, 42, 60, 69, 93, 108, 135, 160, 178, 189, 194, 314, 326, 363
loving God 37, 37, 60, 80, 100, 108, 135, 143, 189, 197, 267, 312, 367

M
manipulation 189
materialism 13, 112, 194, 292, 323, 378
mercy 13, 42, 144, 164, 165, 179, 188, 199, 202, 210, 229, 236, 299, 354, 385
miracles 14, 21, 53, 234, 279, 289, 294, 318, 353

INDEX

mistakes 23, 53, 57, 79, 115, 128, 142, 150, 165, 179, 209, 257, 273, 286, 302, 311, 351, 364, 368
morality 300
mystery 36, 56, 64, 77, 172, 215, 237, 340, 385

O

obedience 250, 334

P

pain 76, 186, 202, 211, 223, 281, 323, 324, 336
patience 47, 173, 366
peace 28, 41, 53, 62, 69, 71, 94, 107, 111, 116, 173, 176, 177, 182, 186, 192, 208, 225, 245, 257, 282, 293, 306, 330, 331, 352, 366, 376
personal relationship with God 185
potential 14, 97, 102, 153, 251, 278
power 12, 59, 84, 101, 126, 128, 244, 330, 357, 365, 378
prayer 60, 130, 144, 187, 206, 230, 251, 258, 293, 332, 368, 384
priorities 22, 60, 75, 96, 116, 132, 148, 152, 184, 198, 247, 249, 262, 263, 310, 374
prisons 229, 292, 304, 323
protection 235, 270, 390

R

rationalization 174, 256, 305, 345
reason 20, 214, 268, 372
redemption 91, 140, 189, 192, 280, 283
regret 12, 58, 241, 299, 356, 364
relationships 18, 30, 47, 60, 112, 116, 146, 171, 231, 245, 324
religion 52, 160, 238, 291, 355, 359
resentment 101, 156, 162, 306, 347
rest 49, 194, 262, 331, 339, 390
resurrection 82, 267, 269
righteousness 31, 56, 99, 102, 119, 186, 204, 210, 229, 343

S

sacrifice 22, 74, 88, 102, 152, 165, 246, 321, 369

safety 357
science 215
Scripture 77, 363
seeking God 34, 56, 60, 84, 177, 183, 214, 230, 264, 291, 300, 333, 352, 377, 379
selfishness 159, 184, 216, 294, 387
self-interest 57, 93, 184, 199, 252
self-reliance 259, 272
self-righteousness 30, 229, 285
service 217, 293
sin 13, 24, 32, 128, 150, 178, 221, 280, 292, 302, 320, 333, 356
small things 174, 277, 369
stubbornness 219, 248, 314, 365
success 17, 69, 86, 94, 95, 124, 190, 212, 228, 235, 303
suffering 64, 77, 80, 323, 337

T

time 109, 112, 134, 138, 147, 163, 178, 226, 253, 287, 331, 374, 376, 383
tolerance 204
transformation 101
trust 49, 56, 59, 70, 86, 91, 110, 115, 116, 122, 196, 204, 208, 219, 270, 294, 309, 321, 323, 335, 346, 371
truth 23, 87, 98, 154, 161, 190, 283, 292, 301, 385, 392
turning to God 372

U

urgency 134

W

weakness 147, 270, 275, 281, 303
wholeness 189
wisdom 172, 173, 190, 198, 215, 274
witness 117, 269, 385
work 51, 109, 131, 212, 288, 378
worry 22, 41, 104, 130, 306, 328, 387
worship 18, 35, 67, 70, 88, 113, 156, 204, 225, 246, 252, 305
worthiness 44

Index by Title

Indicated by date

A bit of bread and fish 1/3
A dollar's worth of Shakespeare ... 3/5
A good day 8/27
A heart for God 11/20
A safe place to stop 8/14
A smaller plate 10/21
A stranger on earth 1/26
A walk to remember 4/30
Above and below 11/17
Aerial coverage 1/15
After the fall 10/1
All eyes 4/21
All lost together 7/27
All that glitters 1/18
All that moves 7/10
All that stuff 2/11
All we ask or imagine 7/17
Annex 11/19
Answers and questions 12/10
Are you sure? 11/18
Away 12/2
Back seat 2/18
Be loved 3/10
Beginnings and endings 9/14
Beneath the surface 5/12
Best-kept secret 6/4
Better 3/25
Better weapons 3/21
Big little words 6/11
Boss as brand 4/16
Broken 4/17
Builder of bridges 4/15
Busting out 10/7
But it's cold out there 2/9
Bye-bye 4/10
Can you describe Him? 4/12
Can't buy me love 8/11
Carrying a torch 7/12
Change the world 11/26
Complete 11/5
Concrete desert 8/18
Dance lessons 3/1
Dare (the) devil act 3/2

Darkness and light 11/12
Day by day 2/17
Disarmament 1/4
Disarming 6/27
Disposable lives 4/23
Do you want to get well? 6/22
Don't blame me 2/27
Down the mountain 1/27
Driving force 1/17
Eclipse 6/19
Elsewhere 5/23
Emergency call 12/7
Empty words 7/30
Ever 2/5
Everything in a box 8/4
Exploring inner space 6/7
Fall 9/21
Fall from space 8/13
Feeding the hungry 6/9
Feeding the volcano 5/1
Filling the glass 11/29
Find some dust 2/3
Finding change 10/19
Finding reverse 3/16
Finding the equator 7/24
Finding the right key 7/13
Fireproof 5/21
Fireworks 7/3
Flowers along the road 5/22
For good 3/7
Forgive us our debts 9/24
Found 9/15
From here (to eternity) 7/31
From the great height 9/19
From the valley 8/6
Getting home 2/24
Getting there from here 12/9
Getting used to it 2/21
Giving and selling 11/9
Giving back 6/21
Giving up the gold 3/13
Giving up the oars 4/6
Glimpses of God 5/4

396 PRACTICALLY HOLY

INDEX BY TITLE

God be with you 5/8
God looks on the heart 5/27
God loves ou 9/3
God with us 12/1
God-finding 4/14
God's echo 7/15
God's pocket 10/12
God's speed 3/26
God's symmetry 10/20
God's toolbox 2/1
God's ways 1/28
Gone too far 9/17
Good and great 5/20
Goodness, greatness 3/29
Grace 1/5
Grand opening 10/5
Grounded 11/28
Grown-up toys 7/7
Hammers and nails 9/6
Happy endings 6/29
Have you ever? 3/17
He is not sleeping 2/6
Healthy hearts 11/8
High definition 11/6
Holding the umbrella 6/24
Holier and Thou 11/30
Home 9/30
Home for Christmas 12/25
Home rage 4/2
Homemade prisons 9/27
Hope rises 3/18
Hopefully 8/31
Human beings and human doings. 6/18
Hungry 2/23
Hunter-gatherers 8/5
I see heaven open 11/1
I wouldn't want to live there ... 3/19
I'd sooner see God 8/1
Identity theft 8/28
If these stones could speak 9/1
In the meantime 1/14
Inclination 5/5
Inevitable crash 10/29
Infrequent flyer 6/14
Inside out 3/27
Is this going to be on the test? ... 3/31
It has my name on it 2/20

It's the mirrors 3/24
Judgment 6/10
Junkers 3/8
Just sitting there 9/16
Keeping out the looters 7/5
Kindling 11/21
Knowing (about) God 6/26
Last wish 12/13
Length of days 4/1
Life eternal 4/3
Like wildfire 8/9
Limping well 11/24
Little sparrows 4/13
Living the Words 8/2
Looking for the light 5/29
Love extravagantly 1/22
Love never fails 7/26
Loving lavishly 4/9
Loving the sad songs 2/15
Low-resolution images 8/7
Matter 1/19
Medicine 1/21
Melting the ice 2/7
Mine 7/11
Missing 5/2
More or less 12/17
Motive 7/23
Moving pictures 11/15
Music of the past 8/26
My own business 8/23
My, my, my 1/7
Mystery lesson 3/4
Nasty little tyrants 4/19
Near and far 6/16
Need to (not) know 8/8
Never again 12/3
New life forms 9/29
No accounting for grace 10/14
No fear 10/31
No simple season 3/30
Noise reduction 12/23
Nothing for something 5/10
Nothing matches 1/31
Offense, defense 3/20
On the side of the law 10/17
One across 5/6
One hundred percent 1/30

INDEX BY TITLE

One in a million 9/18
One perfect gift 12/15
One thing 4/22
Ordnance 9/25
Out of the way 10/13
Overnight sensation 1/6
Paint it black 8/15
Passport 12/16
Perfect pronunciation 2/2
Phone home 7/29
Plans 2/10
Play 10/24
Pleas and thank you 10/3
Please ask for more 11/13
Possibility 5/16
Pounding the rocks to dust 7/1
Prepared for the Lord 12/22
Present 4/29
Present tents 9/7
Preventive medicine 6/17
Prime numbers 1/11
Prints of peace 8/24
Prisoners taking prisoners 7/28
Prisons 10/26
Proportional response 11/14
Put us under 3/3
Random acts 11/25
Range of motion 10/27
Reconciling 2/28
Reflections 5/11
Regaining the joy 5/19
Remade in God's image 5/14
Resurrection 9/4
Return and enter 11/27
Road ends 5/9
Rolling away the stone 4/25
Room to forgive 7/20
Ruby red slippers 2/16
Running backward 9/26
Saturday in the Park 6/25
Saving breath 12/5
Say the Word 5/25
Seeing God's face 4/27
Seen and not herd 12/29
Send pictures 6/20
Shake, rattle, and roll 8/29
Show me a picture 6/13

Silent witness 10/4
Simple 8/30
Singing for God 4/20
Singing lessons 12/14
Skating on the surface 11/16
Sliver of a moon 4/18
Small things 9/12
Sneaking past the filters 8/19
So small 1/2
Soul memory 4/28
Stilling the strings 1/29
Stopped watch 4/7
Stopping along the path 3/23
Storm-chasing 4/26
Stormy weather 6/6
Symptoms 4/11
Tastes like numbers 12/12
Telling the truth 1/12
Temporary housing 7/2
The bearer of all things 9/28
The best of love 10/18
The big event 6/2
The big tip 1/10
The bridge 10/30
The broken key 6/8
The broken seal 5/24
The burden of lost baggage ... 5/28
The charge 10/10
The check 7/6
The chorus 11/23
The day of grace 1/1
The day of small things 12/8
The day the world changed ... 9/11
The desert 8/16
The divine express 9/13
The flow of good(s) and service(s) 7/16
The forest and the trees 5/3
The freedom trail 7/4
The gift of God 12/21
The God particle 12/31
The God rush 10/6
The God-made light 10/28
The grace of God 1/20
The grace of what didn't happen 11/10
The hands that do his work ... 9/23
The heart knows 10/25
The hill teaches 9/10

INDEX BY TITLE

The home team 10/8
The horizon................... 4/4
The identity game 11/3
The jab and the Cross 3/9
The key enemy 8/25
The keys 3/28
The knowledge of the heart 3/14
The lake's secrets 3/11
The least of these 8/21
The living Word 1/16
The Lord rains................ 5/18
The machine 3/22
The mean old man............ 8/22
The mechanic 10/23
The mingling of earth and sky ... 7/19
The mouth of the cannon 9/5
The music of eternity 4/5
The mystery door............. 11/11
The mystery of God's favor 1/25
The narrowest places........... 9/20
The need for speed 8/20
The needy and the greedy....... 5/17
The new old................. 10/15
The open door................ 2/19
The opera singer 9/8
The price 6/28
The price is right............. 12/11
The rain of God................ 8/3
The reality of snow 12/6
The rest of my life............. 11/2
The river 6/30
The road to Jerusalem........... 9/9
The sleeping giant............. 7/22
The small picture.............. 6/5
The sound of thunder 6/12
The strong man 4/8
The temple................... 1/24
The thieves of light 5/15
The tree in the road........... 12/27
The umbrella................. 7/18
The uncashed check 10/22
The unfinished puzzle.......... 2/13
The unruly child 5/7
The unspoken Word 2/12
The weather inside is frightful 2/4
There has been a sighting 5/30
This old thing 8/10

Through the fire 7/8
Throwing away the gift......... 7/21
To be loved is no easy thing 3/6
To the high place.............. 7/25
Today....................... 10/9
Tomb of the unknown.......... 7/14
Too much light 4/24
Tracking..................... 2/8
Transformers 12/30
True love 2/14
Turning point................. 9/22
Twins....................... 1/8
Ugly houses.................. 1/13
Uncertainty 12/28
Unexpected gifts 12/19
Unhappy medium 6/23
Unknown becomes known 12/24
Unlit candles 10/11
Unnamed storms 6/1
Unoriginal sin 5/13
Untoward.................... 5/31
Up, up, and away 2/25
Upstairs, downstairs 8/12
Waiting 3/12
Wanted: Dead and alive 10/16
Wasted space................. 10/2
Wears God?.................. 12/20
Well qualified or not 2/26
What God has done to us 7/9
What I know 5/26
What problems does your fuel cause?. 11/4
What we consume............. 6/15
What we gave away 6/3
What we worship 3/15
What you want 12/26
Whether to laugh or cry 12/18
Why she smiles................ 1/9
Will I recognize Him?.......... 8/17
Winning and loosing 12/4
Without love 11/7
Wounded grace 1/23
Written on human hearts........ 2/22
You are here 9/2
You can go home again........ 11/22

PRACTICALLY HOLY 399

Practically *Holy*

Finding God in the Everyday

by Carol Mead

Ordering Information

Practically Holy is available at selected retailers
as well as directly from the publisher.
Please visit the website at www.holyordinary.com
for prices, specific ordering information,
and details about where the book is available.

Thank you for your interest in the book.

May God bless you and keep you!